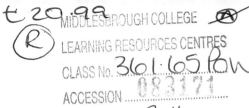

WELFARE STATE AND
WELFARE CHANGE

Martin Powell
and
Martin Hewitt

Open University Press

D0599818

Open University Press
McGraw-Hill Education
McGraw-Hill House
Shoppenhangers Road
Maidenhead
Berkshire
SL6 2QL

email: enquiries@openup.co.uk
world wide web: www.openup.co.uk

and

Two Penn Plaza
New York, NY 10121-2289, USA

First Published 2002
Reprinted 2008

A catalogue record of this book is available from the British Library

ISBN-10   0 335 20516 X (pb)   0 335 20517 8 (hb)
ISBN-13   978 0 335 20516 5 (pb)   978 0 335 20517 2 (hb)

Library of Congress Cataloging-in-Publication Data
   Powell, Martin A., 1961–
   Welfare state and welfare change / Martin Powell & Martin Hewitt.
      p. cm.
   Includes bibliographical references and index.
   ISBN 0-335-20517-8 – ISBN 0-335-20516-X (pbk.)
      1. Public welfare – Great Britain.   2. Welfare state.   I. Hewitt, Martin.   II. Title.
   HV248 .P68 2002
   361.6′5′0941–dc21

                                                            2001059108

Typeset by Graphicraft Limited, Hong Kong
Printed in Great Britain by Bell & Bain Ltd., Glasgow

CONTENTS

8 Social explanations 140

9 Welfare change 166

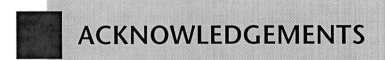

ACKNOWLEDGEMENTS

We would like to thank the combination of support and tolerance on the part of Jacinta Evans and Clara Waissbein at Open University Press.

The views expressed in this book are solely those of the authors and not of their employing organizations.

1 WELFARE STATE

Introduction

What is the welfare state? Do recent changes in social policy suggest that we now have a new welfare state? What forces lead to changes in the welfare state? Such questions are basic issues in social policy. However, many debates on such issues have tended to confuse rather than inform, in that they have often been conducted at a high level of abstraction, with little agreement about basic definitions and terms. Our intention in this book is to provide an accessible introduction to these debates, bringing together basic descriptive, analytical and explanatory material to address basic issues regarding the 'what, when and why' of welfare change. We illustrate these debates by focusing on welfare change and the British welfare state.

Starting with the 'what' question, accounts of welfare change since the 1970s are marked by large disagreements about terminology and chronology. Many colourful terms have been used. The welfare state has been in crisis (Mishra 1984), under threat (Lowe 1999a), in transition (Johnson 1987, Esping-Andersen 1996), resilient or robust (Le Grand 1991), reshaped (Johnson 1990), refashioned (Wicks 1987), restructured (Sullivan 1992, 1996; Wilding 1992), retrenched (Mishra 1990), reconstructed (Johnson 1990), residualized (Digby 1989; Townsend 1995), rolled back (Hay 1996), recast (Fererra and Rhodes 2000), recalibrated (Ferrera *et al.* 2001), transformed (Squires 1990; Sullivan 1992; Holman 1993) and even dismantled (Community Development Project 1977). There appears to be some consensus that the favourite 'r-word' may be 'retrenchment' (P. Pierson 1996; Bonoli *et al.* 2000). The word 'new' has been used almost as much as in Labour Party documents: there is a new era of social policy (Glennerster *et al.* 1991), a new agenda, a new consensus (see Powell and Hewitt 1998), a new order and a new paradigm (Taylor-Gooby and Lawson 1993), and a new politics of the welfare state (P. Pierson 1996, 2001). Similarly, there is talk of post-modernism (Hewitt 1994), post-Fordism (Burrows and Loader 1994), post-welfare state (Smith and Mallinson 1997; Fitzpatrick 2001), post-welfare society (Tomlinson 2001), the end of ideology (again!), the end of history (Fukuyama 1992) and the end of the welfare state (see Powell and Hewitt 1998). More recently, it has been claimed that we have a Schumpeterian post-national workfare state (Jessop 1999). Finally, New Labour claims that its 'third way' policies will lead to a new contract between citizen and state and, eventually, to a new welfare society (Powell 1999a). It is unclear whether this reflects nothing more than elegant variations of change. Esping-Andersen (1990: 22) claims that 'The proliferation of labels, such as "post-modernist", "post-materialist", "post-fordist" or "post-industrial", often substitutes for analysis'. Do these terms from the academic ivory towers of Babel add analytical, as opposed to, literary value? Are the meanings similar or different? Are they more than 'Humpty Dumpty' words? In short, it is generally agreed that 'something happened' (Clarke *et al.* 1994: 1), but there is little consensus beyond this point.

Turning to the 'when' question, writers have dated the end of the classic welfare state as 1973, 1975, 1979, 1981, 1987, 1988 and 1989. Verdicts vary from the mid-1970s Labour government (e.g. Krieger 1986) to an assortment of dates associated with the Conservative government (e.g. Corrigan 1979; Gough 1991; Le Grand 1991). More recently, New Labour is seen to have made significant changes (MacGregor 1999; Powell 1999a). Lowe (1999b) identifies three 'turning points': the Beveridge Report in 1942, the abandonment of the commitment to full employment in 1976 and the introduction of quasi-markets in 1988. These major turning points in post-war welfare policy saw 'the successive promotion of a grand vision, the kicking away of one of its major props and a fundamental restructuring of service delivery' (Lowe 1999b: 8). However, as we saw above, it is possible to identify alternative 'turning points' or indeed no turning points. As the historian Carr (1990) explains, the 'historical fact' that the Battle of Hastings was fought in 1066 is based on two observations. First, it was fought in 1066 and not 1065 or 1067 and, second, it was fought at Hastings and not at Brighton or Eastbourne. However, we are interested in these facts only because historians regard it as a major historical event. Historians have decided that 'Caesar's crossing of that petty stream, the Rubicon, is a fact of history, whereas the crossing of the Rubicon by millions of people before or since inter- ests nobody at all' (Carr 1990: 10). It follows that it is necessary to examine the reasons why particular turning points in welfare history are important.

Finally, addressing the 'why' question, there is a large literature that seeks to explain the development of welfare states (e.g. Carrier and Kendall 1973, 1977; Higgins 1981; Mishra 1981; Jones 1985; Baldwin 1990; P. Pierson 1996; C. Pierson 1998a; Bonoli *et al.* 2000; Scarborough 2000; Alcock 2001; Fitzpatrick 2001; Kennett 2001). As Baldwin (1990: 36–7) puts it,

> Explanations of the origins, rise and development of the welfare state abound. Scores of theories compete to explain why it exists at all, dozens of comparative analyses account for its variations, legions of narratives detail how individual examples contradict or confirm general hypotheses. Industrialisation, free trade, capitalism, modern- isation, socialism, the working class, civil servants, corporatism, reformers, catholicism, war – rare is the variable that has not been invoked to explain some aspect of its development . . . Even the sea- soned observer may be forgiven for occasionally feeling lost in this academic Babel of paradigms, models, interpretations and accounts.

As a discipline, social policy has tended to travel with fairly light theoretical baggage. There are many 'explanations' of welfare change that, on closer inspection, fade into at best functional arguments lacking causal mechanisms or at worst changing descriptive labelling. This is well illustrated by Schwartz (2001), who examines his question of 'who killed the growth of the welfare state' in terms of a fusion between the film 'Casablanca' and the murder-mystery novel. Schwartz first 'rounds up the usual suspects'. The first is the 'external extruder', 'SAM' (low wage Southern competition; technological Advances; Monetary policy). The second is the 'insider job' of ILSA (Inflation control; Low Service sector productivity growth; Ageing). The final suspect is 'RICK' (property Rights; Income streams; Coalitions). As Schwartz argues, it is necessary to examine the traditional elements of motive, opportunity and method. However, while there must be progress on all three elements to secure a conviction, many suspects are convicted simply on circumstantial evidence pointing out a motive in the form of a functional prerequisite. Schwartz (2001: 17–18) points to several problems that have wider applicability:

> causal chains linking the alleged murderer to the copse are missing ... and the variety of weapons is bewildering ... The central mystery in the relationship between globalisation and the welfare state is accurately identifying the victim ... no one is quite sure which dependent variable matters and how it is changing.

While Pierson (1998b: 17) claims that 'no one could argue that we lack a theoretical account of the development of social policy', most are deficient in above terms, being 'non-rival explanatory sketches' rather than explanations *per se* (Schwartz 2001). Nevertheless, the 'explanations' and theories that we present are still useful, as they allow us to examine facts within a framework (Pierson 1998b) or to ask questions more intelligently than we would otherwise ask (Fitzpatrick 2001).

Esping-Andersen (1990: 32) claims that 'a theory that seeks to explain welfare-state growth should also be able to understand its retrenchment or decline'. However, Paul Pierson (1996, 2001) argues that a 'new politics of the welfare state' must be recognized: welfare state retrenchment is not simply the mirror image of welfare state expansion. The variables crucial to understanding expansion are of limited use in understanding retrenchment. In short, 'new times' call for new explanations (cf. Bonoli *et al.* 2000; but see Scarborough 2000).

In short, there are major disagreements about what has changed, when it changed and why it changed. Indeed, in addition to significant differences between accounts, in some cases differences exist between different accounts offered by the same writer. Such disputes about terminology, chronology and explanation appear to be due to varying (and often implicit) definitions of the welfare state, different political perceptions, different criteria and different readings of the evidence. In summary, it remains unclear whether the welfare state has been restructured, the criteria of any restructuring and when it was restructured. In this book, we seek to place the above debates within a wider framework and longer time-scale. We combine descriptive, analytical and explanatory perspectives to focus on the 'what, when and why' of welfare change.

There are clear links between theory and evidence. As Pierson (1998b: 25) points out, 'facts do not speak for themselves' and are always explained within a particular theoretical framework (however implicit and inarticulate). In other words, the features that we stress in Chapters 2–4 have an important impact on the explanations (Chapters 5–8) making some appear more plausible than others. We have examined the evolution of the welfare state in fairly standard and orthodox political-institutional terms (cf. Glennerster 1995; Timmins 1996; Lowe 1999a). Alternative accounts (e.g. Williams 1989; Hughes and Lewis 1998) emphasize different features, which may favour different explanations and lead to different verdicts about periodization. There is no way around this problem, but it is necessary to be aware of it.

Welfare states, welfare societies and welfare regimes

Ideally, there would be a simple and consensual definition of the welfare state against which changes could be examined (cf. Veit-Wilson 2000). However, not only is there no universally agreed definition of a 'welfare state', but some writers prefer to use other terms such as 'welfare society' and 'welfare regime'. In this section, we examine these terms in turn. Our starting point is the most widely used term of the 'welfare state'. At the risk of some oversimplification, we focus on welfare issues beyond the state in terms of welfare society and then discuss broader state concerns in terms of welfare regime.

Many writers have pointed to the problems of defining a welfare state (e.g. Carrier and Kendall 1973, 1977; Robson 1976; Mishra 1981; Jones 1985; Goodin 1988; Spicker 1988; Esping-Andersen 1990; Hay 1996; Page 1996; Lowe 1999a,b). In a recent summary, Veit-Wilson (2000: 1) argues that the welfare state is a 'Humpty Dumpty' term ('When I use a word it means just what I choose it to mean – neither more nor less'), emptied of all explanatory meaning. According to Brown (1995: 1):

'The Welfare State' is a term which for more than 50 years has been used in various contexts, including historical analysis, without any clear agreement as to its meaning. It is impossible to define precisely and equally impossible to do without it, even though its use has invariably involved implicit or unstated assumptions, which in the face of efforts to clarify them remain vague or can even seem incompatible. This lack of clarity tends to be acknowledged but discounted in writing on the British Welfare State.

Lowe (1999a: 14) claims that a widely endorsed definition of the welfare state is that of Asa Briggs, who wrote that:

A 'Welfare State' is a state in which organized power is deliberately used . . . in an effort to modify the play of market forces in at least three main directions – first, by guaranteeing individuals and families a minimum income irrespective of the market value of their work or property; second, by narrowing the extent of insecurity by enabling individuals and families to meet certain social contingencies (for example, sickness, old age and unemployment) which lead otherwise to individuals and family crisis; and third, by ensuring that all citizens without distinction of status or class are offered the best standards available in relation to a certain agreed range of social services.

Briggs' definition appears also in Spicker (1988: 76), Flora and Heidenheimer (1981: 29) and Goodin (1988: 7). Brown (1995: 5) argues that Briggs' definition is as good as any, but provokes many questions. In many ways, it is more of a description than a definition and defies simple operationalization. It is not clear on the purpose of the welfare state because, as we shall see later, it is possible to argue that the emphasis given to the three directions has varied between different governments. Neither does Briggs' definition offer much guidance on the scope of the welfare state. Many textbooks focus on the 'big five' services of health, education, housing, social security and personal social services. However, long before the suggested enlargement of scope associated with the 'new social policy' (Cahill 1994), Robson (1976) discussed the environment, leisure and recreation and town and country planning, while Le Grand (1982) suggested transport.

The term 'welfare society' is equally problematic. The term implies a changed focus from the state towards society. However, this can take several forms, with different variants of the broad welfare society model.

The dominant model is based on welfare pluralism or the mixed economy of welfare (see Johnson 1987, 1999), which points out that there are sources of welfare outside the state. Klein (1985) asks us to consider a mythical country whose government decides to keep public expenditure below 25 per cent of gross national product. Instead of introducing a social security scheme or a national health service, it makes it mandatory for every firm to insure its employees and their families. Instead of building motorways, it offers generous tax concessions to turnpike trusts. Instead of subsidizing jobs to prevent unemployment, it offers legislation forbidding companies to dismiss anyone. Instead of spending money on pollution control, it compels the private companies to clean up the polluted air and rivers that they have created. This country has virtually no welfare spending as measured on the conventional public expenditure statistics. Klein goes on to say that the country is mythical, but the instances are actual, reflecting Japan, France, Italy and Sweden, respectively. Rose and Shiratori (1986) argue that 'total welfare' is the sum of state, market, voluntary and informal sources. The welfare mix varies between countries, which means that an *etatiste* definition of welfare, which assumed that the only welfare in society was that produced by the state, is misleading. A crisis of the welfare state is not a crisis of welfare in society. Criticizing this view, Mishra (1990) claims that a focus on 'total welfare' is not simply the 'sum of the parts'. The mix in the 'mixed economy of welfare' cannot be ignored, as the parts 'cannot simply be regarded as functional equivalents', since they are based on different principles and they differ in scope. It is important to distinguish between means and ends. For example, a transfer from state to informal (read: female) care leads to increasing gender inequality and ignores entitlement (citizenship), as there exists no 'right' to charity. In short, it is more than a 'mere rearranging of furniture in the drawing room'.

Some British historians point out the importance of non-state welfare. According to Harris (1992), legislation after the Second World War created in Britain one of the most uniform, centralized, bureaucratic and 'public' welfare systems in Europe and, indeed, in the modern world. Yet a social analyst of a hundred years ago would have observed and predicted the exact opposite: that the provision of social welfare in Britain was and would continue to be highly localized, amateur, voluntaristic and intimate in scale by comparison with the more coercive and *etatiste* schemes of her contintental neighbours (in particular imperial Germany). Daunton (1996) argues that a characteristic feature of Britain in the nineteenth century was the extent to which the provision of welfare, education and culture was left to voluntary societies such as friendly societies and voluntary hospitals. When services were left to public bodies, their finance and administration were usually local, whether boards of guardians with responsibility for the poor, orphans, the old and sick; school boards for elementary education; or borough and county councils for technical schools, asylums and infant welfare. In Victorian Britain, both the expenditure and personnel of voluntarism were greater than those of the central and local state, and those of the local state exceeded those of the central state. According to Lewis (1995), it may be necessary to rethink the nature of the 'welfare state'; rather than seeing the story of the modern welfare state as a simple increase in state intervention, it is more accurate to see Britain as always having had a mixed economy of welfare, in which the voluntary sector, the family and the market have played different parts at different times.

There has been a reaction to the 'whig' account of welfare history in which greater state intervention is seen as inevitable (Finlayson 1994; Daunton 1996; Green 1996; Johnson 1996). Thane (1996: 277) has protested that 'although this was once the ruling paradigm of welfare state histories in the optimistic 1950s and 1960s . . . in the mid-1990s it is difficult to think of a serious historian who has written in this mode for at least twenty years'. She is correct to point out that, since the Conservative government of 1979, greater state intervention is no longer seen as *inevitable*. However, many writers, whether implicitly or explicitly, regard it as *desirable*. Similarly, Finlayson (1994) clearly distinguishes between the arguments that welfare agencies outside the state 'could not cope' and 'should not cope'. In other words, the debate about the appropriate role of the state is a normative one, with traditional disagreements between the political right and left.

Welfare society is a term usually associated with the political right, and is generally associated with a decreased role for the central state. For example, the Institute of Economic Affairs (IEA 1967) produced a report entitled 'Towards a Welfare Society'. This report rejects the monopoly of state welfare, arguing that governments should not provide welfare services that people can provide for themselves. State welfare has reduced individual responsibility. 'The doctrines of state paternalism, equal social benefits and the badge of citizenship teach that a man with a broken leg should be given larger and stronger crutches as society advances. The opposite view is that unless he is allowed and encouraged to put his leg to the ground, tentatively at first but with increasing strength, it will atrophy' (IEA 1967: 19). There should be a greater use of market, charitable and family resources. The report points out that rather than a free, national food service, people are given cash benefits to allow them choice. Likewise, instead of relying on state services in kind, poor people should be empowered by being given cash or vouchers that will allow them greater choice and will restore individual responsibility.

For a time, long or short, there will remain people who are deprived, irresponsible, short-sighted, ill-informed, malleable or gullible. Their children will need protection from them. But the conclusion is that social policy should not treat all citizens as subnormal. It is rather that each individual or family should be socially enfranchised as soon as he or it is capable of exercising responsibility, decision-making and choice.

(IEA 1967: 19–20)

Similarly, Seldon (1996) argues that people should be liberated from the welfare state. Welfare should be re-privatized after 'the lost century' of state control provided inferior welfare as compared to what would have developed with market and charitable alternatives.

A less extreme version of this thesis suggests that the state may reduce its role in the direct provision of services, but still have a role in funding or regulating them (e.g. Burchardt *et al.* 1999). In economics, Keynes (for example, in Pierson 1998a: 26) argued that the state could manage the economy without the need for socialization, as in the form of national-ization as advocated by traditional socialists. This form of Croslandite revisionism (Crosland 1964) has now become part of the Labour Party's revised Clause 4 of their constitution. Like its Conservative predecessor, the current New Labour government sees a larger role for welfare beyond the state (Johnson 1999). For example, the Welfare Green Paper (DSS 1998) hints at a welfare society, stressing a greater role for partnerships between public, private, voluntary and community sectors. This is in line with recent calls to reinvigorate civil society (Blair 1998; Giddens 1998), with a greater role for mutual organizations (Hirst 1994; Green 1996; Pestoff 1998; Field 2000).

A further variant of the welfare society thesis is provided by Robson (1976: 7), who claims that 'The welfare state is what Parliament has decreed and the Government does. The welfare society is what people do, feel and think about matters which bear on the general welfare'. He continues that there is often a yawning gulf between public policy and social attitudes. Unless people generally reflect the policies and assumptions of the welfare state in their attitudes and actions, it is impossible to fulfil the objectives of the welfare state. He concludes that we cannot have a genuine welfare state without a welfare society as its counterpart. So far, we have achieved only limited success in building a welfare state because there are so many elements in our society and our policies that are in conflict with that aim. Robson's focus, then, is on the 'fit' between state policies and public values. It has been claimed that some policies are based on outdated values and assumptions, such as the male breadwinner model (Daly 2000). Some conservatives argue that policies have changed values, such as making single parenthood and withdrawal from the labour market more acceptable (Murray 1996). Field (1996) argues that no welfare system can function effectively if it is not based on a realistic view of human nature. As self-interest, not altruism, is humankind's main driving force, welfare has to reflect the pivotal role that self-interest plays within our motivations and reward good behaviour. In this way, it should enhance those roles that the country values.

A concept that is not usually discussed in the context of a welfare society, but for convenience will be discussed here, is the social division of welfare. This was developed by Richard Titmuss in a lecture in 1956; it was written as a response to those who were arguing that the welfare state was associated with excessive taxation of the rich and the indiscriminate and excessive delivery of benefits to the poor. Titmuss (1963) pointed out that welfare was delivered by fiscal and occupational mechanisms in addition to the more familiar 'social services'. Fiscal welfare refers to benefits delivered through the taxation system, such as tax relief on mortgages and later private pensions and health insurance. Occupational welfare refers to the 'fringe benefits' of employment, such as subsidized pensions, health insurance, mortgages and company cars. Titmuss argued that fiscal and occupational welfare were clearly regressive in nature in that they gave most to those with the higher incomes. In other words, critics of excessive redistribution focused on the 'narrow' welfare state of social welfare and ignored the wider picture that also included fiscal and occupational welfare.

Despite its traditional identification with the political right, a welfare society clearly has a variety of meanings. Consequently, progress towards a 'welfare society' means different things to authors such as the IEA (1967), Titmuss (1968), Robson (1976) and Pestoff (1998).

Following the work of Esping-Andersen (1990), much attention has been paid to the concept of welfare regimes. Esping-Andersen (1990) points out that the welfare state has been approached both narrowly and broadly. The former examines 'the traditional terrain of social amelioration: income transfers and social services, with perhaps some token mention of the housing question' (pp. 1–2). The latter often frames its questions in terms of political economy, including issues such as employment, wages and overall macro-economic steering of the economy within the broad framework of the 'Keynesian welfare state' or 'welfare capitalism'. Welfare state regimes are based on the 'big picture' and seek to offer a reconceptualization and re-theorization of the welfare state in terms of issues such as de-commodification, social stratification and employment (Esping-Andersen 1990). Esping-Andersen (1990: 19–22) suggests a 'content' rather than a 'quantitative' view of the welfare state. He rejects a focus on welfare state spending, arguing that all spending does not 'count equally'. As he points out, 'Few contemporary analysts would agree that a reformed poor-relief tradition qualifies as a welfare-state commitment'. It is important to examine the 'content' of welfare states: targeted versus universal programmes, the conditions of eligibility and services and, perhaps most importantly, the extent to which employment and working life are encompassed in the state's extension of citizen rights. As Myles (1998) points out, a focus on regimes takes us beyond the 'narrow world' of social spending and turns our attention to the larger institutional complex in which social spending takes place (Castles and Mitchell 1992). This broad context involves an examination of types of capitalist system, such as Anglo-American shareholding, European stakeholding, Rhenish and East Asian (Ebbinghaus and Manow 2001). It brings the often neglected world of work, including issues such as industrial relations and minimum wages, into social policy (Whiteside 1996; Cressey 1999; Crouch 1999). Myles (1998) makes the important point that countries with otherwise similar welfare state regimes differ dramatically in programme design (see P. Pierson 1994) and the models they use to finance and distribute benefit. For example, American social security is more similar to that of continental Europe than that of the UK (Myles 1998). However, beyond this example, there is little empirical justification for this assertion. In general, the relationship between the shell and kernel is unclear; for example, do we expect liberal social policy in a liberal welfare regime? (cf. King 1999).

Due to its established position within the literature, we propose to continue with the term 'welfare state' for all its problems. However, we tend to consider the term in its wider context, bringing in features of welfare societies and welfare regimes (cf. Mishra 1990). Although space does not permit a detailed examination, we discuss briefly at various points aspects of employment, taxation, the mixed economy of welfare and the social division of welfare.

In search of the welfare state: the inductive route

Despite the existence of terms such as welfare societies and welfare regimes, most writers, often with reluctance, caveats and inverted commas, use the term 'welfare state'. However, as we have seen, there is no clear, universal definition of a welfare state. In this section, we examine the inductive route, distilling out criteria of welfare states from an examination of the comparative and historical literature.

The comparative literature illustrates that many different states count as 'welfare states'. A crude distinction may be made between the 'wide' and 'narrow' or 'thick' and 'thin' perspectives of the welfare state. At one extreme, the 'historical, comparative, quantitative' literature appears to have a very lenient definition of a welfare state. Orloff and Skocpol (1984: 726) claim that 'Britain was a pioneer in launching a modern welfare state. Before World War I, it instituted workers' compensation, old age pensions, health insurance, and the world's first compulsory system of unemployment insurance'. By 1919, Britain had initiated 'all the key programs of what would later come to be called a modern welfare state'. Similarly, according to Korpi (1989: 310), 'the break between the old poor laws and the new welfare state was based precisely on the introduction of social rights via social insurance'. Finally, Alber (1988) clearly dates the beginning of the welfare state to the end of the last century. It follows that the British welfare state is located in the reforms of the Liberal government of 1906–14. According to this approach, then, 'welfare states' predated the popular birth of the term, and the 1940s saw the development rather than the birth of the welfare state. For example, Flora and Heidenheimer (1981) suggest that modern welfare states developed in the twentieth century. They see three broad stages of welfare state development – experimentation, consolidation and expansion – with the 1940s seen as the consolidation stage (see also Heclo 1981). Pierson (1998a) sets out a similar thesis. Broadly speaking, the 'birth of the welfare state' is located in the period 1880–1914, in terms of criteria such as the introduction of social insurance, the extension of citizenship, the depauperization of welfare and the growth of social expenditure. Welfare states consolidated and developed up to the 1940s, arguably reaching their 'golden age' in the period after the Second World War.

Very crudely, this approach appears to have two key characteristics. First, social insurance is seen as a vital mark of the welfare state, while universality is seen as marking the transformation to a consolidated or mature welfare state. Second, welfare state expenditure is a key measure, and the rise in expenditure suggests earlier origins and continuous development rather than a discrete historical moment.

On the other hand, the broad perspective moves away from definitions based on services and focuses on the 'big picture' of political economy, including issues such as employment. According to some, there is a range of 'welfare states' from the USA to Sweden, which may be displayed either on a quantitative continuum or within a typology (Esping-Andersen 1990; Pfaller *et al.* 1991; Abrahamson 1999). This method generally confirms that 'The Nordic model has commonly been regarded as the embodiment of the highest stage of the welfare state's evolution' (Baldwin 1990: 43). Conversely, Britain and the USA tend to do badly. In short, they are poorly performing welfare states. However, for others, very few countries deserve the term of welfare state. As Furniss and Tilton (1977) put it, only Sweden qualifies as a welfare state, with the USA and Britain being termed a positive state and social service state, respectively. Basing the definition of a welfare state on the criteria of a commitment to full employment, and state responsibility for providing a comprehensive range of universal welfare benefits and services, 'Few would apply the term to Japan . . . and it is doubtful whether it can now be applied to Britain. Only Sweden . . . can still be said to meet the requisite criteria, and that may not be for much longer' (Gould 1993: 3).

The comparative literature has only limited relevance in the debate on the new welfare state in Britain. This is because of the extraordinary elastic use of the term. At one extreme, it has been applied to a multitude of different contexts in time and space (see, for example, Schottland 1967): almost every state is a welfare state. As Hubert Humphrey (in Schottland 1967: 160) claims, 'the welfare state has been an American objective ever since the Constitution was adopted'. On the other hand, there are hardly any welfare states. Comparison with an ideal type means that all existing welfare states will inevitably fall short of perfection. Moreover, countries such as Britain and the USA, to some observers very different, emerge with very similar 'welfare scores'. Indeed, the comparative literature reinforces the anglocentric frame of reference. As there is an extraordinary range of welfare states or welfare regimes, the answer to the question of whether Britain has a new welfare state should be examined not with reference to generic welfare states, but in the context of the British welfare state.

The consensus of the historical literature is that the welfare state in Britain emerged around the time of the Second World War (Marsh 1980; Hage *et al.* 1989; Sullivan 1992; Gladstone 1995). However, in some of these accounts, it remains unclear *precisely* what makes the Beveridge Report or 5 July 1948 the magic ingredient or the philosopher's stone that turns the base metal of the 1930s into the golden age of the welfare state.

In search of the welfare state: the deductive route

It has been shown that it is extremely difficult to reach a consensus on the key characteristics of a welfare state from the inductive route. We now turn to the deductive route, where the welfare state is compared with a range of conceptual criteria. For example, Jones' (1985) study of comparative social policy is based on the questions: what counts? what for? for whom? on what terms? by what means? and to what effect? Mishra (1981) considers criteria such as the state's responsibility in meeting need, the range of statutory services, the population covered by those services, the use of means tests and the status of clients and the proportion of state expenditure spent on state services. Alber (1988) suggests criteria such as the scope, range, quality, instruments, financing, benefit type and redistribution associated with the welfare state.

Perhaps the most interesting approach is that of Johnson (1996), who focuses on four distinct attributes of welfare instruments: the type of risk pool, the nature of redistribution, the nature of entitlement and the structure of management. Their polar types range from comprehensive to exclusive, intrapersonal to interpersonal, solidaristic to contractual, and local to national and private to public, respectively. For the moment, the exact details are not important, but it illustrates the 'multidimensional character of welfare instruments' (Johnson 1996: 231). Using this framework, Johnson finds no simple transition in Britain between 1879 and 1939 from private to public, from 'individualism' to 'collectivism', or from solidaristic to contractual insurance. The picture of a progressive evolution of welfare provision across the twentieth century becomes blurred. The Victorian poor law, for all its faults, was based on the idea of a comprehensive risk pool, of a solidaristic rather than a contractual system of entitlement, and on substantial interpersonal redistribution. The combination of social insurance and social assistance since the Second World War has, in the main, continued to be comprehensive, solidaristic in practice and broadly supportive of interpersonal redistribution. But the Edwardian development of national insurance was a move towards an exclusive risk pool, towards contractual entitlement and towards a self-financing system of interpersonal redistribution. Viewed from this perspective, 'the neat lineages of welfare development from the poor law to Beveridge are seen to be an erroneous historical construct' (Johnson 1996: 245–6).

Perhaps the simplest conceptual framework is to view the welfare state as a production process in which a given structure is meant to produce given policy goals (cf. Castles and Mitchell 1992; Powell 1997a; Glennerster and Hills 1998). Just as a factory produces a given product by spending money on certain production processes, welfare states have goals and attempt to turn inputs into outcomes. This production process model is useful as a heuristic device. This clearly distinguishes means and ends and suggests that the same goals can be met with different means (e.g. a change in structure or expenditure) and that the same means may combine to produce different ends. This framework forces attention at a basic, but usually implicit, question: Is the essence of a welfare state to be found in its aims, its structure, its inputs or its outcomes?

These approaches examine stated aims and objectives. In other words, they are based on 'intrinsic evaluation', examining performance in the institution's own terms (see Powell 1997a, 2002). They cannot say much about the 'hidden' or 'real' aims of policy. For example, Marxists would argue that the state's real aims are to maintain capital, while feminists would argue that the state's real aims are to maintain a patriarchal society. Concentrating on stated aims, our approach is 'narrow' rather than 'broad' and tends to focus on 'governments' rather than 'states'.

We claim that ends are more important than means: the choice of objectives is of primary importance, while the mechanisms of achieving objectives is secondary (cf. Crosland 1964). However, pinpointing the stated goals of welfare states is problematic. This is partly because there is no coherent social theory of welfare (Barry 1999). Goodin (1988: 3) claims that the welfare state is a political artefact, the product of historical accretion and political compromise. Different bits have been added over the years by different people with different purposes in mind. It is not a single unified, unambiguous entity, but rather a ragbag of programmes, only vaguely related and imperfectly integrated. In other words, there is no one overall aim or principle underlying the welfare state. Different services have different aims and objectives. It is of little value searching for the pedigree of the welfare state as it is a mongrel. It is hardly surprising that there is continuing debate about the objectives and principles of welfare state programmes (see Le Grand 1982; Powell 1995a). It remains difficult to distil clear operational goals from the often vague and vacuous soundbites of political pronouncements (Powell 1997a;

Glennerster and Hills 1998). As Goodin (1988) argues, there is no way around this impasse, but it is important to be forthright.

One basic debate revolves around minimum standards (Crosland 1964; Robson 1976; Furniss and Tilton 1977; Glennerster 1995; Powell 1995a) or equality (Le Grand 1982; Bryson 1992)(see George and Wilding 1984). As noted above, there is no overall design principle and some services such as the National Health Service (NHS) tend more towards equality, whereas others such as social security tend more towards minimum standards (e.g. George and Wilding 1984; Powell 1995a). In other words, unpacking the welfare state shows that its different component parts have different aims and mechanisms.

There are two issues that may be thought of as both means and ends. Perhaps the core of the British welfare state is the universalism of its major services in kind. This may be viewed as the means to the end of the universal national minimum (Marshall 1963) and a proxy for achieving the integrative, altruistic society sought by Titmuss (1968; Page 1996). Similarly, full male employment was considered as a means and an end. In the narrow sense, it may be seen as a prop for a contributory insurance scheme. In the wider sense, it is a vital part of the 'welfare regime', with a complete fusion between work and welfare (Esping-Andersen 1990).

Analyses based largely on inputs or expenditure trends are fraught with difficulty (Esping-Andersen 1990; Mishra 1990; Bonoli 1997; Pierson 1998a). As Carrier and Kendall (1986) ask, how much welfare is needed to justify the term 'welfare state'? For example, when the cost of the Old Poor Law rose to almost one-fifth of public expenditure in Georgian England, did that make the state a welfare state? The conceptual problems are that a narrow focus on expenditure might suggest that there was more spending on social security ('good'), but from the wider perspective this can be seen as failure resulting from increases in unemployment (Commission on Social Justice 1994; Blair 1998). It also misses the point that objectives can be achieved in other ways; for example, an active labour market policy may be more efficient and effective than passive financial relief. There are also empirical problems. It is often not clear whether expenditure is nominal, real, volume terms, or adjusted for need/demand/expectations (Hills 1997). Outputs and outcomes have greater direct impact on people than inputs (Hills 1997; Powell 1997a). Taken to its logical conclusion, the idea that a sole focus on expenditure implies greater efficiency – the same provision from less expenditure – is not desirable.

We argue that the structure and mechanisms of the welfare state are more important than aggregate spending. The qualitative issues of the 'texture' or 'character' of the welfare state are more important than quan-titative inputs. One important criterion is whether welfare measures tend to cover everyone or whether they are targeted at poor people. The wel-fare state in Europe tends to include more of the population than that of the USA. A more specific contrast may be made between the universal NHS in Britain and the health programmes in the USA, which are aimed at the elderly and poor people. In theory, council housing in Britain is open to all, whereas there are strict upper income limits on welfare housing in the USA. The arguments favouring universality or inclusion are traditionally based on giving all citizens – rich and poor – a stake in the welfare system. It has been claimed that residual services often become 'poor services' for 'poor people' (Titmuss 1968: 134). A social mix in housing, health care and education delivers equality of status between citizens (Marshall 1963; Crosland 1964; Titmuss 1968; Bevan 1978; Powell 1995a). However, this may disguise a 'false' universalism and an exclusive rather than an inclusive citizenship inherent in the post-war welfare state (Williams 1989; Clarke and Newman 1997; Hughes and Lewis 1998).

Welfare instruments include universalism, selectivity and social insur-ance. Universal services are open to all. The NHS is usually given as an example of a universal service, while child benefit is often an example of a universal benefit. On the other hand, selectivity or means testing delivers the benefit or service after an individual test of means. In Britain, the left has traditionally been opposed to means testing (Titmuss 1968; Field 1996). Many means-tested benefits have low rates of uptake, meaning that some who are judged to need the benefit go without it. However, it is unclear whether this is necessarily the result of means testing or whether it is linked with the particular historical contexts such as the Poor Law and the Household Means Test of the 1930s in Britain. For example, means-tested student grants had a near universal take-up rate in Britain. Means testing is much more acceptable in coun-tries such as Australia. A further problem of means testing is the poverty trap. Benefits are often linked together so that a benefit such as income support acts as a passport to other benefits such as housing benefit, free school meals and free prescriptions. This means that there may be little incentive to take a job, a slightly better paid job or extra earnings through overtime, as the extra income may be outweighed by the loss of total benefit, making the individual worse off. Social insurance is similar in one way to private insurance in that it is a contributory benefit. Only those who have contributed into the scheme may take benefits out. Just as those who have no contents insurance cannot claim if they suffer a fire or theft, only those who are in regular employment and contribute into social insurance are covered in times of sickness or unemployment.

Welfare systems can be measured on their degree of redistribution and de-commodification. Redistribution depends on the relationship between what people pay in and get out. In other words, while distribution depends on the level of benefits and services (Le Grand 1982), the degree of redistribution also takes taxes into account. In this sense, the welfare state in Britain is redistributive, as final income is more equal than initial income (Hills 1997). However, there is some trade-off between redistribution and inclusion (above). As rich people are eligible for the NHS, state education, the state pensions and child benefit, there is inevitably less redistribution than if such benefits were restricted to the poor, which would mean a sharp division between a 'paying class' and a 'benefiting class'. The form of the British welfare state gave a higher priority to inclusion than to redistribution (Powell 1995a).

For Esping-Andersen (1990: 37), the key concept is de-commodification, 'the degree to which individuals or families can uphold a socially acceptable standard of living independently of market participation'. The level of de-commodification depends on structural issues such as the stringency of eligibility rules, the level of income replacement and the range of entitlements. In general, both benefits in cash and services in kind can be de-commodified. An example of a de-commodified cash benefit may be a pension based on citizenship rather than one based on contributory insurance. Esping-Andersen (1990) does not deal in any detail with services, but it may be suggested that services in kind are de-commodified if they are open to all citizens and are free at the point of use. In the view of writers such as Marshall (1963, 1981) and Crosland (1964), free services or de-commodified provision is of secondary importance; a means to an end rather than as an end in itself. Free services cannot be the hallmark of the classic welfare state because some charges came into existence in 1948 and more emerged in the next few years (Powell 1997a). On this reading, it is not the existence of charges themselves that matters, but the implications of those charges. Charges that 'bite', that cause hardship or deter, are important.

The final part of the production process is outcomes. Welfare states may be judged by their population's levels of health or education. As we know little about the production process, it is best to judge by results rather than processes. For example, Rose and Shiratori (1986) point out that, despite relatively low levels of state welfare, Japan is well educated, well housed and healthy.

Finally, it is important to specify the scale of analysis. Analysis of 'the welfare state' as a whole may miss important variations among constituent parts. A welfare state may have a good health policy, but a poor housing policy. Disaggregation shows that change may vary by sector. A focus on the welfare wood may hide changes in individual trees.

Conclusions and plan

There is little consensus beyond 'something happened' in the debate about welfare change. Most writers point to some degree of change in the form of 'restructuring' or some variant of the 'r-word'. However, the debate tends to be conceptually and empirically limited. This is illustrated by different conclusions with different timings. There has always been change in welfare. The question is whether change is sufficient to merit a new label: is there a 'watershed' or a 'new historical moment'? There is a need for greater rigour, particularly with respect to the definitions and concepts of the welfare state, and criteria, measures and parameters of change (see Mishra 1990). In crude terms, the restructuring debate may be characterized as rhetoric in search of rigour, description of policy change in search of a framework and answers in search of questions. It is clear that the debate on welfare change needs an agreed vocabulary and grammar to discuss which indicators and what degree of change should count as decisive. In simple terms, debate requires a dialogue rather than a monologue to talk to, rather than past, each other.

The rest of this book sets out to provide an introduction to this vocabulary and grammar of welfare change. Focusing on the British welfare state, it aims to integrate three main perspectives of description, analysis and explanation. First, there is some descriptive material on welfare change. This is fairly brief, containing just sufficient material to understand the analytical and explanatory material. This brief walk through the welfare woods provides limited detailed descriptions of the individual trees. Readers who are coming to this material for the first time may need to fill in some of the detail from other accounts (see 'Further reading'). Second, the analytical perspective focuses on definitions and measures of welfare change. It aims to throw some light on issues such as how and when basic dimensions of welfare changed. Third, the explanatory perspective considers the competing explanations of welfare change. Which explanations seem to have the greatest coherence? Do new circumstances require new explanations?

There is no fourth perspective of evaluation. We do not set out to judge explicitly which welfare state is 'best'. This is partly because of space constraints, partly because we do not yet have the tools to do so (Thane 1996; but see Lowe 1999a: ch. 11; Powell 2002; Powell 1997a for the NHS) and partly because this question depends on value judgements. In particular, value judgements differ between individuals (even between co-authors) and over time. Very different answers may result if values of contemporaries are compared against those of hindsight. For example, today the harshness of the Victorian New Poor Law may appear very different to contemporaries; and different between pauper and taxpayer then.

Chapters 2–4 describe and analyse the classic, restructured and modern welfare states, respectively. As a heuristic device, we discuss the classic welfare state from the 1940s to the 1970s, the restructured welfare state from then until the 1997 general election, and the modern welfare state from then until the present. These are useful terms to examine periods, but the labels are to some extent arbitrary. The classic and restructured welfare states are in widespread use, and the modern welfare state is New Labour's favoured term to differentiate it from earlier Conservative restructuring. In each of these chapters, we describe the main welfare changes of the period and then discuss whether any significant changes can be detected in terms of aims, mechanisms or inputs, outputs and outcomes.

Chapters 5–8 outline theories of welfare state development and discuss how these theories relate to welfare change. In particular, we search for any breaks of slope associated with our three welfare states. In other words, can the theories account for the classic, restructured and modern welfare states? For convenience, we divide explanations using the concept of welfare settlements. Hughes and Lewis (1998; cf. Hay 1996) break up the 'monolithic welfare state' into four welfare settlements – political, economic, social and organizational – that emerged in the post-war period in the UK. We discuss economic, political, social and organizational explanations.

Finally, we bring the different strands of the book together in Chapter 9. We recognize that this preliminary attempt to focus on the 'what?', 'when?' and 'why?' questions of welfare change covers a great deal of ground. At times readers may feel that our interpretations are at best oversimplified and at worst incorrect. Nevertheless, we feel that our attempt to integrate descriptive, analytical and explanatory dimensions covers important and largely neglected issues in social policy.

Further reading

Cliff Alcock, Sarah Payne and Michael Sullivan (2000) *Introducing Social Policy*. Harlow: Pearson.
Examines recent policy trends that go beyond the 'big five' services, but also has sections on history and the wider context and theory of social policy. Part 3 on theory is particularly useful.

John Baldock, Nick Manning, Stewart Miller and Sarah Vickerstaff (eds, 1999) *Social Policy*. Oxford: Oxford University Press.
A wide-ranging and accessible introductory text. Chapters on policy trends in a wide range of services are at the core of the book, but there are also sections on the history and politics and social and economic context of social policy.

Peter Baldwin (1990) *The Politics of Social Solidarity*. Cambridge: Cambridge University Press.
This is an impressive discussion of the rise of European welfare states from 1875, showing a significant command of detail for individual countries. It is useful to place the British welfare state in a wider comparative context. This book remains the level that comparative writers aspire to, but it is not an easy read.

Tom Burden (1998) *Social Policy and Welfare: A Clear Guide*. London: Pluto Press.
More of a sourcebook than a textbook, but provides brief accounts on a wide range of material in a structured and cross-referenced fashion. Not a book to read from cover to cover, but useful to dip into using the contents pages and the 'hypertext' links in the book.

2 THE CLASSIC WELFARE STATE

Introduction

The period after 1945 has often been termed the 'classic welfare state' (Digby 1989; Lowe 1999a). The term implies that it was perfect. However, Glennerster (1995) argues that the classic welfare state achieved its perfect form in 1948 is a myth (cf. Raban 1986). In this chapter, we describe and analyse the classic welfare state. Was it different from earlier periods? Was it based on a coherent framework? How much did its form vary? We first examine the evolution of the classic welfare state, which, by definition, must be 'pre-classic'.

Pre-classic welfare states

Nineteenth-century welfare

The accounts of Midwinter (1994) and Jones (2000) begin in Medieval Britain, pointing out the contribution to welfare of the church and the early voluntary hospitals such as St Bartholomew's ('Barts') in London. Focusing on the statutory sector, Fraser (1984: 31) begins his 'evolution of the British welfare state' in the fourteenth century, with the paternalistic state's attempts to introduce wage control with the Statute of Labourers of 1351 and the Poor Law Act of 1388. In 1536, parishes were authorized to collect money to support the impotent poor who would thus no longer need to beg: 'The state was thus acknowledging some minimal responsibility for those who were unable to work' (Fraser 1984: 31). Many accounts stress the centrality of the Poor Law. The Poor Law Act of 1601, the '43rd of Elizabeth', codified and superseded all earlier legislation. The key to the Elizabethan Poor Law was classification into three different sorts of treatment for three different sorts of pauper. The first group, the impotent poor (people who were aged, blind, chronically sick and 'lunatics'), were to be accommodated in 'poor houses' or 'almshouses'. The second, the 'able-bodied', were to be set to work in a 'house of correction', not at first residential. Finally, the 'vagrants' were to be punished in the house of correction. As the Poor Law was decentralized and based on the parish, large variations between places existed, making the Poor Law 'a tool of social policy of infinite variety and unlimited versatility' (Fraser 1984: 35). Increasing strains were put on the Poor Law, which was designed for an agricultural economy, by the 'industrial revolution' with its rapid increases in industrialization, urbanization and population growth from about 1800 onwards. The population of Britain doubled between 1801 and 1851 and doubled again in the next 60 years. Decenniel increases of over 40 per cent were common in some of the rapidly expanding towns, such as Manchester, Leeds and Glasgow. Most relief was given to people in their own homes and was termed 'outdoor relief'. There were growing criticisms of outdoor relief, of which the most celebrated, but by no means the sole, form was the Speenhamland system, where wages were supplemented from the poor rates in accordance with the size of the family and the price of bread. Criticism centred on the growing cost of the system, which was thought to undermine work incentives and create a 'dependency culture'.

In 1832, a Royal Commission on the Poor Laws was set up. Its report 2 years later, 'a classic document in the history of English social policy' (Fraser 1984: 41), formed the basis for the 1834 Poor Law Amendment Act and marked the break between the 'Old' and the 'New' Poor Law. The principles of the New Poor Law were 'less eligibility', the workhouse test and administrative uniformity. The main problem of the Old Poor Law was that it was seen as giving paupers on poor relief a higher standard of living than those on the lowest wages. In other words, the system gave perverse incentives, in that workers were, in the words of the Report:

> under the strongest inducements to quit the less eligible class of labourers and enter the more eligible class of paupers . . . Every penny bestowed, that tends to render the condition of the pauper more eligible than that of the independent labourer, is a bounty on indolence and vice . . .
>
> (in Fraser 1984: 258)

The solution was simply to reverse the incentives by ensuring that paupers were always less eligible than the lowest independent labourer. Outdoor relief for the able-bodied would be abolished and genuine need would be established by the workhouse test. Those applying for poor relief would be offered entrance to the workhouse, which would provide basic subsistence but at the cost of a harsh, deterrent regime that included a loss of liberty, family break-up, only minimal food, hard work and uniforms. The smaller parishes were amalgamated into Poor Law Unions, which would provide roughly equal treatment across the country. The system was based on the assumption that people chose not to take available jobs. This assumption clearly broke down in times of economic depression. However, the New Poor Law was never fully implemented. Outdoor relief was never abandoned. In 1846, of 1.3 million paupers, only about 200,000 were 'in', of whom only about 80,000 were able-bodied. Conversely, of the 1.1 million 'out' paupers, nearly 300,000 were able-bodied (Midwinter 1994). Nevertheless, the new regime was successful on its own terms as the costs of poor relief fell.

Another area of state intervention may be seen in public health. Beginning in 1848, a series of Public Health Acts was passed to deal with the public health problems in the rapidly growing towns. These Acts were largely permissive in character. In general, they permitted, but did not force, local areas to carry out environmental or sanitary reform in the shape of the civil engineering solutions of supplying fresh water and sewerage, and some basic building standards for housing. A later extension of public health measures included the Housing of the Working Classes Act of 1885, which accepted the notion of state intervention (Hennessy 1992).

As suggested above, other components of the mixed economy of welfare – voluntary, commercial and informal – pre-date state intervention. Voluntary action is often regarded as being composed of the areas of philanthropy and mutual aid. The scale of philanthropy was significant. For example, in 1861 there were about 640 charities in London with an annual income of £2.5 million, more than that spent by the national Poor Law (Laybourn 1995). Schools were provided by the rival religious organizations representing the established Anglican Church and 'Dissent' associated with the chapels. The government began to give some financial assistance to these organizations in 1833. However, in the 1870 Education Act, the government considered it necessary to fill the gaps with state education. The Act set out to provide elementary schools throughout the country for children up to the minimum age of 10 years. These schools were run by elected school boards. Education became compulsory in 1880 and free in 1891. In some cases, charity tended to provide a parallel system to the Poor Law. For example, voluntary hospitals were financed by the rich to provide a service for the 'deserving poor' (not the 'undeserving poor' of the Poor Law). Indeed, some saw the role of the Charity Organization Society as attempting to provide a filtering role, separating the wheat for the mill of philanthropy from the chaff destined for the poor law (see Laybourn 1995; Lewis 1999). This was later termed a 'parallel bars' system in which the two groups were kept apart. On the other hand, mutual aid consisted largely of the efforts of the skilled working class to help itself. The most notable example was the Friendly Societies, which were based on the principle of contributory benefits. Members paid in contributions each week and were entitled to benefits in times of need, such as sickness and unemployment (Green 1998). Building Societies were another example of mutualism. Those not covered by mutualism were forced to buy certain services such as the services of a 'general practitioner'. By its very nature, informal care tends to be hidden outside the formal system. For example, there are few statistics concerning the hours of care given. However, although difficult to quantify, it is likely that informal care has always been significant (Lewis 1999).

Liberal social reforms

The early years of the twentieth century saw a number of significant moves in welfare. Concerns about the physical fitness of volunteers in the Boer War (1899–1902) led to the setting up of the Interdepartmental Committee on Physical Deterioration. Its report in 1904 suggested that school meals and medical inspection should be undertaken within the state educational system. These were introduced in 1906 and 1907 respectively. A Royal Commission on the Poor Laws (1905–09) issued a Majority and Minority Report. Both reports agreed on some matters, such as the abandoning of the harsh 'principles of 1834' and the transfer of functions from the Poor Law Guardians to the local authorities. The Majority Report was based on 'orthodox' opinions and on views of the Charity Organization Society. Those who signed the Minority Report included the Fabian Beatrice Webb and the future leader of the Labour Party, George Lansbury. Although the aim of the Majority Report was to bring all paupers under the auspices of a single committee of the local authority, the Minority wished to 'break up the poor law'. This would mean treating all citizens under committees based on functions such as health and education, rather than a separate committee dealing solely with the client group of paupers.

After their landslide election victory in 1906, the Liberals introduced some significant welfare measures. In 1908, the Old Age Pensions Act introduced a non-contributory pension for the 'very poor, the very respectable and the very old' (Thane 1996: 77). In 1909, the Chancellor, David Lloyd George, introduced his 'People's Budget', 'the most famous in modern English History' (Fraser 1984: 156), which levied progressive income tax and heavy duties on unearned income such as sales of land. Lloyd George termed it a 'War Budget': 'It is for raising money to wage inplacable warfare against poverty and squalidness'. As Fraser (1984) comments, it was frankly and overtly redistributing wealth through taxation, seeking to raise revenue by taxing the wealthy few for the benefit of the penurious many. In contrast to the non-contributory pension of 1908, the most notable feature of Liberal social policy was the emphasis of the contributory principle of social insurance. The 1911 National Insurance Act was composed of two parts. The first, associated with Lloyd George, was concerned with health insurance and essentially nationalized the insurance schemes operated by the Friendly Societies. All workers earning less than £160 a year were required to contribute a flat rate amount of 4 pence a week into the scheme. This entitled them 'as of right' to sick pay of 10 shillings a week and the services of a doctor selected from a panel. The second part of the Act, associated with Winston Churchill, was concerned with unemployment insurance. It forced workers from certain industries to pay a contribution of $2\frac{1}{2}$ pence a week. In return, they were entitled to receive unemployment pay at 7 shillings a week, up to a maximum of 15 weeks, and one week's benefit for every 5 weeks of contribution.

By their nature, contributory insurance schemes gave benefits only to those who had contributed. This shows a clear division between benefits directed at workers and at citizens. Contributory schemes largely operate on the assumption of a 'male breadwinner model', where the male worker brings home the family wage and women and children benefit by their attachment to the male worker (Williams 1989; Hughes and Lewis 1998; Daly 2000).

Inter-war social policy

Welfare reform continued during and after the First World War. At this time, approximately 90 per cent of all households rented their accommodation from private landlords. During the First World War, some landlords attempted to increase rents while the workers' income was largely static. This led to industrial action by munitions workers in Clydeside, which is generally seen as the reason for the government introducing rent control in 1915. In 1918, Fisher's Education Act raised the school leaving age to 14. With Lloyd George's slogan of 'Homes fit for heroes', the Housing and Town Planning Act of 1919, associated with Christopher Addison, gave local authorities the duty of building council houses, which was to be subsidized by a central grant. Reconstruction measures were curtailed by the expenditure cuts of the 'Geddes Axe' in 1922. In 1925, contributory pensions that delivered a pension between the ages of 65 and 70 were grafted onto the existing non-contributory scheme, resulting in a complex system (Fraser 1984).

However, unemployment – or, more specifically, male unemployment – was to become the central problem of the inter-war period (Fraser 1984; Crowther 1988). From the end of 1920 until the Second World War, unemployment was never below one million and at times was above three million. The National Insurance Scheme struggled to cope with the structural unemployment of the inter-war years, where large areas, particularly in Scotland, Wales and northern England, saw the collapse of basic industries such as coal, steel and shipbuilding. Mass unemployment caused a decline in the numbers in work paying contributions and a rise in the numbers out of work and receiving benefit. In addition to the financial problem of paying the legitimate benefit of insured workers, there was the political problem of dealing with those who had exhausted their benefit or who had never earned the right to benefit. Most of the inter-war period saw the almost annual juggling of levels of contributions and benefits and the grafting-on to the insurance scheme of a series of devices that sought to preserve the fiction of insurance, but in reality were a system of thinly disguised outdoor relief (Fraser 1984). The problem of unemployment is often associated with the collapse of the Labour government in 1931, when the Labour Prime Minister Ramsay MacDonald agreed to head a national government. The national government cut insurance benefits by 10 per cent, standard benefit was limited to 26 weeks and transitional benefit was to be administered by the Public Assistance Committees of the local authorities, which were empowered to administer a stringent household means test. This meant that an unemployed man, who prided himself on being the traditional bread-winner of the family, could find benefit refused and being told to rely on a few pennies earned by a child's paper round. In effect, unemployed people were thrown back to the *de facto* Poor Law. However, there were wide local variations in the generosity of the Public Assistance Committees. In particular, some Labour councils made great efforts to protect unemployed people from the worst effects of the Depression. The 1934 Unemployment Act attempted to remove unemployment from inconsistent local control. The responsibility for those without entitlement to insurance benefit was effectively nationalized, being handed over to the national Unemployment Assistance Board. In this way, the local 'Poor Law' lost its responsibility for able-bodied adults.

Welfare outside the state continued (Lewis 1999; May and Brunsdon 1999). Those such as women and children, largely excluded from the National Health Insurance scheme, continued to rely on mutual and private sources. Health care, to some extent, remained a purchased commodity, with services ranging from spectacles from 'Woolworths' to health insurance from organizations such as BUPA. Housing remained 'the most important form of commercial welfare' (May and Brunsdon 1999: 279). As Hennessy (1992) puts it, housing was one of the few success stories of interwar Britain: 'more homes were built for the heroic (and the less heroic) than in any comparable period in British history' (p. 169). A major part of this growth was in owner-occupation. Between 1914 and 1938, the number of owner-occupied houses quadrupled and owner-occupation rose from 10 to 32 per cent of the housing stock. Verdicts on the buoyancy of the voluntary sector remain mixed (Finlayson 1994), but most accounts stress that the relationships between the statutory and voluntary sectors changed over time. Beveridge pointed to a 'perpetually moving frontier for philanthropic action' (Finlayson 1994: 259–60), while Macadam (1934) argued for a 'new philanthropy' based on a partnership between statutory and voluntary sectors.

The classic welfare state

The Second World War brought changes such as evacuation, food rationing, the abolition of the household means test and greater planning for both the economy, such as the manufacture of armaments, and welfare, such as the Emergency Medical Scheme (Titmuss 1950; Hennessy 1992; Page 1996: ch. 3).

The Beveridge Report of 1942 is often seen as a historical moment of wartime reconstruction and the blueprint of the welfare state. Beveridge saw the problem as defeating the 'five giants' of want, disease, ignorance, squalor and idleness. At the heart of his solution was a flat rate social insurance scheme. This means that all workers paid in a flat-rate contribution and received a flat-rate benefit in times of need. This was underpinned by means-tested national assistance, designed to deliver the universal 'national minimum'. Above the minimum, Beveridge considered that individuals should build their own extension ladder of private and voluntary welfare above the state minimum. For the scheme to work, the assumptions of full (male) employment, a national health service and family allowances had to be in place. As with the previous insurance schemes, Beveridge assumed a 'male breadwinner model' in which it was expected that married men would work to bring home the family wage, while married women would not generally engage in paid work. In Beveridge's famous words, 'she has other duties', which were largely in terms of unpaid care in the household (see, for example, Williams 1989; Hughes and Lewis 1998).

Planning for post-war reconstruction commenced during the war under the coalition government, following the broad outlines of, although not the exact shape of, Beveridge's vision (Hewitt and Powell 1998). The coalition government produced White Papers on education, health, employment and social insurance and produced the Butler Education Act 1944. After Labour's election landslide in 1945, Acts followed on health, national insurance, national assistance, industrial injuries, family allowances and housing. On 5 July 1948, the appointed day, the whole apparatus of what came to be called the welfare state moved into operation.

It is generally claimed that the years to the 1970s saw few *major* changes, being marked by continuity and incrementalism (e.g. Glennerster 1995; Timmins 1996). There was a bi-partisan or 'Butskellite' consensus about the broad shape of the welfare state, the mixed economy and full employment. After Labour was defeated in 1951, there were Conservative governments until 1964, which critics saw as 13 wasted years. Labour was in office in the period 1964–70, followed by the Conservatives in 1970–74.

Although the Labour government implemented the main structures of the Beveridge Report, there were some differences on matters of detail. In particular, Labour was more generous in promising full pensions at the inception of the scheme, rather than allowing entitlements to build up over the next 20 years, but less generous in deciding on levels of benefit that appeared to be lower than those deemed adequate (Glennerster 1995; Hewitt and Powell 1998; Lowe 1999a). In the 1950s, the Conservative government accepted a report that regarded an adequate pension for all as an 'extravagant use of the community's resources'. This meant that, rather than withering away as desired by Beveridge, means-tested assistance benefits expanded to become the base of the national minimum. In this sense, one of Beveridge's main aims, adequacy of benefit 'as of right', was abandoned (Glennerster 1995). Far from being slain, Beveridge's giant of want re-emerged in the 'rediscovery' of poverty in the 1960s. Similarly, there were bi-partisan moves away from the Beveridge flat rate package towards a graduated structure of contributions and benefits, where those who paid in more got higher benefits in return. Although agreed on the general principle of graduation, the 1970s saw Labour and Conservatives developing conflicting detailed plans on pensions, with one of the main points of difference being the Conservatives' emphasis on occupational pensions (Glennerster 1995; Hewitt and Powell 1998; Lowe 1999a).

In education, the major debates centred around comprehensive as opposed to selective education, and the role of private education. Some writers argue that Labour was conservative in following the Butler 1944 Education Act, resulting in a 'tripartite system' of grammar, technical and secondary modern schools. Critics argued that a child's destiny was often determined by performance on a single day on the '11+ test', with those that 'passed' going to grammar schools and the 'failures' consigned to the more poorly resourced secondary moderns. The Labour Minister of Education, Tony Crosland, issued Circular 65/10 'requesting' local authorities to present schemes to move to comprehensive education. When the Conservatives returned to office, Margaret Thatcher withdrew Crosland's circular, but it was too late to stem the comprehensive tide, which appeared to be little influenced by the political party in office at either central or local level. Thatcher, as Secretary of State, presided over a period when the number of comprehensive schools rose more rapidly than at any other time. By the time she had left office, the proportion of children attending comprehensives had doubled to over 60 per cent (Sullivan 1996). In the 1960s, Labour set up the Public Schools Commission, which issued two reports, neither of which led to much action before Labour left office in 1970 (Glennerster 1995). Mrs Thatcher's period as Education Secretary was a 'masterpiece in contradiction' (Sullivan 1996: 159). After opposing comprehensive education, she abolished free milk for schoolchildren, which saved about £8 million per year, and became popularly known as 'Margaret Thatcher, milk snatcher'. Yet, she became 'a conventional expansionary education minister' (Sullivan 1996: 159), raising the school leaving age and saving the Open University from closure. She issued a White Paper entitled 'Education: A framework for Expansion', which called for 90 per cent of 4-year-olds to be in nursery education, 40 per cent more teachers and a 60 per cent growth in places in higher education within the next 10 years.

In housing, owner-occupation and council housing continued to expand while private renting continued to fall. As the minister responsible for housing in 1945, Aneurin Bevan insisted on high standards in council housing, hoping that this would attract the social mix that high-quality health care had attracted to NHS hospital wards (Powell 1995a). However, ministers later sacrificed quality for quantity, which resulted in housing being a 'numbers game' in which stress was placed on the number of houses built rather than the quality of homes. This trend was accelerated by the move towards tower blocks that won architectural awards, but became unpopular to live in. The Conservative goal of a 'property-owning democracy' slowly became Labour policy in the light of electoral realities. Lubricated by tax relief on mortgages (an excellent example of fiscal welfare), owner-occupation became the 'normal', majority tenure. However, moves to promote the market in private renting were less successful. The Conservatives attempted to reverse the decline in private renting through the 1957 Rent Act, 'the most contentious and bitterly fought legislation of the period' (Glennerster 1995: 83). The Conservatives argued that private renting was in decline because of a shortage of supply. Rent control meant that landlords were not able to get an 'economic rent' for their properties and so rents were deregulated. After the 1964 election, Labour repealed the Act and replaced it with 'fair rents'. In 1972, the Conservatives attempted to redirect housing subsidies away from buildings and towards people. This meant examining the whole area of housing subsidy across council housing and private renting, but not the mortgage tax relief associated with owner-occupation. In practice, this focus on equity across the two tenures meant that rent for council houses tended to rise.

The area of health care saw a major hospital building programme. The 1962 Hospital Plan was designed to achieve an equal distribution of hospital beds across the country, located in new district general hospitals. It was also a period of reorganization. Most commentators agreed that the tripartite system in the NHS was far from ideal. However, while there was general agreement on the diagnosis, there was little on the solution. Labour issued two Green Papers in 1968 and 1970. However, the Conservatives brought forward a different reorganization in 1973 that was due to be implemented in 1974.

Similar structural issues were debated in social services. Following the Seebohm Report of 1968, the previous departments in local authorities dealing with children and elderly people were brought together in unified social service departments, forming the 'Fifth Social Service' (Hill 1993; Glennerster 1995; Timmins 1996; Lowe 1999a).

Accounts of the classic welfare state generally give limited attention to other parts of the mixed economy of welfare (but see Finlayson 1994; Johnson 1999; Lewis 1999; May and Brunsdon 1999). However, private services continued in areas such as health and education and, as we have seen, debates around the role of the state versus the market were central to housing. Owen (1965: 527), in a famous phrase, termed the voluntary sector the 'junior partner in the welfare firm', with its role to supplement and complement state provision (Lewis 1999). Some voluntary organizations adapted to new roles. From the 1960s, a new generation of volunteers set up self-help and campaigning bodies such as Shelter and the Child Poverty Action Group. The role of informal care, by family, friends and neighbours, began to be increasingly recognized. In particular, feminists pointed out the gendered assumptions in caring, exposing the vast amount of unpaid care that borders on 'compulsory altruism'. Similarly, greater attention was directed at fiscal and occupational welfare. Mortgage tax relief has already been mentioned. Perhaps the most obvious example of occupational welfare is occupational pensions, which perpetuate inequality during work into 'two nations in old age' (Titmuss 1963: 74).

In search of the classic welfare state

This section examines whether the classic welfare state was different from previous periods and whether it remained constant until the 1970s. Some writers see the Old Poor Law as a 'welfare state in miniature' (Thane 1996: 278). Similarly, it is clear that the New Poor Law catered for a wide range of circumstances (Johnson 1996). Writers such as Sullivan (1996: 4) view Liberal social policy as 'the embryonic welfare state'. Thane (1996: 90) points to a 'quite remarkable shift in social action by the British state in the period between 1906 and 1914'. As shown in Chapter 1, some comparative writers see the emergence of the welfare state in this period (see, for example, C. Pierson 1998a).

Some argue that the welfare state was present before the Second World War. For example, Gilbert (1970: 308) claims that, by 1939, 'the British State had committed itself to the maintenance of all its citizens according to need as a matter of right'. Similarly, according to Political and Economic Planning (PEP 1937), 'Never before have the public services of the state been so continuously and intimately bound up with the family life of *ordinary* citizens as they have been in recent years' (p. 10, emphasis added). Some argue that municipal welfare or the local welfare state was significant. As early as 1889, Sidney Webb observed that municipal services impinged on many areas of life (in Fraser 1984: 112). The phrase 'cradle to grave' is often used in connection with the period after the Second World War, but a Labour MP argued in 1945 that 'local government touches our lives at all stages from the cradle to the grave' (Powell 1995b: 361; see also Powell 1998; Powell and Boyne 2001).

However, Gladstone (1995) and Sullivan (1992) write that there is general agreement that Britain's classic welfare state was established in the 1940s. According to Hage *et al.* (1989), the historical moment is the Beveridge Report and the 1945 Labour government. As Marsh (1980) considers that there seems to be a widely held view that it was born on 5 July 1948 (cf. Laybourn 1995), 'The fifth of July 1948 was welfare state day . . . one of the great days in British history' (Hennessy 1992: 174, 143).

It is often argued that the classic welfare state as part of the Butskellite consensus lasted into the 1970s (see Hewitt and Powell 1998). For example, Gough (1991) writes that over the next three decades, there were many changes in the welfare state, but only SERPS involved fundamental reform, all others were 'incremental encrustations on the basic Beveridge/Butler/Bevan edifice' (p. 135). Taylor-Gooby (1988: 1) asserts that 'The British welfare state developed for some three decades more or less consistently within a framework laid down at the end of the Second World War'. Glennerster (1995: 2–3) contends that the social legislation of 1944–48 'does constitute one of the most coherent and long-lasting institutional legacies in modern British history ... Although many adaptions were made to this design in the next forty years, it was not really until the late 1980s that a similar concentration of social legislation was to occur that had a similar coherence'. On the other hand, some writers claim that significant changes occurred before the 1970s (Webster 1994; Brigden and Lowe 1998). For example, Glennerster (1995) claims that the period 1951–64 had a distinctive Conservative face. This is particularly the case for housing – 'to suggest that it had no distinctive policy is simply incorrect' (Glennerster 1995: 74) – and for education – 'The Conservative Party in 1951 therefore came to power with a distinctively Conservative liberal agenda on social policy. It had not accepted the 1945 Labour institutions or indeed those of the Second World War "consensus". It had its own coherent, and arguably far-sighted, set of policies' (Glennerster 1995: 75).

These views are examined in a little more detail using the analytical framework developed in Chapter 1 of aims, mechanisms, and inputs, outputs and outcomes.

Aims

At the risk of some oversimplification, there are two broad approaches that examine the aims of the classic welfare state. 'Hard' or 'maximalist' accounts examine welfare aims in terms of citizenship or equality (e.g. Le Grand 1982). 'Soft' or 'mimimalist' accounts point to a more limited agenda of the national minimum or 'mimimum universalism' (Powell 1995a; Tomlinson 1998). Both are partially correct (and incorrect), as the term classic welfare state conflates very different parts with different aims. In crude terms, the welfare state is a hybrid of a Beveridge welfare state for benefits in cash and a Marshall welfare state for benefits in kind. The former aimed to produce a national minimum (Crosland 1964; Robson 1976; Furniss and Tilton 1977; Marshall 1981; Glennerster 1995; Powell 1995a) using an extension ladder. There was to be little clear redistribution other than across the life cycle and within classes rather than between classes. Want was one of Beveridge's giants; inequality was not (Bradshaw and Deacon 1986). This conception of freedom from want fits well with the concept of absolute poverty. Beveridge (1942) considered that benefits should rise periodically in line with prices. However, it was no business of the government to provide for more than a subsistence minimum (Glennerster 1995; Hewitt and Powell 1998; Lowe 1999a). This fits well with Esping-Andersen's (1990) characterization of Britain as a 'liberal welfare state'.

However, services in kind were based on the Marshallian concept of citizenship or the optimum rather than the minimum. For example, the NHS clearly de-commodifies and, consequently, fits with Esping-Andersen's (1990) notion of a social democratic welfare regime. It is more reasonable to view equality as an aim for services in kind, but it is clear that at one level the British welfare state was never intended to deliver more than a limited notion of 'equality of entitlement' or status (Marshall 1963; Crosland 1964; Powell 1995a). On the other hand, the radical nature of fellowship (Tawney 1964) and Bevan's social mix in health and housing (Bevan 1978; Powell 1995a) have not been achieved. This agenda of qualitative socialism, Christian socialism and English ethical socialism has not been fully recognized (but see Harris 1987; Powell 1995a).

In spite of their vital importance, the distinction between the 'national minimum' and 'guaranteed minimum', 'floor level' and 'voluntary action', 'extension ladder' and 'superstructure' (Beveridge 1942; Marshall 1963) are little discussed in many standard accounts. In other words, it was not clear exactly what was part of the base and what was part of the superstructure. For the base, national minimum benefits in cash could be defined precisely in pounds, shillings and pence. But benefits in kind given to individuals because of their particular needs and capabilities, as in health, social care and education, were less clear. If the problem of defining the base, platform or minimum in the 1940s was difficult (Marshall 1963), then it is more so today in a much more complex world, with its greater life-span, affluence, widening inequalities, consumer expectations and medical technology.

The Beveridge and Marshall tradition was clear on the importance of the national minimum. Any provision outside the state was in addition to the minimum and formed part of the superstructure enhancing individual choice and protection beyond what the state provided. However, there appears to be a contrast between their positions on the relationship between the floor and superstructure. Marshall (1963) considered that in some sectors such as health care, the guaranteed minimum has risen to such a height that the term 'minimum' becomes a misnomer, with the intention to make it a reasonable maximum so that the extras which the rich are able to buy will be no more than frills and luxuries: 'The provided service, not the purchased service, becomes the norm of social welfare' (Marshall 1963: 108). Subsequent social democrats like Crosland (1964) considered that social equality mainly required the creation of standards of public health, education and housing so high that no marked qualitative gap remained between public and private provision. The position of Beveridge is less clear. While Beveridge (1942, 1948) is clear on the importance of voluntary action with respect to cash benefits, supporting a significant extension ladder leading to a large cash difference between the state minimum and the voluntary maximum, he was more ambivalent concerning benefits in kind. On the one hand, he talks of a comprehensive state health service (Beveridge 1942), but on the other hand saw old people's homes as an area for voluntary action, a need that would remain in a 'social service state' and, by implication, not part of the state minimum (Beveridge 1948). As Williams and Williams (1987) comment, Beveridge supposed that whereas the state provided money, voluntary action could provide services (see Beveridge 1948: 319–24, especially p. 320: 'the State is or can be master of money, but in a free society it is master of very little else'). Williams and Williams continue that his position on voluntary action remains unclear. However, Beveridge considered that the relationship between state and voluntary action, and by implication between national minimum and extension ladder, would not be static. In a famous phrase, he talked to the 'perpetually moving frontier for philanthropic action' (Finlayson 1994: 259–60). In spite of the many problematic points of detail, it may be possible to tentatively advance potentially important differences in the degree of class abatement (Marshall 1963) or social equality (Crosland 1964) between the Beveridge and Marshall welfare state (see Hewitt and Powell 1998).

Some see moves towards equality later in the period of the classic welfare state (Glennerster 1995; Hewitt and Powell 1998; Powell and Hewitt 1998). If this analysis is correct, it follows that there was a major, and largely unheralded, change in ends. As the emphases changed from the national minimum to equality, 'the old politics of social policy began to give way to the new in the 1960s' (Glennerster 1995: 98). Concern shifted from absolute to relative poverty. In other words, while the traditional meaning of poverty meant freedom from want, the new conception was concerned with the position of poor people in relation to the wider population. In other words, inequality, like poverty, was rediscovered when the original Beveridge goal posts were shifted. Digby (1989: 74) argues that:

> Some commentators have effectively replaced the objectives of the welfare state of the forties with those stemming from socialistic

egalitarianism, and a relativistic conception of poverty based on quite different tenets of Edwardian Liberalism; Beveridge may have had more sympathy with New Right than left in the 1980s . . . The egalitarian welfare ideals of the sixties seem . . . to have become practically obsolete to a greater extent than the more limited ones of the classic welfare state of the forties.

Mechanisms

Midwinter (1994) argues that the scenario of the 1945–51 welfare state as a novelty is a false one. It is the strength of the consolidation that should be stressed. Many of the mechanisms were similar. For example, Butler saw his Education Act as merely 'codifying existing practice' (Digby 1989: 57). Midwinter (1994) notes that the notion of a national scheme of contributory social insurance dated back to 1878. However, this understates the importance of the classic welfare state. Some of the mechanisms were old, but the aim of universalism was original, and the key to the classic welfare state may be seen in the new relationship between ends and means. The whole was more than the sum of its parts. As Marshall (1970: 76) argues, 'We adopt the term "Welfare State" to denote this new entity composed of old elements'. As Beveridge put it, 'The scheme proposed here is in some ways a revolution but in more important ways it is a natural development from the past. It is a British revolution' (in Marshall 1970: 76).

The classic welfare state contains two key differences with respect to means (cf. Gladstone 1999). First, it is based on a 'cradle to grave' universalism. As Briggs (1961) points out, it is the third part of his definition, embracing the *de facto* universalism of social citizenship, that marks the distinctive characteristic of a welfare state (Spicker 1988; Lowe 1999a). 'By the outbreak of the Second World War, Britain's welfare system remained residual and partial and directed almost exclusively at the working class' (Gladstone 1999: 31). 'A decade later the "classic" welfare state was both more universal in its coverage of the population and more comprehensive in the range of the services it provided'. 'If the essential theme of the 1930s had been selectivity, that of the 1940s was universalism' (Fraser 1984: 207). It was the universality of provision that constituted the claim of the post-war Labour governments to have established something qualitatively new or a 'welfare state'' (Thane 1996; see also Marshall 1970; Spicker 1988). Second, it uses the 'full use of the powers' of the state to maintain full (male) employment. This illustrates the importance of Keynesian demand management to the classic welfare state.

The classic welfare state made two sharp breaks. First, it completed the Liberal agenda of divorcing provision from the Poor Law. At one level, the Poor Law was comprehensive and universal (Johnson 1996). A person who was sick, hungry, unemployed or old could turn to the Poor Law, but the shame of being a pauper hid, in the words of Lloyd George, 'a mass of poverty and destitution which is too proud to wear the badge of pauperism' (in Fraser 1984: 154). Two methods emerged from the shadow of the Poor Law, undercutting its client base and beginning to make it wither on the vine. The first method was insurance for health, unemployment and pensions. The different eligibility and different character of policy meant that old age pensions were not simply a nationalization of outdoor relief (Midwinter 1994). This new birth-right, a part of citizenship, not a deprivation of it, paid 'as of right', set the Liberals firmly on a course which was to involve basic departures in social policy (Fraser 1984). As Lloyd George noted (in his diary):

> Insurance necessarily temporary expedient. At no distant date hope state will acknowledge full responsibility in the matter of making provision for sickness, breakdown and unemployment. It really does now through Poor Law, but conditions under which this system has hitherto worked have been so harsh and humiliating that working-class pride revolts against accepting so degrading and doubtful a boon. Gradually the obligation of the State to find labour or sustenance will be realised and honourably interpreted. Insurance will then be unnecessary.
>
> (in Fraser 1984: 163)

As Fraser (1984: 175–6) puts it, 'one cannot escape the conclusion that Liberal social policy before the First World War was at once at variance with the past and an anticipation of radical changes in the future'. The classic welfare state completed the agenda of twentieth-century social policy through adding dignity to security (Hennessy 1992). Welfare subjects were citizens rather than paupers or non-citizens associated with the Poor Law (Marshall 1963). In other words, Esping-Andersen's (1990) stress on de-commodification is historically inaccurate, as welfare states tended not to rescue citizens from the market, but from the Poor Law. It follows that more accurate terms may be destigmatized or depauperized. However, as we have noted, there is a problem in using the language of citizenship as some benefits were tied to contributory insurance and given to workers rather than citizens. Critics have argued that this created a false or nominal universalism, in which some social divisions such as race and gender were associated with second-class citizenship (e.g. Williams 1989; Hughes and Lewis 1998).

Second, the classic welfare state was largely national in character. Previously, local welfare states varied from place to place (Powell 1995b). The inter-war period is often regarded as the high water mark of local autonomy (Powell and Boyne 2001). 'Some policy was innovatory, particularly in council housing and in a hospital system which relied neither on charity nor the Poor Law' (Crowther 1988: 73). However, 'the years of depression from 1929 reinforced the centralising tendency of social policy' and 'In their tendency to centralise policy, interwar governments moved closer to the Welfare State' (Crowther 1988: 59, 73). As Fraser (1984: 154) puts it, 'Much of the social policy on the twentieth century road to a Welfare State has been concerned with removing categories of need from the remit of the Poor Law and providing socially more acceptable alternatives'. From this perspective, municipal- and insurance-based welfare carried a symbolism that far outweighed any evaluation based on expenditure or welfare effort.

There appears to have been some variation in means over time. For example, Bridgen and Lowe (1998) claim that the period of Conservative rule between 1951 and 1964 was not quite the pedestrian period of consensus; beneath a broad agreement over means and ends, there remained considerable differences between the major parties and within the Conservative Party itself. Some believed that the state should be 'rolled back', including education vouchers, student loans and hospital 'hotel charges', which were to enter the policy debate again after 1979. Bridgen and Lowe (1998) see the Conservative term of office as setting the people free (1951–58) and creating an opportunity state (1958–64) as opposed to a welfare state.

On the other hand, the 1964–70 and 1974–79 Labour governments (see Chapter 3) attempted to 'complete the post-war agenda' and introduce a new social policy agenda (Glennerster 1995: chs 5–7). These governments are often given little credit (e.g. Townsend and Bosanquet 1972, Bosanquet and Townsend 1980). Certainly, their success may have been limited and their tendency to be blown off course by economic difficulties started to look like an unfortunate habit. Nevertheless, they had clear aims and mechanisms that do appear to be distinctive from the restructured welfare state (Chapter 3).

The character of the classic welfare state changed over the 30 or so years from 1948. There were moves from a flat-rate to a graduated social insurance scheme. Means tests moved centre stage to become a permanent fixture rather than declining over time as intended by Beveridge. The balance between public and private and that between base and superstructure varied over time (Hewitt and Powell 1998). However, the main structures from 1948 were still clearly in place.

Inputs, outputs and outcomes

At a general level, it may be claimed that the twentieth century has seen more or less continuous increases in welfare inputs, outputs and outcomes. A more detailed analysis may show variations from year to year and between services, but the overall picture is clearly one of increasing expenditure, staffing and a more healthy and educated population (Hills 1997; Glennerster and Hills 1998). Two issues must be briefly addressed. First, the links between these concepts are far from clear. Although welfare expenditure or 'welfare effort' is commonly regarded as a basic indicator of welfare statism, our knowledge of the 'production process' or 'what works' remains limited (e.g. Davies *et al.* 2000). The old assumption that more spending automatically leads to better outcomes has been subject to criticism from both academic (Esping-Andersen 1990; Bonoli 1997) and political quarters (Commission on Social Justice 1994; Blair 1998). Second, it is not clear whether a 'break of slope' can be detected. In other words, one method of distinguishing the classic welfare state may be based on dating its inception with a significant increase of expenditure and its demise with a plateau or fall in spending increments. This is a complex exercise, but there is probably more justification for detecting a break signalling its inception in the 1940s than for its demise (Hills 1997; Glennerster and Hills 1998; Gladstone 1999: ch. 5).

Conclusion

We have argued that it is possible to point to the emergence of the classic welfare state, which is distinctive in terms of aims and mechanisms, in the 1940s. It is marked by a universal national minimum outside the Poor Law. It is important to stress its hybrid nature, with different aims and mechanisms for services in cash and in kind. Critics have pointed out that in theory and in practice some were more equal than others and that there were second-class citizens (e.g. Williams 1989; Hughes and

Lewis 1998). We do not deny these points, but still claim that historically – with all its faults – the classic welfare state marked a major advance. We have claimed that the classic welfare state was more limited in conception than is sometimes claimed, approximating to the minimalist rather than the maximalist version. As Sullivan (1996: 75) puts it, Labour's welfare state was 'ameliorative, rather than egalitarian, in intent as well as in outcome'. Nevertheless, this limited notion of citizenship did constitute an important, albeit incomplete, break with 'pre-classic' welfare states. This may be minimized by critics with the benefit of hindsight (e.g. Hay 1996), but any historical analysis based on the symbolism for contemporaries and the 'emotional factor in history' (Hennessy 1992) points to a significant break. The classic welfare state did experience some major changes in the 30 or so years under review but none was significant enough to change its fundamental character. In the next chapter, we examine the question of whether the classic welfare state was restructured.

Further reading

Derek Fraser (1984) *The Evolution of the British Welfare State*, 2nd edn. Basingstoke: Macmillan.
Written by a 'real' historian, with useful documents given in the appendix. It is particularly strong on the period before the 1940s that we have termed the 'pre-classic welfare state'. This authoritative account has become a standard text that has been reprinted many times.

Howard Glennerster (2002) *British Social Policy Since 1945*, 2nd edn. Oxford: Blackwell.
Covers a wide range of issues and is particularly strong on the classic welfare state. It provides authoritative yet accessible arguments by an author who was an active participant in many of these debates that shaped the classic welfare state.

Robert Page and Richard Silburn (eds) (1999) *British Social Welfare in the Twentieth Century*. Basingstoke: Palgrave.
This contains excellent accounts of the main state services of the classic welfare state, as well as material on the often neglected areas of commercial, occupational, voluntary and informal welfare.

Nicholas Timmins (2001) *The Five Giants*, 2nd edn. London: Harper Collins.
Written by a journalist, this is the most readable 'biography of the welfare state'. It covers everything you want to know about the British welfare state from Beveridge to Blair, with extensive bibliographical notes and an index as well as photographs. Perhaps not quite beach reading, but this is one of the most exciting books available on social policy.

3 THE RESTRUCTURED WELFARE STATE

Introduction

This chapter examines the restructured welfare state, focusing on the period from the mid-1970s through the Conservative governments of 1979–97. The term 'restructured' is no more than a convenient term in fairly common currency to describe recent welfare change. As there is a continuing debate about the extent and timing of restructuring, we examine welfare change under the Labour governments of 1974–79 and the Conservative governments of 1979–97, subdividing the latter into the first two terms in office of 1979–87 and the last two terms of 1987–97. Does this period show a new and distinctive welfare state? If so, does the turning point come in the 1970s under a Labour government or later with the Conservatives?

Restructuring the welfare state

Labour 1974–79

The Labour government of 1974 under Harold Wilson was constrained by a narrow Parliamentary majority and by economic difficulties. The period was also marked by problems of industrial relations. As Timmins (1996) points out, the Labour government came to power in the aftermath of the miners' strike against the previous Conservative Heath government. The Labour government would be defeated after the 'winter of discontent'. The Labour government attempted to make a 'social contract' with the trade unions. In return for an increased 'social wage', the unions would moderate their wage demands. This meant 'an initial flurry of action on social policy' (Hill 1993: 108). The period was later described by Joel Barnett, the Chief Secretary to the Treasury, as 'spending money which in the event we did not have'. He continued that, 'the only give and take in the social contract was that the Government gave and the unions took' (in Timmins 1996: 316). The wider economic context saw the end of the long period of economic growth that caused problems for social democratic governments such as 'Old Labour'. The main problems included concerns with public expenditure, rising unemployment and the co-existence of inflation and economic stagnation that was termed 'stagflation' (see, for example, Dell 2000; Thomson 2000; C. Pierson 2001).

A major area of activity fell within the province of Barbara Castle, Secretary of State at the Department of Health and Social Security (DHSS). Her immediate problem was to decide what to do with legislation pending from the previous Secretary of State, Sir Keith Joseph, on pensions and NHS reform. A major NHS reorganization was scheduled within about a month of coming to office. Labour, in opposition, had voted against these reforms. However, as Castle put it in her diary, 'it was too late to unscramble Sir Keith's eggs' (Powell 1997a: 71) and some minor changes were made to make the structure more democratic. However, on pensions, Castle rejected Joseph's scheme that was on the statute book waiting to be implemented. Labour dusted down their 1960s files and, according to the Permanent Secretary at Social Security, attempted to 'design a new plane from the models that have crashed on the runway'. This model combined the best of Crossman and Joseph, in a way acceptable to the Conservative opposition and the occupational pensions lobby (Timmins 1996). Under this 'last great bipartisan social security development' (Timmins 1996: 347), state earnings related pensions (SERPS) were to build up over 20 years, with full pensions being paid in 1998. This graduated scheme would be built on an individual's best 20 years of earnings, with recognition of caring resulting in being 'the most advanced in the world in terms of equal rights for women and carers' (Glennerster 1995: 114). The basic state pension was to be uprated annually to the higher of increases in prices or earnings. A further bipartisan measure, although one which would cause internal divisions within the Labour Party, was child benefit. This universal benefit would usually be paid to the mother and would replace the tax allowance that previously went to the male earner. This led to a battle between 'purse and wallet', with some in the party arguing that this transfer might lose male votes. Similarly, both parties were turning away from Beveridge's adequacy based on insurance and acknowledging a larger role – arguably reluctantly for Labour, more enthusiastically for the Conservatives – for social assistance. In 1978, a DHSS document frankly admitted that little could be done to stem the growth of means testing. In the words of Timmins (1996: 352), this meant that 'Beveridge's minimal safety net was now formally acknowledged as a permanent and "mass" part of the scene'.

In the NHS, Labour recognized different types of inequalities (Powell 1997a). It introduced a formula that reallocated NHS funds from 'overprovided' areas such as London to 'underprovided' areas such as the North and Midlands. A document on 'priorities' attempted to steer more resources to the 'Cinderella groups', such as the mentally ill, mentally handicapped and elderly patients in long stay hospitals, 'the slum of the NHS'. A committee was set up to investigate inequalities in health. However, the most visible aspect of Labour's health policy was its ideological crusade to phase out private practice or 'pay beds' from the NHS. This was seen by the Labour left as removing one of Bevan's compromises that was perceived to be a blot on the NHS landscape. A prolonged period of industrial unrest involving the consultants and NHS ancillary staff led to a reduction in pay beds. However, this led to an increase in private insurance and the number of beds outside the NHS. 'By an awful irony, Barbara Castle had become the patron saint of private medicine' (Timmins 1996: 340).

Labour's first act on housing was to freeze council house rents. It then passed the 1975 Housing Act, which amended the 1972 Act, returning to local authorities the power to set their own rents and so essentially 'a return to the status quo before 1972' (Hill 1993: 119). This period also saw the Housing (Homeless Persons) Act of 1977. This was the result of a Private Member's Bill rather than being the direct result of government legislation. It gave local authorities the responsibility to provide accommodation for certain priority groups such as families with children.

Labour wanted to end privilege and selection in education. Its principal targets were the direct grant schools and the remaining grammar schools. The Conservative council of Tameside refused to comply with Labour's 'requests' to go comprehensive. In a legal battle, the Law Lords decided in Tameside's favour. This prompted Labour to change from its previous 'circular route' to direct legislation. The 1976 Education Act ended direct grants to the private grammar schools and compelled the remaining grammar schools to go comprehensive. Of the remaining 150 direct grant schools, 51 became comprehensive schools; the rest became independent. 'If Mrs Thatcher had been responsible for overseeing the biggest growth in comprehensive education, Labour now found itself creating more independent schools than any government in living memory' (Sullivan 1996: 160). As Timmins (1996: 20) puts it, 'In one of those ironies which litter the tale of the welfare state [compare health, above], a move aimed at reducing divisions in the state sector in fact enlarged the private one'. In 1976, James Callaghan, the new Prime Minister, made a speech at Ruskin College, calling for a 'great debate' on education. He argued that education was failing to provide the skills needed for a modern economy and that there should be a move towards technical and vocational education. His 'Ruskin speech' criticizing the producers of education, in particular the teaching unions, marked a break with Labour's relationship with the producers and set a tone that was to become clearer under the Conservatives and New Labour.

Most social policy accounts see the later years of the Labour government as a disappointment (e.g. Bosanquet and Townsend 1980). According to Hill (1993), it is tempting to analyse the 1974–79 Labour government in terms of pre- and post-IMF, or Wilson and Callaghan as Prime Minister. Glennerster (1995) claims that most of Labour's period in office after the IMF visit in 1976 was concerned with the battle with inflation, the statutory limits to pay and cuts in public expenditure. However, Timmins (1996: 317) argues that 'the 1974–9 government saw a period of much light and shade; of marked progress as well as distinct setbacks, not all of which fall neatly into pre- and post- the IMF crisis'. Many on the Labour left saw it as a betrayal, which led to the lurch to the left of the party and the defection of some Labour MPs to the newly formed (and short-lived) Social Democratic Party (SDP). It is clear that, 'By July 1978, the thirtieth anniversary of the welfare state, the Labour Government was plainly running out of steam' (Timmins 1996: 353). As Shaw (1996) puts it, the government gave an impression of struggling to do its best in extremely bleak conditions, where the familiar landmarks were vanishing, and where few of the levers used in the past to control events worked any longer. With all its policy eggs in the Keynesian basket broken, Labour had few answers to problems of employment or inflation. As Glennerster (1995) puts it, with no new policies or a new strategy, the government tightened its belt and hoped for the best.

Conservatives 1979–87

The first sentence of the first Conservative White Paper on public spending stated that 'Public expenditure is at the heart of Britain's present economic difficulties' (in Timmins 1996: 371). This view implied that the welfare state was a parasite, sucking the lifeblood from the more productive parts of the economy. This meant that the balance of public and private spending had to be changed through tax cuts and rolling back the state. Chancellor Geoffrey's Howe's first budget of 1979 reduced the top and standard rate of income tax. It also announced the breaking of the link between pensions and earnings. Further chipping away at public spending included a series of cuts in social security benefits, an attack on benefit fraud and a freeze in child benefit. These cheese-paring cuts failed to halt the rise in the social security bill. This is hardly surprising as, unlike other services, social security could not be cash limited. In particular, the large rises in unemployment meant that the cost of unemployment benefit spiralled. A review of social security was set up. As the opening sentence of the resulting 1985 Green Paper put it, 'To be blunt the British social security system has lost its way'. The Minister, Norman Fowler, had styled his review as a 'New Beveridge', but it fell well short of this claim in terms of reception and coherence. Most responses to the Green Paper disagreed with its proposals. Many of these proposals involved some rebadging and retrenchment of benefits. According to Timmins (1996), the most important change was the initial attempt to abolish SERPS, which became a dilution of the scheme. There were also several highly symbolic changes. Instead of meeting 'exceptional needs' with grants, the 'Social Fund' gave loans from a local capped budget as a last resort after approaches to the voluntary sector had failed. Similarly, the symbol of the 'cradle to grave' welfare state was ended with the termination of maternity grant and death benefit, which had limited monetary value as they had withered on the vine for many years (Timmins 1996).

In education, the government attempted to reduce local authorities' obligations to provide school meals and transport. The latter was defeated in the House of Lords. R.A. Butler, in his last intervention in public life, defended the provisions of his 1944 Act, arguing against the government's attempts to break his 36-year-old promise (Timmins 1996). The same legislation introduced greater choice in education. Parts of Labour's 1976 Act were abolished, allowing local authorities the choice to retain selective education. Instead of being based on school catchment areas on a map in the town hall, parents were allowed a greater say in the choice of their children's schools. The Assisted Places Scheme allowed children to attend independent schools using means-tested public money. Termed elitist and divisive by the Labour opposition, the commitment to abolish the Assisted Places Scheme was one of the few to survive the transition from Old to New Labour (see Chapter 4). In 1986, city technology colleges were introduced. They were intended to specialize in technological subjects. Industry would work in a partnership with government, providing some funding. Very few city technology colleges developed.

The NHS underwent a further reorganization in 1982, only 8 years after the last one. A greater market orientation inside and outside the NHS was sought (Powell 1997a). Inside the NHS, Roy Griffiths, the managing director of 'Sainsburys', was asked to conduct a review of NHS management. The resulting Griffiths Report, a 24 page letter, led to 'the most important single change to the NHS since 1948' (Timmins 1996: 409). Griffiths argued that the NHS needed a clearer management and more attention to the needs of its patients or 'customers'. General managers, the counterparts of industry's managing directors, were appointed at all levels of the NHS. They were to make use of performance indicators to see how well they were performing. The market orientation was also clear in the policy of compulsory competitive tendering. NHS hospitals were forced to put their 'hotel services' such as laundry, catering and cleaning out to tender. The 'in-house' workers were forced to compete with private companies. The lowest tender would normally win the contract and any savings were to go to patient care. Optical and dental services drifted into the realm of the market. Those who were formerly entitled to NHS spectacles were given vouchers that they could use in the market. Proponents argued that this policy would extend choice for customers and enforce competition among producers. In many parts of the country, it was difficult to find a NHS dentist as adults were 'encouraged' to take out a dental insurance plan. Outside the NHS, the Conservatives encouraged private practice in word and deed. Some people felt pushed into the arms of the private sector as pieces such as dentistry fell off the edge of the NHS, and government ministers stressed the pressures of the NHS and the attractions of private medicine. Perhaps the most serious piece to fall was in the area of continuing care, where it became increasingly clear that the NHS was pulling out of long-term care and 'persuading' elderly people that they should move to long-term residential care that was means tested rather than free and, in the case of the richer residents, was to be financed through selling their homes.

In most of the areas discussed above, the welfare state was chipped away rather than being rolled back. Although new principles such as choice and competition were stressed, the main elements of continuity were still visible. However, two areas that arguably show the most important changes in the first two Thatcher governments were housing and employment.

The 1980 Housing Act contained provisions to increase the market in private renting through creating 'assured' tenancies, which allowed landlords to charge 'market rent' for new dwellings, and 'shorthold' tenancies, which limited the time of the rental contract and allowed the landlord to repossess the property at the end of this term. The aim of these measures, like the 1957 Rent Act, was to stimulate the private rented sector by swinging the pendulum back towards the landlords. However, the most important provision of the Act was in public housing, where council tenants were given the right to buy their properties. There was a generous scale of discounts based on the length of tenure. Long-standing tenants could buy at about half market value. Council house sales were termed 'the biggest single privatisation of the Thatcher era, raising £28 billion over thirteen years – more than the sales of gas, electricity and British Telecom put together' (Timmins 1996: 380). This 'Sale of the Century' was selective in that the richest tenants tended to buy the best houses in the most desirable areas. This produced a residualization effect whereby the remaining properties tended to be houses or flats in the least desirable areas housing the poorest people. Bevan's dream of a high-quality, mass tenure of socially mixed tenants was becoming a nightmare of 'no go areas' of tower blocks and estates plagued by crime and unemployment.

Unemployment had been for many years a key issue for governments. As we have seen, it was a major concern for inter-war governments leading to the collapse of the 1929 Labour government. After 1945, governments of both parties attempted broadly to maintain full (male) employment using a variety of techniques. The Conservative opposition criticized the rise in unemployment under the Labour governments of 1974–79, culminating in the 1979 election slogan 'Britain isn't working'. However, in government, the Conservatives refrained from intervention in the economy, viewing the market as the medicine to remedy the 'British disease' and transform industry into a leaner, more competitive alternative. Unemployment increased, prompted in 1981 by 'Howe's most vigorously anti-Keynesian Budget yet' (Timmins 1996: 388). The unemployment total hit three million, with the result that unemployment benefit contributed to the spiralling social security budget. Glennerster (1995: 177) sums up this period of the first two terms of Conservative government with the words 'containment, continuity and tentative change'.

Conservatives 1987–97

Mrs Thatcher claimed that the Conservative 1987 election manifesto was the 'best ever' (Glennerster 1995). The third Thatcher government (1987–90) is often regarded as the most radical. In social policy, the most notable feature was the introduction of internal or quasi markets, which separated the financing from the production of welfare.

Education was one of the first areas of social policy to be examined after the 1987 election. Education Secretary, Kenneth Baker, introduced a wide-ranging 'Great Education Bill'. Baker's GERBIL, as it became known, contained many broad areas: sweeping changes to schools, the introduction of a national curriculum and testing, changes to universities and polytechnics, and abolition of the Inner London Education Authority. According to Timmins (1996: 442), 'No legislation since Bevan's NHS had aroused so much professional opposition. No measure had taken so much parliamentary time'. The proposals contained a mix of centralization and decentralization. A greater proportion of education expenditure was to be devolved to the school, reducing the power and expenditure of the local education authority (LEA). Some schools, termed grant-maintained schools, were able to opt out of LEA control, following a ballot of parents. The idea was that parents, rather than the LEA, would have greater power in choosing schools for their children. Funds would be determined by the number of children that the schools attracted. The idea was that schools would compete for pupils. The best schools would get more pupils and more money. As with city technology colleges, relatively few grant-maintained schools developed. On the other hand, there was some centralization in the introduction of a national curriculum and national tests. The polytechnics were removed from the LEAs. Under appointed local boards, they were re-named universities. There was a determined attempt to tackle student finance. It was pointed out that the UK was one of the few countries to give grants to students. In 1990, the student grant was frozen and 'top-up' loans were introduced.

In housing, the policy of individual council house sales was beginning to run out of steam, as the best buys and the richest tenants had long since disappeared. The level of individual discounts was increased, but attempts to get the state out of landlordism now switched from a retail to a wholesale concept, from individual sales to block transfers. Tenant's Choice allowed 'social' landlords to take over estates or a whole local authority's stock of council housing. Housing Action Trusts were allowed to take the most rundown estates over. After repairing the estate, the trust would dispose of the properties. There was yet another attempt to revive the individual private landlord. The tenancies created in 1980 were extended, tilting the scales further towards the landlord in terms of level of rents and the length of tenancy. Glennerster (1995: 196–7) points out that, despite the radicalism of the housing policy, much of it remained 'a dead letter' as 'no market for poor tenants' custom existed'.

Similar radical intentions were apparent in social security, where John Moore was appointed Secretary of State. Despite a manifesto commitment that 'child benefit will continue to be paid as now', it was frozen in 1987 and 1988. As Timmins (1996) points out, freezing universal benefit pushes more people into 'dependency' of means-tested benefits. The right to income support for 16- and 17-year-olds was withdrawn as part of the government's guarantee of a Youth Training Scheme place to all those not in work or education. The theme of 'responsibility' permeated a number of policies. First, the Child Support Agency (CSA) was created in 1990 with the aim of recovering maintenance costs from absent fathers. It is based on the principle that fathers should not be able to escape their responsibilities and pass the costs of raising children totally to the taxpayer. Although there was widespread support for this principle, the CSA became one of the biggest administrative fiascos in the history of the welfare state. Second, paying the interest on a mortgage in the first months of unemployment was transformed from a public to a private responsibility. Individuals were encouraged to take out private insurance to cover such an eventuality. This essentially marked the end of the state basic minimum for housing support. The third policy of 'jobseeker's allowance' emerged later in John Major's period as Prime Minister (see below).

There was little in the Conservative manifesto about the NHS. However, the NHS was widely perceived to suffer a funding crisis in the winter of 1987–88. Mrs Thatcher surprised almost everyone, including by many accounts her Cabinet, by announcing on the 'Panorama' TV programme a fundamental review of the NHS. From this review evolved the quasi market in health care. Health authorities would be 'purchasers' and hospitals would become 'providers'. Health authorities would contract with providers to fulfil the needs of their residents. General practitioners could choose to become general practitioner fundholders (GPFH), essentially providers of GP services and 'mini-purchasers' of secondary care for their list of patients. At the margins, there were moves from the state towards the market. Tax concessions for elderly people to purchase private health insurance were introduced. Free eye tests and dental checks were withdrawn.

Glennerster (1995) states that the community care reforms had little to do with community care as such and a lot to do with saving public expenditure. Old people with limited assets were entitled to have their fees in residential homes paid by public money. This 'almost perfect voucher scheme' paid for by 'an open cheque book' led to the spiralling of expenditure in the 1980s. It also had the perverse effect of paying for an expensive option that many old people did not want, while no money was available to support many old people's preferred option of remaining in their own homes. Roy Griffiths was persuaded to produce a Report, which is often known as the 'Second Griffiths Report'. He argued that local authorities should be given the role of 'enabling', although not necessarily providing community care. Care managers, in consultation with their clients, would purchase a package of care from a variety of sources, although the government ensured that much of this would come from the private sector. This would ensure that people's choices were met from a level playing field between community and residential care.

The field of local government finance, traditionally not an area of 'high politics', was an unlikely one to contribute to Mrs Thatcher's resignation. The Conservatives had long regarded the local rates or property taxes as unfair and unaccountable, as only a small percentage of the local electorate paid full rates. They argued that this led to the problem of 'free riders', as many local voters could vote for high-spending parties (read: Labour, especially in some large cities) and receive the benefits of local services without paying the full cost. In other words, the situation was the reverse of the famous slogan of the American Revolution. Americans complained that they were taxed without representation. The Conservatives argued that many local voters were represented without being taxed. They proposed a flat rate local 'community charge' that soon became known as the 'poll tax'. Mrs Thatcher's association with the unpopular poll tax was soon to be a major reason contributing to her resignation as Prime Minister in 1990.

It is difficult to sum up the policy direction of the new Prime Minister, John Major. On the one hand, Major is said to have consolidated the Thatcher agenda (Hay 1996). For example, the replacement of unemployment benefit with the jobseeker's allowance in 1996 may be seen as part of moves towards greater responsibility and conditionality. Timmins (1996: 515) notes that this was the 'first time entitlement to a weekly national insurance benefit to which people had contributed had been cut back'. Unemployed people are given an allowance, but in return they have to show what steps they are taking to find work. King (1999) regards this contractarian or quasi-workfare scheme as 'the biggest change in the dole system since 1948' (p. 248). On the other hand, Major allowed some significant increases in NHS spending, presided over a large expansion in higher education and abolished the poll tax. His 'big idea' was the Citizen's Charter. This gave citizens a set of rights in services as diverse as health, education and transport. However, many of these rights turned out to be largely empty, consisting of a consumerist charm offensive and more related to an individual consumer's or citizen's rather than a collective citizens' charter. Major unexpectedly won the 1992 election. However, he had little opportunity to stamp his identity on policy as the Conservatives lurched from a recession in the south to the farce of 'Black Wednesday' when almost hourly rises in interest rates could not prevent an eventual withdrawal from the European Exchange Rate Mechanism. From then onwards, Citizen John increasingly looked like the manager of a losing team, with its only policy of grimly hanging on to power until the voters put it out of its misery at the following election.

In search of the restructured welfare state

Some writers suggest that the mid-1970s saw the end of the classic welfare state (e.g. Krieger 1986; Sullivan 1992; Hill 1993; Glennerster 1995; Lowe 1999a). Pierson (1998a) sums up this line of argument that, in more or less apocalyptic terms, 1975 [or 1976] is often seen to mark the end-point of nearly 100 years of welfare state growth and to bring the threat or promise of its imminent dismemberment. Some precise timings have been offered for the ending of the classic welfare state. According to Timmins (1996), the defining moment came on 28 September 1976 when Chancellor Denis Healey, due to fly to an international conference, returned from Heathrow to face a financial crisis where the pound was falling fast against the dollar. Next day, the Labour government applied to the IMF for a loan, which was granted with conditions of cuts in public expenditure. On the other hand, attention has been focused at Prime Minister Callaghan's speech at the 1976 Labour Party conference, announcing the formal break with Keynesianism. Callaghan stated that: 'We used to think that you could spend your way out of recession . . . I tell you in all candour that option no longer exists . . . The cosy world . . . where full employment would be guaranteed by a stroke of the Chancellor's pen cutting taxes, deficit spending – that cosy world is gone'. According to Timmins (1996: 315), 'It was the moment which marked the first great fissure in Britain's welfare state'. On this view, the election of the Conservative government in 1979 merely accentuated and exacerbated existing trends (Raban 1986).

On the other hand, some writers seek to 'play up' 1979 (e.g. Corrigan 1979; Leonard 1979; Loney 1986; Wicks 1987). For example, Walker (1997) views 1979 as a 'watershed in social policy'. Continuing our 'choose-a-date' chronology, Gough (1991: 123) argues that 'It was the 1981 budget which more than any other signalled a shift in the responsibilities of government in guaranteeing the welfare of its citizens'. He continues that 'in some ways 1981–1982 marked a watershed' (p. 124). Similarly, Mishra (1990: 30–1) quotes the *Guardian*, which saw the1988 budget that lowered the top rate of tax to 40 per cent representing 'the final disappearance of the last vestiges of the post-war consensus'. Yet more writers emphasize the 'resilient welfare state': the first two terms of Conservative government were not associated with significant changes to the welfare state (Taylor-Gooby 1988; Le Grand 1991; Glennerster 1995; but see Page 1995, 1996). However, some authors claim that the welfare state did change in the third term of Conservative government. Conservative Minister, David Willetts, saw 1988 with the Education Reform Act, the NHS Review, the (second) Griffiths Report and the Housing Act as the *'annus mirabilis* of social policy' (Timmins 1996: 433). Gough (1991: 135), with his third bite at the chronological cherry, claims that 'In retrospect, 1988 may mark the year when the British "welfare statism" was finally and radically restructured'. Le Grand (1991: 351) views 1988 as the year that may come to be seen as 'the one when the dog finally barked'. Some authors continue to view the welfare state as resilient. For example, Riddell (1991) claims that most parts of the welfare state basic principles remain largely intact. According to Gladstone (1995: 1) there are significant continuities: 'Fifty years on, the essential features of the classic welfare state are still visible'. C. Pierson (1994) writes that British social policy is marked quite as much by long-term continuity as by radical change. Klein (1993) argues that the Keynesian welfare state emerged virtually intact from the 1980s, discomforting those who had written its obituary. There were no dramatic changes in welfare state institutions, policies and programmes. Marsland (1996) regrets that the current reforms leave the fundamental *status quo* of the welfare state largely intact. No privatization has been introduced and the state retains its monopoly.

Aims

There are some clear differences between the Labour and Conservative governments in this period. Labour made genuine efforts to reduce inequality in several areas through both progressive taxation and specific policies in areas such as the NHS. In contrast, the Conservative government's accepted and promoted inequality, radically reducing the highest rate of income tax, and prioritizing efficiency over equity in many policy areas. For example, according to Digby (1989), the 1988 budget rejected the tradition of progressive taxation as a tool for equality since the budget of 1909. She goes on to record that this strikingly regressive 1988 budget was seen by Mrs Thatcher as 'an epitaph for socialism'. The Conservatives linked benefits to prices rather than earnings, which 'effectively rejected the idea of relative poverty' (Timmins 1996: 376). This is because as earnings generally increase more than prices, benefits linked to prices mean that no-one is worse off in an absolute sense, as their benefit allows them to buy the same shopping basket of goods as the previous year. However, there will be a growing gap between the living standards of workers and those on benefits, making the latter worse off in a relative sense to the rest of society. Some commentators have raised the spectre of a residual welfare state. Digby (1989) claims that, with the election of successive Thatcher governments after 1979, the Butskellite consensus on welfare ended, with the long-term aim of replacing what remained of the universality of the classic welfare state by state welfare of a more residual kind. Wicks (1987: 89) points to the 'Conservative strategy' of moving towards a residual welfare state, a return to Poor Law principles and an increase in alternative sources of welfare – 'the ideological trinity of market, voluntarism and family'. Townsend's (1995) attempt for the prize for dramatic overstatement is the claim that Britain is already close to becoming a residual welfare state. There is little doubt that the welfare state has become more residual over time. There is no longer *a* national minimum, but a series of residual minima, associated with different groups and with different levels of conditionality (Powell and Hewitt 1998). There are more and larger holes in the safety net, but to claim that it closely resembles the Poor Law regime or the American welfare state owes more to melodrama than analysis. Indeed, in *some* ways the Conservatives moved towards our 'minimalist' conception of the classic welfare state. The link of bene-fits to earnings and the state earnings related pension (SERPS) are not timeless features of the classic welfare state, but innovations of the 1970s. Ironically, they date from a time that some commentators regard as being after the classic welfare state.

Similarly, the Conservatives' stress on private insurance *may* be com-patible with the concept of the national minimum and the extension ladder. The problem involves making a clear distinction between the base and the superstructure. Even if this was clear in 1948, there is no reason why the division remains static over the next 50 years. Some Conservatives wished to replace the welfare state by a 'welfare society' of the future where 'an increasing share of provision will be made by indi-viduals, families and companies' (Lilley, in Timmins 1996: 514). Sim-ilarly, John Moore argued (using words that could easily be those of Tony Blair; see Chapter 4) that '1987 is very different from 1947 ... Life has changed, people's expectations have changed and it's necessary for what we call our welfare state to change as well ... away from dependency and towards opportunity' (Digby 1989: 109). In short, the death of redistributive politics (Mishra 1990; Gough 1991) and increasing inequality (Johnson 1990; Wilding 1992) may be evidence that the welfare state might be retreating back to its more limited Beveridge agenda.

Mechanisms

Several writers focus on the changing structure of the welfare state in terms of the mixed economy of welfare or welfare pluralism (Wilding

1992) or privatization (Ruane 1997). Johnson (1990) argues that the welfare state has been reconstructed, with a reduced role for the state and increases for private, voluntary and informal welfare: 'The main pillars of the welfare state have been, or are in the process of being, transformed' (p. 220). However, it is unclear whether this refers to the role of state funding, provision or regulation. Is the concern associated with a move away from state provision *per se* or is welfare pluralism seen as a Trojan Horse for decreasing state funding? Similarly, according to Sullivan (1996), quasi markets are seen to insert market mechanisms and concede the principle of the mixed economy of welfare. Their introduction has 'moved the NHS nearer to the private model and 'has made the privatisation of the service in the future a much shorter step' (p. 115). In this view, quasi markets are not seen as a neutral technique to achieve ends, but as distributional mechanisms whose operation has to be located in political space (Cutler and Waine 1997).

As we saw above, private protection has a significant place in the restructured welfare state. It is used for pensions, long-term residential care, mortgage insurance and dental insurance. However, there is no clear argument of principle about its use. Although it is possible to argue that pensions above a basic minimum were not part of the classic welfare state, NHS dentistry certainly was. There has been no debate that 'dental health' is not part of the NHS. Similarly, the trend towards means testing in social security is a clear break with the classic welfare state.

The mid-1970s abandoned one of the major assumptions of the Beveridge Report as full employment, one of the original props of the welfare state, was kicked away (Lowe 1999a). Lowe (1999a) argues that the main casualty of the classic welfare state was the commitment to full male employment; throughout this carnage, the social services remained largely unscathed. Put simply, this is essentially Beveridge without Keynes (Sullivan 1996). While both governments appear to have abandoned Keynesianism, Mishra (1990) argues that it is a mistake to overlook important differences between the Callaghan and Thatcher governments. The new Conservative government 'introduced a qualitatively new dimension to the picture' as basic objectives and methods of the welfare state were abandoned. In other words, it is necessary to look beyond outputs to intentions and objectives. Mishra appears to be arguing that abandoning full employment is different if forced by external forces or chosen as a matter of policy. Moreover, is full employment possible with the new pressures and external forces of globalization? (P. Pierson 1994; Esping-Andersen 1996; Taylor-Gooby 1997; Mishra 1999). To equate the classic welfare state solely or largely with the era of full male employment runs the risks of two possible errors. First, it assumes that full employment could be fully explained by the successful application of Keynesian economic management; a result of deliberate government action as opposed to the happy coincidence of sustained economic growth. Second, it relegates all other activities of the welfare state in importance and ignores the contribution of the welfare state in times of recession (see Hills 1997).

Inputs, outputs and outcomes

Many early discussions of restructuring focused on expenditure and, in particular, on 'the cuts', placed firmly in inverted commas to emphasize the complexity and contestability of the concept (Wilding 1992). Labour Cabinet Minister Tony Crosland's claim in 1975 that 'The party is over' implied a clear discontinuity in public spending. The share of the nation's resources going to social policy was to stabilize and then decline in the period 1981–90, the first time this had happened in the twentieth century except as a consequence of war (Glennerster 1995). Some of the early studies cried wolf at a declining rate of increase of expenditure (Pierson 1998a). Many of these cuts were in fact no more than reductions to previously planned increases in spending, but a sharp psychological shock to the world of incremental growth (Glennerster 1995). We have already noted that analyses based largely on expenditure trends are fraught with difficulty (Esping-Andersen 1990; Mishra 1990; Pierson 1998a). It is necessary to examine spending by sector. Aggregate cash transfers increased, but in a world of mass unemployment and an ageing population this is inevitable. A series of cuts in eligibility attempted to rein back individual entitlement, but the aggregate social security bill increased as it covered a lot more individuals. Apart from public housing, expenditure on most areas of service provision increased. However, most individuals judged services not by their increase in cash terms, but whether the spending was sufficient. For example, in the NHS demographic push, technological pull and growing expectations meant that the real increases in NHS expenditure were not judged sufficient and led to the perceptions of a service in crisis (Powell 1997a). Similarly, most indicators of outputs and outcomes continued to increase (Glennerster and Hills 1998). There is little evidence to support Gough's (1991: 147) claim that 'welfare statism has been rolled back over the past decade and a half in respect of inputs, outputs and outcomes'. According to Le Grand (1991), contrary to popular perception, indices of welfare inputs, outputs and outcomes in key areas such as education, health care and community care had either remained constant or had actually risen over the period, even when changes in need were taken into account. There were significant exceptions, notably in housing and in some areas of social security, but the overall picture was one of a possibly surprising degree of resilience. Glennerster (1995) writes that it suits both left and right to foster the myth that the state was rolled back by Mrs Thatcher. However, as we saw above, while this is valid in quantitative terms, the extent of changes to the character of the welfare state in terms of aims and mechanisms are less clear.

Conclusion

The debate about the restructured welfare state remains confused. Early verdicts of substantial change have largely been replaced by accounts that stress greater continuity (cf. Ferrera *et al.* 2001; Leibfried 2001; P. Pierson 2001). Reports of the death of welfare are premature (Timmins 1996; Powell and Hewitt 1998). This general verdict hides much variation between areas. Timmins (1996) argues that only in pensions and housing was the state rolled back. If housing provided both one of the sharper policy breaks as well as the biggest single instant cut in welfare state expenditure, 'education policy initially continued largely down the 1970s road. It did so, however, on a less lavishly provided highway' (Timmins 1996: 382). In short, we have a resilient welfare state that is not reduced in scale, but is reduced in scope. In terms of our criteria, we conclude that the aims of the restructured welfare state are not radically different from those of the classic welfare state. However, this hides the distinction between the frustrated egalitarian and redistributive agenda of Labour in the 1970s and the Conservatives. There has been a major shift on means, with both governments moving away from Keynesianism and universalism. However, while this was a matter of policy choice for the Conservatives, for Labour it was more due to being adrift in uncharted waters, battered by financial problems where the old policy levers seemed no longer to work. Finally, inputs, outputs and outcomes do not appear to clearly mark the boundaries of the classic and restructured welfare state. Although it is difficult to pinpoint a single historical moment of transition, we consider that the most important changes came in the Conservative period of office, notably the third term of 1987–92, rather than during Labour tenure.

Further reading

Mark Drakeford (2000) *Privatisation and Social Policy*. Harlow: Longman.
Covers many aspects of the Conservative's restructured welfare state, with some briefer material on New Labour.

Howard Glennerster and John Hills (eds) (1998) *The State of Welfare*, 2nd edn. Oxford: Oxford University Press.
Examines the main welfare services since 1974. It is loosely based around the production process model of welfare, with a common chapter structure that examines goals and policies, expenditure trends, outputs and outcomes. It stresses a quantitative perspective and presents a wealth of data in many tables and figures.

Gordon Hughes and Gail Lewis (eds) (1998) *Unsettling Welfare: The Reconstruction of Social Policy*. London: Routledge.
Discusses the political, economic, social and organizational settlements that form the basis for the explanatory chapters in the present book. It examines changes in the main policy areas, with particular emphasis on 'new social divisions' such as race and gender. It is an Open University set text, and uses devices such as document extracts, activities and comments. It contains many figures, tables and cartoons.

Paul Pierson (1994) *Dismantling the Welfare State?* Cambridge: Cambridge University Press.
Not an easy read, but a text that made important conceptual advances in a discussion of welfare state restructuring in the UK and the USA. It suggests that welfare retrenchment is not simply the mirror image of welfare growth and that there are significant political and institutional factors limiting retrenchment. The answer to the question of the title is that the welfare state was not dismantled.

4 | THE MODERN WELFARE STATE

Introduction
Modernizing the welfare state
In search of the modern welfare state
Aims
Mechanisms
Inputs, outputs and outcomes
Conclusion

Introduction

It is generally accepted that, after its election defeat in 1979, the Labour Party moved towards the left. Labour suffered its worst ever defeat at the 1983 general election, with its manifesto being termed by a member of the Shadow Cabinet 'the longest suicide note in history' (see, for example, Powell 1999a: 6). The Party underwent renewal under the leadership of Neil Kinnock and John Smith, culminating in the move to 'New Labour' under Tony Blair. Most commentators argue that Labour and Conservative policies tended to converge (Hewitt and Powell 1998; Hay 1999; Powell 1999a; Burden *et al.* 2000; Heffernan 2000). Writing before the

1997 election, McKibbin (1997) argued that if Labour won, it would do so for two reasons: because it was not the Conservative Party and because it was not very different from the Conservative Party.

The 1997 election manifesto (Labour Party 1997) claimed that 'We will be the party of welfare reform'. The manifesto concluded with five pledges on education, health, employment, crime and taxes. In the Queen's Speech debate, Blair launched a crusade for welfare reform, singling out modernization of the £90 billion a year 'welfare' (i.e. the social security) system as the 'big idea' of the government. Frank Field was appointed Minister of Welfare Reform with a brief to 'think the unthinkable' (see Powell 1999a).

In this chapter, we briefly outline the modern welfare state being developed as part of New Labour's third way (for more details, see Powell 1999a, 2002; Burden *et al.* 2000; Jones 2000: ch. 15; Glennerster 2001; Rake 2001; Rawnsley 2001; Savage and Atkinson 2001; Toynbee and Walker 2001). The term 'modern welfare state' is a convenient label with which to examine the changes since 1997. It is one of the government's favoured terms, although it sometimes also uses an 'active' or 'new' welfare state, and clearly relates to New Labour's agenda of 'modernization'. However, it does not bear any necessary relationship to the 'modernity' debate in academic terms (see Chapter 8). Do changes consolidate or reverse Conservative measures? How new is the new welfare state?

Modernizing the welfare state

One of the most notable changes from Old Labour was in the area of taxation and public expenditure (Burchardt and Hills 1999). After its unexpected loss in the 1992 general election, the Party decided that its tax policy had to change. One of the main components of New Labour's 'newness' was an attempt to shed the 'tax and spend' image of Old Labour (Gould 1998; Rawnsley 2001). To this end, a key manifesto pledge was not to increase direct taxation in the form of the basic and higher rates of income tax. This meant that significant redistribution was ruled out in the hunt for the Middle England vote. However, it has found a number of ways to increase the overall tax burden, which has been termed 'redistribution by stealth'. These 'backdoor tax increases' include changing the tax dividends on pensions and increasing stamp duty for higher priced house sales. The 1998 and 1999 budgets were mildly redistributive (e.g. Glennerster 1999, 2001; Toynbee and Walker 2001), with stronger redistribution towards poorer families (Blackman and Palmer 1999) and more redistributive than the budgets of the French socialists (Sassoon 1999). On spending, Labour would be 'wise spenders not big spenders'. This 'prudence for a purpose' included a comprehensive spending review, in which the main result was to increase 'good' spending or 'investment' at the expense of 'bad spending' or the 'bills of economic failure' such as benefit payments (Burchardt and Hills 1999).

The 1997 election manifesto claimed that 'Education is the Government's first priority' (Labour Party 1997; see Tomlinson 2001). New Labour has in particular targeted the early years of education, with promises of a free nursery place for every 4-year-old whose parents want it (now extended to 3-year-olds in the 2001 manifesto) and a reduction in class sizes in primary schools. It emphasizes educational standards and has 'zero tolerance of failing schools', which can be 'named and shamed' and failing LEAs can be replaced. It has retained the central place in educational policy occupied by the inspectorate, Ofsted. This is complemented by a newer option of 'marketization' (Gewirtz 1999; Whitty and Power 1999), which includes merit pay – 'payment by results' for teachers and the use of private providers to run schools and whole LEAs. As part of its agenda to improve employability through training and skills, Labour is committed to 'lifelong learning', which involves 'second, third and even fourth chances'. Traditional support for the Open University is supplemented by a new 'University for Industry' and individual learning accounts. Similarly, it wishes to increase the participation ratio in higher education to 50 per cent. However, this is to be partly financed by a reform of student finance that goes beyond the policies of the Conservatives. In England and Wales, student grants have been replaced by loans and means-tested tuition fees have been introduced in higher education. However, in Scotland, one clear outcome of devolution is a different package of student finance. It will increasingly be the responsibility of students to invest in their own human capital. Similarly, the responsibility of parents in areas such as truancy has been emphasized. New Labour is aware that its first term concentrated on primary education. In a second term, the focus would move to the secondary level. A Green Paper, 'Schools – Building on Success' (Department for Education and Employment 2001), announced a major extension of diversity in the secondary school system. The education service must move from a 'one size fits all' model to a more flexible system where every school has a distinctive mission and ethos. This could mean developing specialisms in areas such as science or schools being run by faith groups or private companies. Put bluntly, Blair admitted that comprehensives have failed. Even more bluntly, the Prime Minister's Press Secretary Alistair Campbell referred to 'bog standard comprehensives'. This gives rise to two spectres for the left of specialization and selection and of privatisation (see Tomlinson 2001).

Like education, health has been a favoured area in increased public spending. Labour wishes to create a 'new NHS' (Department of Health 1997) by abolishing the Conservative internal market and replacing competition with collaboration and partnership. It has replaced the general practitioner fundholding (GPFH) scheme based on individual practices with new Primary Care Groups, covering an average population of about 100,000. It hopes to retain the advantages of GPFH, without the disadvantages. It has introduced Health Improvement Programmes, where rather than simply being in a purchaser/provider relationship, the partners will plan together. Within hospitals, clinical governance has been introduced to improve quality. Labour's health policy includes a mix of devolution and centralism. Although it has promised that there will be no return to the hierarchical command and control of Old Labour, it has introduced new institutions of the National Institute for Clinical Excellence, which will set standards, and the Commission for Health Improvement, which will enforce them at local levels. The Secretary of State has taken increased reserve powers. Labour set up the Acheson Committee to examine inequalities in health and has emphasized fairness and a 'one nation' NHS. The National Institute for Clinical Excellence will end two-tierism and postcode prescribing. There are concerns to set national standards and attention has been drawn to variations in the quality of provision in hospitals, including waiting lists, cleanliness and post-operative mortality rates. The first national target for reducing health inequality was outlined (Department of Health 2000). On the other hand, there has been some devolution of powers to the Scottish Parliament and Welsh Assembly, resulting in free long-term care in Scotland and free prescriptions for those aged under 25 in Wales. Local targets have been stressed and Health Action Zones have been given freedoms. The NHS is to be modernized by walk-in centres and a telephone help line, NHS Direct. The Private Finance Initiative will deliver the greatest hospital building programme ever seen in the NHS. The NHS Plan (Department of Health 2000) claims to be the most fundamental reform of the NHS since 1948. It significantly increases the spending on the NHS, but this investment has to be accompanied by reform. The NHS is described as a 1940s system operating in a twenty-first century world. The Plan represents a package of reforms to address the systematic weaknesses inherent in the NHS since 1948. Boundaries between professionals and organizations must be broken down. The NHS must develop better partnerships between both local authorities and the private sector. According to some commentators, this concordat with private medicine 'crosses the Rubicon' and ends the class war that Old Labour waged against the private sector. However, the Plan also proposes that newly qualified consultants should not be allowed to engage in private work in the first 7 years of appointment, which quickly prompted medical leaders to suggest that perhaps MPs ought not to be allowed to combine their public role with lucrative private work. There has been an increased emphasis on public health, with a Green Paper, 'Our Healthier Nation' (Department of Health 1998), and a White Paper, 'Saving Lives' (Department of Health 1999). Labour claims that the Conservatives' view of public health was focused only at the individual level, blaming individuals for their own ill health. Labour recognizes structural influences on health and has policies in place to deal with unemployment and poor education. Labour's 'joined up government' is, in some ways, an updated version of Beveridge's Giants. Like Beveridge, it claims that it is impossible to attack any 'giant' in isolation: 'Disease' is intimately linked with other giants such as 'Want' and 'Idleness'. However, Labour also recognizes the importance of agency. It has set up a 'three-way contract' between central government, local agencies and individuals in which all recognize their responsibilities as well as their rights.

The main theme in social security is 'work for those who can; security for those who cannot'. This consists of a rights and responsibilities discourse. Those who cannot work have a right to security. However, for those who can work, the right to benefit is more conditional. The basic philosophy is that work is the best route out of poverty. This consists of carrots and sticks. 'Making work pay' includes a national minimum wage, tax reforms such as the working family tax credits and nursery credits, which increase the return from low paid work and reduce the poverty trap. The government aims to achieve full employment. However, this does not signal a return to the 'full (male) employment' associated with the Keynesian demand management of the classic welfare state, which is regarded as not possible in a globalized world. The government's objective is more ambitious in that it stresses full employment for all rather than simply full male employment. However, in terms of mechanisms, it concentrates on the 'supply side' of 'employability'. Instead of merely paying people in poverty more benefit, New Labour will redistribute opportunities and take a preventive approach, giving people the skills to escape poverty.

The government provides the framework for economic growth with active rather than passive labour market policies, with a lightly regulated, flexible labour market. The centrepiece of this employment-centred social policy is the 'New Deal' programmes. The carrots and sticks vary for different groups. For example, young unemployed people are offered four choices – a subsidized private sector job, education, a voluntary sector job or an environmental task force. If they refuse all of these options, there will be no 'fifth option' of staying at home on benefit as benefits will be reduced. On the other hand, single parents will be invited in for an interview, to make them aware of opportunities but, unlike some States in the USA, there are no penalties if they decide not to take paid employment. In addition to being responsible for acquiring skills and work, people are to be more responsible for their actions. In particular, Labour is improving the administration of the Child Support Agency, emphasizing that absent fathers will no longer be able to escape their responsibilities for their children. Labour has suffered its two largest backbench revolts in the area of social security, with significant votes against the government on benefits for single parents and disabled people. Labour has made an ambitious promise to end child poverty within 20 years (Walker 1999b).

In the area of pensions in the short term, Labour continued to uprate basic state pensions by prices rather than earnings. In the year 2000, this led to an increase of 75 pence a week, although the poorest pensioners have a means-tested minimum pension guarantee that was tied to increases in earnings. This has two implications. First, it represents moves from universalism towards selectivity. Second, it means that over time pensioners will continue to fall behind workers. The new agenda is clearly a return to preventing absolute rather than relative poverty for some pensioners. Beyond this minimum, supplementary pensions come from a number of sources. There will be a 'state second pension' that will be more generous to the low paid than the SERPS scheme that it replaces. Outside the state, the government is setting up stakeholder pensions. The government regards stakeholders as a 'public–private partnership'. However, they may more accurately be seen as moves towards privatization and regulation rather than a direct providing and financing role for government in pensions. The maximum level of charges of 1 per cent for stakeholders are well below the much higher levels often found for private pensions. However, in return for this regulation, Labour wishes to reverse the balance of funding from 40 per cent private and 60 per cent state to the converse. It remains to be seen if this overall coherent scheme will be blown off course by the political whirlwind that blew up after the 75 pence rise. The government has admitted that this was politically disastrous and, in the run up to what was widely seen as a general election, the next annual uprating was by £5 a week, which was more than the amount that uprating by prices or earnings would suggest.

Labour has made fewer changes in the areas of personal social services and housing. Communitarianism has a particular relevance for personal social services, with a stress on communities and civil society, including voluntary organizations and mutual aid. Responsibility in the area of the family is also a key theme. Modernizing social services (Department of Health 1998) emphasizes partnership and regulation. Labour set up a Royal Commission on long-term care. Its report (Sutherland 1999) recommended that 'treatment' and 'nursing' costs should be free, but that 'hotel costs' should be means-tested. In England, the government refused to accept its recommendations, largely apparently on the grounds of costs. For all but the poorest, long-term care is clearly seen as a private rather than a public responsibility. Like the Conservatives, it is hyper-critical for New Labour to preach thrift and responsibility and then penalize 'the responsible' in their old age (cf. Field 2000).

New Labour has made few significant policy changes in housing, but the main themes include a greater acceptance of the market, strengthening communities and encouraging greater responsibility of tenants. Owner-occupation is viewed as the normal tenure, although mortgage tax relief has finally been phased out. The government is continuing the Conservative policy of large-scale voluntary transfer or 'demunicipalization' of dwellings from local authorities to social landlords. This is happening faster than it did under the Conservatives, leading to 'Britain's biggest sale of homes' that constitutes 'as big a housing revolution as the laws passed in the 1920s that saw municipal housing providing the homes fit for the heroes returning from the battlefields of the Somme' (*Economist*, 5 May 2001: 33–4). Housing policy blends with communitarian themes in the work of the Social Exclusion Unit on the worst estates (Social Exclusion Unit 1998) and the New Deal for Communities. Only those tenants deemed to behave in a responsible manner will be tolerated in public housing. A greater conditionality has appeared in the form of 'probationary tenancy periods' and 'mutual aid clauses' (Dwyer 2000) and rules against racial harassment. Critics may attack this 'moral stance' and 'authoritarianism', but this view may not be shared by victims of harassment who live in areas where they have suffered racist graffiti and attacks (cf. Field 2000). Dwyer (2000) found strong support for probationary tenancy periods in his focus groups.

In addition to the emphasis on responsibility in the areas of work, education and community life, there is now a responsibility to save. The government has proposed child trust funds and savings gateways in an attempt to spread assets throughout the population (HM Treasury 2001). Despite the proximity to a general election, the government denied that it was trying to bribe the electorate by adding a new financial premium to the 'cradle to grave' welfare state. Moreover, the government will help those who help themselves by matching funds to the amounts saved by those on low incomes.

In search of the modern welfare state

New Labour's third way claims to be different from both the Old Left and the New Right, from Old Labour and the Conservatives. In the previous chapter, we examined whether the changes of the Conservatives were distinctive from the classic welfare state. New Labour's rhetoric suggests that its policies are different from *both* the classic welfare state and the restructured welfare state.

New Labour claims that its basic values and the main aims of the welfare state have not changed. However, Labour wishes to develop a more rational welfare state. Blair, in the introduction to the Welfare Green Paper (DSS 1998: v) states that 'We must return to first principles and ask what we want the welfare state to achieve'. According to Miliband (1994: 88), 'we need to redefine welfare, and turn our understanding of the role of the welfare state . . . on its head'. The modern welfare state will be intelligent, active, conditional, inclusive and based around work (cf. Commission on Social Justice 1994; Blair and Schroder 1999; Green-Pedersen *et al.* 2001).

Aims

Blair (1998) claims that the third way rests on four basic values: equal worth, opportunity for all, responsibility and community. White (1998) suggests real opportunity, civic responsibility and community. Le Grand (1998) offers CORA – community, opportunity, responsibility and accountability – while Lister (2000) suggests RIO – responsibility, inclusion and opportunity. There are clear similarities between these summaries, as well as others (Giddens 1998, 2000; Vandenbroucke 1999; see Driver and Martell 2000). Blair (1998) insists that policies flow from values: policy aims remain constant, but means will be flexible.

Commentators note that some of these values and aims appear to have been redefined. The most significant criticism is that New Labour has moved from equality to inclusion and from equality of outcomes to equality of opportunity, meaning that the importance of redistribution has declined (Lister 2000). Certainly, the third way tends to stress inclusion more than equality (Giddens 1998, 2000). Blair (1998: 12) argues for a 'diverse but inclusive society', while Wright (1996: 143) argues that New Labour must be 'egalitarian enough to be socially inclusive'. In other words, some degree of income equality is compatible with inclusion (see Levitas 1998). Levitas (1996, 1998) discusses the differences between a redistributive, egalitarian discourse (RED), a social integrationist discourse (SID) and a moralistic, underclass discourse (MUD). She suggests that New Labour tends to abandon RED in favour of MUD and SID, viewing inclusion through paid work as the key strategy that reduces the importance of unpaid work (cf. Lister 2000). According to Land (1999), at least care at home was valued in the Beveridge version of the male breadwinner model. She notes that in some ways, such as reduced eligibility for widows' pensions, women are not even second-class citizens. However, Glennerster (1999) has criticized the critics, arguing that paid work brings dignity and respect (cf. Field 1996, 2000). Moreover, viewing inclusion solely through work understates the importance of services in kind. While the route to inclusion in social security may be new, the 'Strategy of Equality' or more accurately the 'Strategy for Fraternity' of Tawney (1964; see Le Grand 1982; Powell 1995a) is traditional. To some extent, this links with the citizenship agenda of Marshall (1963) and the equality of status sought by Crosland (1964): unequal private incomes are underpinned by a platform of social income.

New Labour claims that it has moved from fiscal redistribution through the tax and benefit system to an emphasis on redistributing opportunities or assets (Brown 1999). This has tended to be dismissed as being linked with a change from a social democratic emphasis on equality of outcomes to a liberal emphasis on equality of opportunity (Lister 2000). However, it can be argued that the classic welfare state was concerned more with minima than with equality (Glennerster 1995; Powell 1995a). Moreover, this argument neglects the emphasis on national standards and greater equality in areas such as health and health care. In particular, New Labour's targets on reducing health inequalities, *if* achieved, would be a significant step towards greater equality of outcome. The major problem is that equality of opportunity can have very different meanings, ranging from the liberal abolition of barriers to a more social democratic equalization of circumstances and life chances (Giddens 1998, 2000; White 1998; Brown 1999), and it is not yet clear whether New Labour tends towards the 'maximalist' or 'minimalist' version.

New Labour claims that whereas the right tended to stress the duties of citizenship and the left tended to stress the rights of citizens, the third way involves a modern welfare state based on rights and duties. In line with communitarianism, responsibilities are seen to be indivisible from entitlements. In short, the third way of citizenship move from 'dutiless rights' towards 'conditional welfare'. The main area concerns paid work (King 1999), but the rhetoric of responsibility permeates many other areas (Lund 1999; Dwyer 2000; Lister 2000). In many ways, this is not new, reflecting the deep division between the 'deserving' and 'undeserving' poor in the Poor Law (King 1999) and the Beveridge Report (Hewitt and Powell 1998; Glennerster 1999). Certainly, if Dwyer's (2000) focus groups are in any way representative, 'ordinary people' are more in line with New Labour than some of their academic critics (cf. Mandelson and Liddle 1996; Gould 1998).

Some of the objectives have not changed. New Labour, like Old Labour, claims to want to end child poverty (Walker 1999b) and achieve full employment. In some ways, the full employment target is more ambitious. New Labour has moved from the traditional male breadwinner model that saw 'full employment' in terms of full *male* employment to full employment for all. As Land (1999) puts it, tax and social security systems have been reformed to assist mothers to behave more like fathers (i.e. as workers), and 'paid work is the only badge of citizenship'. In conclusion, although aims have changed, they may have changed less than some commentators have suggested. In some cases this results from overstating the aims of the classic welfare state, and in others by neglecting potentially radical aims such as reducing health inequalities. However, as we shall see below, the mechanisms have changed substantially.

Mechanisms

New Labour claims that the welfare system must change because the world has changed. These changes include changing work, working women, changing families, an ageing society and rising expectations (DSS 1998; cf. Hills 1997; Giddens 1998; see Chapter 8). New times call for new policies. Realistic and feasible answers require adherence to our values but also a willingness to change our old approaches and traditional policy instruments (Blair and Schroder 1999). New Labour wishes to promote an active, preventive and intelligent rather than a passive welfare state that encourages people to realize their full potential rather than being chained to passive dependency. Miliband (1994) states that the traditional welfare state was socially active when citizens were economically passive. Today's welfare state must be active throughout people's lives. Welfare has to be preventive rather than ameliorative. For example, a modern health policy is concerned with ensuring people do not fall ill in the first place. While the traditional NHS was largely concerned with 'repair', the 'new NHS' will be more active in preventing illness (Department of Health 1998, 1999). Welfare must be economic as well as social: the most potent social policy is a successful economic policy. Economic and social policy are seen as different sides of the same coin. 'The Government's aim is to rebuild the welfare state around work (DSS 1998: 23). This work-based social policy explains the special emphasis given to education, which Blair has termed the best economic policy we have: 'Welfare is not only about acting after events have occurred . . . the welfare system should be proactive, preventing poverty by ensuring that people have the right education, training and support' (DSS 1998: 20).

The modern welfare state seems to redraw the boundaries between the individual and the state. There may be a reduced role for the state and an increased role for private and mutual organizations. The third way 'is about combining public and private provision in a new partnership for the new age' (DSS 1998: 19). A key principle is that 'The public and private sectors should work in partnership to ensure that, wherever possible, people are insured against foreseeable risks and make provision for their retirement' (p. 33). It is claimed that 'occupational pensions . . . are arguably the biggest welfare success story of the century'. Pensions are the most developed and most successful example of a public–private partnership (p. 34). However, it is noted that this partnership has failed to deliver a decent standard of living for all pensioners. The basic pension – increased at least in line with prices – is the foundation of pension provision (pp. 36–8). This is a very clear return to Beveridge subsistence, rejecting later bi-partisan agreements on increasing pensions in line with the higher of rises of earnings or prices (Hewitt and Powell 1998). Basic or subsistence needs will be met by the state. There will be a state second pension, but for those at and above average earnings the market will provide an extension ladder.

New Labour has selectively and pragmatically embraced the private sector (cf. Glennerster 1999, 2001). On the one hand, it has abandoned some Conservative initiatives to promote private welfare, such as nursery vouchers, the assisted places scheme and tax relief on private medical insurance for those aged 60 and above. On the other hand, it has continued the Private Finance Initiative, indicated that it wishes to change the overall pension burden from public to private funding, and has allowed 'privatization' of education services in some areas. For example, while Conservative education policy was largely based on an *internal* market, extending choice from public providers, New Labour allows private for-profit companies to run schools and even whole LEAs. Many critics argue that there is a thin line between public/private partnerships and 'privatization': in 'Nixon goes to China' fashion, New Labour has privatized, but disguised this by terming it a public/private partnership.

There will also be increasing partnerships within civil society, where the 'community' appears in a number of initiatives (Wright 1996; Blair 1998; Giddens 1998). This may involve a revival of mutual aid, with a more localized and community-based civic society (Field 1996, 2000) or associational welfare (Hirst 1994). The exact role of the state in finance, production and regulation remains unclear, but there may be greater scope for 'DIY welfare' (Klein and Millar 1995; Grice 1997). The government is expanding the scope of the regulatory state (Moran 2001). It is continuing the model of the Conservatives for the regulation of privatized utilities (e.g. OFTEL for telecommunications) and regulation, inspection and audit have been extended to many areas such as health (Commission for Health Improvement) and education (Ofsted, Quality Assurance Agency (QAA)). The Financial Services Agency (FSA) was set up to be the single regulator for all financial businesses in the UK. In its short life it has examined the mis-selling of private pensions that occurred in the late 1980s and early 1990s, the possible shortfall in endowment mortgages and the fiasco of the 'Equitable Life'. The 'Equitable Life', the largest life office in Europe, has been experiencing serious financial problems resulting in the depletion of its policy holders' assets. The government's attempt to regulate the financial market has come in for criticism, particularly over the FSA's handling of 'Equitable Life'. There has been greater stress on fiscal welfare (Titmuss 1968) with the model being the tax credit schemes in the USA (Land 1999; Deacon 2000; McLaughlin *et al.* 2001; Rake 2001). More broadly, Blair has proposed that citizenship should involve each individual being educated in personal financial responsibility, in effect creating a new concept of 'financial citizenship' (White in press).

This has clear links with the new stress placed on responsibility. Le Grand (1998) notes the strong link between opportunity and responsibility. People are urged to become more responsible and make provision for the risks facing themselves and their families. The notion of a 'contract' is mentioned in a number of documents (DSS 1998; Department of Health 1999). This may be seen as a tentative move from a patterned to process distribution. Welfare is not solely dependent on patterned criteria such as 'need', but will partly be linked with process – the behaviour that led to that pattern. Taken to its logical conclusion, the old divide between the 'deserving' and 'undeserving' poor will be mirrored in a moral discourse of a new divide between the 'responsible' and the 'irresponsible'. 'Security for those who cannot' (DSS 1998) must mean no security for those who 'can' but 'do not'. The 'responsible', those who 'do the right thing' (Heron and Dwyer 1999), are to be included, while those deemed 'irresponsible' are to be subject to varying degrees of authoritarianism (Driver and Martell 1998; Levitas 1998). A necessary corollary of greater responsibility in welfare must entail more severe consequences for failure: there must be some stick with which to beat the 'irresponsible' – and their families. It is difficult to see how the circle linking responsibility and inclusion can be squared. The possibility of 'regulatory failure', let alone the Conservatives changing the rules of SERPS and New Labour changing the rules on the taxation of pension dividends, make DIY welfare a risky business. As Hewitt and Powell (1998) warn, like all DIY jobs, it can go disastrously wrong.

Government will be 'joined up', as it is recognized that complex problems require joined-up solutions. At the centre, this means different departments working to a common agenda. At the periphery, it means governance between different agencies. The rhetoric of partnership is also common in areas such as the NHS, where New Labour rejects the command and control of Old Left and competition of New Right and favours partnership and cooperation. It is pledged to abolish the Conservatives' internal market in the NHS and replace compulsory competitive tendering with a new, wider regime of 'best value' in local government. However, in both areas, it is probably true to say that competition is being reduced and redefined, but not abolished. According to Rod Rhodes (2000), New Labour advocates joined-up government or delivering public services by steering networks of organizations where the currency is not authority (bureaucracy) or price competition (markets) but trust. He claims that this is the third way in action and exemplifies the shift from the providing state of Old Labour and the minimal state of Thatcherism to the enabling state. However, this ignores the fact that the enabling state was a major element of Conservative discourse. However, the government has come close to admitting that 'partnership' may fail, as it has introduced some new integrated structures such as new Care Trusts (Department of Health 2000). Instead of health and social care agencies working in partnership, these new organizations contain both services. This looks more like a takeover rather than a partnership and might, in the long term, lead to the demise of local Social Services Departments. Moreover, local 'partners' may be subject to significant central control. The locus of power under New Labour is unclear. On the one hand, there have been some moves towards greater devolution such as in Scotland and Wales, and a greater stress on local targets in area-based policies such as Health Action Zones. There are signs that this may lead to some policy differentiation in areas such as student finance and long-term care in Scotland and free prescriptions for those aged under 25 in Wales. On the other hand, in a number of areas there are the opposite signs of centralization, such as new central institutions and greater central powers for the Secretary of State. Blair's (1998: 16) phrase of 'intervention in inverse proportion to [centrally determined] success' is merely an elegant way of emphasizing Stalinist central control. Rod Rhodes (2000: 360–1) warns of the danger of a 'command operating code in a velvet glove', pointing out that New Labour lacks the trust it seeks to inspire. It fears the independence it bestows.

The means to full employment is not to be achieved via the Old Left solution of Keynesian demand management, which is regarded as not feasible in today's global economy (Blair 1998; Blair and Schroder 1999). The gold watch at the end of the '40 hours a week for 40 years' with the same company has disappeared. The rise of more flexible, part-time employment has shifted the emphasis to supply side solutions of 'employability' (Blair and Schroder 1999; Lister 2000). Specifically, welfare is redesigned along 'productivist' lines to move people from welfare to work. There are different 'New Deals' with varying bundles of carrots and sticks for different groups. At present, the largest sticks are for the young unemployed, and there have been few moves towards the 'workfare' schemes in some States of the USA that require single parents to take up work or training when their children are as young as 12 weeks old. However, Land (1999) notes that initial promises that interviews for single parents to discuss work opportunities would not be compulsory have been broken. Affordable child care remains a major barrier to work opportunities for many single parents (Land 1999; Rake 2001).

In social security, Labour is moving from universalism towards selectivity (Field 2000). Lister (2000: 15) quotes *The Economist*, that the government has 'crossed the Rubicon from . . . the left bank of welfare-for-all to the right bank of means-testing'. In addition, there is targeting via area-based policies (on positive discrimination, see Titmuss 1968). An optimistic interpretation may emphasize moves from the old nominal universalism to difference and particularism (Thompson and Hoggett 1996; Ellison 1999; see Chapter 8).

Inputs, outputs and outcomes

To distance itself from its old 'tax and spend' image, New Labour promised that it would not raise income tax during the Parliament and would stick to Conservative spending limits in the first 2 years. As the traditional resort of increasing inputs was ruled out, the solution was to achieve greater returns of outputs and outcomes from the same level of inputs. This greater efficiency would be achieved through abolishing the inefficient internal market. New Labour rejects high spending as a measure of policy success and will be wise spenders, not big spenders. This appears to have two main elements. First, 'investment' in services such as education and health is 'good'. However, part of the social security budget is 'bad' – 'the bills of economic and social failure'. According to the Commission on Social Justice (1994: 104), 'A higher social security budget is a sign of economic failure, not social success'. Second, the level of public spending is no longer the best measure of the effectiveness of government action in the public interest. It is what money is actually spent on that counts, not how much money is spent (Blair and Schroder 1999).

A further strand is the stated non-dogmatic view of private as opposed to public finance. For example, the Private Finance Initiative (PFI) is set to achieve the largest hospital building programme in the NHS. There is a promise or aspiration to increase NHS spending to the European average. While the debate on the merits of PFI may be conducted at a high level of technical sophistication, the implications of the assumption that there is little difference between public and private inputs into pension funding is readily apparent to all. Moreover, critics have detected in areas as varied as air traffic control, the London Underground and PFI, a dogmatic and ideological view of 'public bad, private good'.

The comprehensive spending review suggests a greater rational, rather than incremental, basis for expenditure. Instead of merely spending extra increments to achieve 'more of the same', there is a nominal return to first principles, to re-thinking objectives. Apart from justifying re-source shifts from passive 'relief' to investment in health and education, there are few signs of a comprehensive implementation of this principle.

After the initial 2 years of staying within Conservative spending plans, New Labour has substantially increased spending in favoured areas such as health, leading to critics from the right arguing an Old Labour 'return to spender'. It recognizes that more inputs are required, but requires better outputs and outcomes in return. This fits with the emphasis on evidence-based policy, results and 'what counts is what works' (Davies *et al.* 2000). This accounts for the stress on performance indicators, per-formance assessment frameworks, public service agreements and SMART targets. The government claims great success in its annual reports, pro-viding progress on the achievement of the 177 manifesto pledges of 1997. Critics dismissed some of the pledges said to be 'done' or 'on course' and suggested that two of the five key pledge card promises (on class sizes and speeding up youth justice) were unlikely to be met. In some areas, there was re-writing of promises (e.g. *Daily Telegraph*, 11 January 2001). For example, instead of '14 days to save the NHS', the government stressed the obvious that it takes time to train doctors and nurses and to build hospitals. Some targets, such as reducing child poverty and health inequalities, are long term. It is probably too early to come to any clear verdict on outcomes, but the early picture is rather mixed (Toynbee and Walker 2001).

Conclusion

Most commentators point to both continuities and discontinuities with the Conservatives, but generally argue that the former outweigh the latter (Burden *et al.* 2000). There have clearly been some changes in social policy, but progress has been far from uniform both between and within service sectors. Progress has been faster in areas such as employ-ment than in others such as housing and personal social services. There has also been some variation between aims and mechanisms. We have argued that aims have changed, but not to the extent that they have sometimes been portrayed. In some ways, there has been a return to a more limited agenda of the Beveridge Report and the Beveridge philo-sophy, rejecting the implementation of the Report in the 1940s and subsequent changes (Hewitt and Powell 1998). Glennerster (1999) has termed this 'retreating to the core'.

The changed means, such as a greater use of the market and civil society and a greater stress on partnership, joined-up government, fiscal welfare, conditional welfare, supply-side initiatives and means testing, have generally been noted (Powell 1999a; Burden *et al.* 2000). However, the more limited rejection of the market and a focus on some aspects of equality has largely been neglected. This fits with the notion of a non-dogmatic, non-ideological stress on delivery: what counts is what works (Powell 2000a,b) New Labour's policies include something old, something new, something borrowed and something blue. This search for shiny policy objects has been termed 'jackdaw politics' (Powell 2000b). It follows that policy adoption is a more suitable term than policy convergence. New Labour did not attempt to return to 1979, to unscramble the eggs in the Conservative omelette. It pragmatically accepted the new political landscape and attempted to reform the Conservative reforms. As Crouch (1997) notes, it is more accurate to compare New Labour not to 'Old Labour' in 1945, but to the Conservatives in 1951, who showed that they could work to an agenda that was not of their making.

Academic verdicts on New Labour have generally been critical (Hay 1999; Burden *et al.* 2000; Heffernan 2000; but see Glennerster 1999, 2001; Toynbee and Walker 2001). While these are correct to stress the substantial shifts in mechanisms, they arguably miss some moves in the opposite direction, such as reducing *some* market mechanisms and increasing emphases on *some* aspects of equality. Moreover, there is perhaps a little misplaced nostalgia for a 'golden age' of welfare, and also insufficient recognition of the economic, social and political constraints on governments (cf. Marquand 1992). As Rawnsley (2001) argues, compared with many governments, New Labour has a well above average record. However, by the measure of the expectations aroused by the size of the majority, New Labour's transformatory rhetoric and the ambitions that Blair had trumpeted, the government looks less impressive (cf. Toynbee and Walker 2001; Powell 2002).

Further reading

Anthony Giddens (ed.) (2001) *The Global Third Way Debate*. Cambridge: Polity Press.
Presents largely friendly reactions to the editor's notion of the 'third way', with useful material on the broad concepts and developments in the welfare state in Britain and in other countries.

Martin Powell (ed.) (1999) *New Labour, New Welfare State?* Bristol: Policy Press.
This was one of the earliest and most detailed accounts of New Labour's early welfare reforms and of the 'third way' in social policy.

Martin Powell (ed.) (2002) *Evaluating New Labour's Welfare Reforms.* Policy Press: Bristol.
This extends the discussion of social policy to the end of New Labour's first term of office. It also provides an evaluative dimension focusing on how the government's achievements matched their stated aims.

Stuart White (ed.) (2001) *New Labour: The Progressive Future?* Basingstoke: Palgrave.
Examines New Labour and the third way in Britain and places this material in a wider international context.

5 ECONOMIC EXPLANATIONS

Introduction

This chapter focuses on economic explanations for the welfare state. We review the older explanations of Marxism, industrial theories, and economic growth and the Keynesian welfare state, as well as the more recent explanations of globalization, post-industrialism and post-Fordism. While economic forces are clearly associated with welfare change and there are a number of similarities between the explanations, no fully coherent and comprehensive economic explanation emerges.

Marxist theories

Marxist theories explaining the development of the welfare state, like Marxist theories *per se*, are multifaceted and complex. We have included them in our economic account because of the emphasis on the economic base that heavily influences events in the superstructure (Gough 1979). George and Wilding (1993) state that Marxist explanations of the development of the welfare state are rooted in the Marxist analysis of how capitalism as an economic system functions. At the heart of this thesis is the capitalist mode of production. The economic base, or structure, of society influences and eventually determines the nature of other institutions in society that form its superstructure. The nature of the political system, the dominant ideology, the family, the social services and other institutions are largely, but not totally, determined by capitalism as a mode of production. As a vast oversimplification, capitalists own the means of production with the aim of making profit, while workers have to sell their labour power and are necessarily exploited.

The original writings of Marx and Engels took place in the nineteenth century, in the era of the Factory Acts and the New Poor Law. However, other writers have produced Marxist accounts of the welfare state (see, for example, Mishra 1981; Deacon 1983; George and Wilding 1993; O'Brien and Penna 1998; C. Pierson 1998a). At the heart of most accounts is the problem of explaining a 'welfare state' in a 'capitalist society'. Most Marxist writers prefer to use the term 'welfare capitalism'. O'Connor (1973) points out that the capitalist state is involved in two contradictory functions of accumulation and legitimation. Accumulation involves the profitability of industry, adequate investment and economic growth. Legitimation is concerned with maintaining social harmony by giving the appearance that the capitalist social order is in the best interests of the workers. O'Connor divides state expenditure into three categories: social investment increases the productivity of labour; social consumption lowers the reproduction costs of labour; and social expenses that are necessary for social stability. Gough (1979: 11) asks whether the welfare state is an:

> agency of repression, or a system for enlarging human needs and mitigating the rigours of a free market economy? An aid to capital accumulation and profits or a 'social wage' to be defended and enlarged like the money in your pay packet? Capitalist fraud or working-class victory?

He replies that it contains at any one time elements of both. 'In other words it is not the Marxist analysis of the welfare state that is contra-dictory, but the welfare state itself' (p. 11). Offe (1982: 11) claimed, in a famous phrase, that 'while capitalism cannot coexist with the welfare state, neither can it exist without the welfare state'.

A crude Marxist account that focuses on the economic base might claim that the nineteenth-century industrial revolution with its 'dark satanic mills' is essentially the same as today's microprocessor industry, as they are both capitalist. However, other accounts point to 'varieties of capitalism' across time and space. Commentators have pointed out that economic activity is institutionally and socially embedded in different countries. National models of capitalism include Rhenish (e.g. Germany), Confucian (e.g. Japan) and Anglo-American models (Thomson 2000; Ebbinghaus and Manow 2001). As Ebbinghaus and Manow (2001) note, although there are some striking similarities between the 'varieties of capitalism' literature and Esping-Andersen's (1990) 'three worlds of wel-fare capitalism', the links between particular forms of social protection and specific economic systems have yet to be adequately examined. While such a task is of great importance for comparative research, our focus here is whether capitalism in Britain has changed over time. Writ-ing in the 1950s, Crosland (1964: 42) argued that the definition of capit-alism in terms of ownership was no longer the clue to the total picture of social relationships. The proper definition of the word capitalism was a society with the essential social, economic and ideological character-istics of Great Britain from the 1830s to the 1930s, and the Britain of the 1950s was no longer capitalist.

Subsequent writers have argued that capitalism has not disappeared, but has changed over time. Some commentators have used the terms 'monopoly capitalism', 'finance capitalism', 'state-monopoly capitalism' or 'late capitalism' (see Lash and Urry 1987). Lash and Urry (1987) criticize these accounts and present their own periodization (see O'Brien and Penna 1998). Their influential account distinguishes the period of liberal or *laissez-faire* capitalism (mid-eighteenth to mid-nineteenth century), the period of organized capitalism (late nineteenth to mid-twentieth century) and the period of disorganized capitalism (mid-twentieth century to the present). They concentrate on the move from organized to dis-organized capitalism, which they claim took place in Britain from the 1960s. They differentiate between changes 'at the top', including the con-centration of industry, and organization 'at the bottom', which includes the development of national trade unions, working-class political parties and the welfare state. Disorganization includes the shift from Taylorist to 'flexible' forms of work organization, the growth of new social movements that increasingly draw energy and personnel away from class politics and the appearance of postmodernism. They suggest that the implications for the welfare state include a limit on increasing the share of national income and moves away from universalism and class-based redistribution towards less bureaucratized, more decentralized and in some cases more privatized forms, resulting in two-tiered provision (Lash and Urry 1987).

Some Marxist and non-Marxist critics point out that there is a limited role for agency in many accounts. Mishra (1981) claims that there is a tendency among Marxists to ascribe the development of the welfare state largely to the functional necessities of capitalism. Lavalette and Mooney (2000) state that class and class conflict are largely invisible in many accounts. The importance of agency was emphasized in 'one of the earliest and finest Marxist analyses of the welfare state (Mishra 1981: 75) by the British historian, John Saville. Saville (1983) sees the development of the welfare state as a result of the interaction of three main factors: the struggle of the working class against their exploitation; the requirements of industrial capital for a more efficient environment in which to operate; and the recognition by the propertied classes of the price that has to be paid for political security.

There are many critiques of Marxist explanations, ranging from the sympathethic (e.g. Mishra 1981; Deacon 1983; O'Brien and Penna 1998; C. Pierson 1998a) to the merciless (e.g. Saunders 1981; Klein 1993). The latter are more entertaining. Saunders (1981) argues that there is a tautology at the centre of Marxist analyses; for example, the 'logically impeccable yet politically absurd thesis that, say, council houses with garages, language teaching in schools, free meals in hospitals, a rising level of pensions and a multitude of other social provisions made by the state in Britain during this century are all "in fact" in the interests of the capitalist class' (p. 209). In contrast to the claim of Gough (above), Saunders argues that Marxist accounts themselves are contradictory. Klein (1993) puts together an amalgam of arguments from O'Connor, Gough and Offe to form 'O'Goffe's tale'. Mullard and Spicker (1998: 46) write that 'There is so much wrong with the Marxist analyses of society that it can be difficult to see why it should have exercised such an influence'.

Marxist accounts do not appear to offer any great purchase on explaining welfare change. Although they are useful in pointing out the broad limits of welfare in a capitalist economy, they have more difficulty in accounting for more specific changes. At one level, crude Marxist explanations suggest continuity. While economies may appear to change, they remain capitalist. Governments and technologies may come and go, but there can never be a proper welfare state under capitalism (Deacon 1983). The 'varieties of capitalism' literature suggests differences over time and space. Although there are still many unanswered questions, the links between different types of capitalism and welfare states have been considered (Esping-Andersen 1990; Ebbinghaus and Manow 2001). The links over time within one country are less developed. It is difficult to disentangle many of the arguments of disorganized capitalism (Lash and Urry 1987) from wider theories of post-Fordism and postmodernism (Kumar 1995; see Chapter 8).

Industrialization theories

According to Higgins (1981), in the 1960s welfare states were found in all industrialized, urbanized societies. The logic of industrialism explains the nature and development of welfare in terms of the 'pull' (requirements or functional imperatives) and the 'push' (consequences) of an industrial technology and society (Mishra 1981: 39). According to Chris Pierson (1998a), the most authoritative advocate of this industrialism thesis has been Wilensky (1975: xiii), who argued that:

> economic growth and its demographic and bureaucratic outcomes are the root cause of the general emergence of the welfare state . . . such heavy brittle categories as 'socialist' versus 'capitalist' economies, 'collectivistic' versus 'individualistic' ideologies, or even 'democratic' versus 'totalitarian' political systems . . . are almost useless in explaining the origins and general development of the welfare state.

He continued that 'over the long pull, economic level is the root cause of welfare-state development'. Its effects are expressed 'chiefly through demographic changes . . . and the momentum of programs themselves once established' (p. 47). This argument is clearly functionalist in tone. Industrial society created new needs – functional imperatives – that forced the state to act. It is also linked with convergence theory: as the problems of industrial society became increasingly similar, the solutions also converged. Wilensky (1975) argues for a convergence thesis: economic growth makes countries with contrasting cultural and political traditions more alike in their welfare state strategy. As Galbraith (1967: 396) puts it, 'Given the decision to have modern industry, much of what happens is inevitable and the same'.

The chronology also fitted with the end of ideology (see Chapter 6). Bell (1960: 402–3) claimed that there is today, 'a rough consensus among intellectuals on political issues: the acceptance of a welfare state; the desirability of decentralized power; a system of mixed economy and of political pluralism'. This thesis has reappeared in the work of Fukuyama (1992: xi), who claims that liberal democracy represents 'the end point of mankind's ideological evolution' and the 'final form of human government'.

Chris Pierson (1998a) assesses the industrialism thesis. He points out the problems with empirical studies, notably the reliance on the dependent variable of 'welfare effort' – the amount of state spending on welfare. As we have already seen in Chapter 1, this is a problematic measure. Pierson (1998a) concludes that while it is clear that industrialism did lead to massive changes in society, explanatory accounts are weakened by their deterministic nature: 'Too often, the "logic of industrialism" has been seen as a sufficient explanation of the rise of welfare state institutions, without identifying the political and historical actors/forces which were to make such changes happen' (p. 19) Higgins (1981) rejects convergence theory: the 'end of ideology' and 'convergence' theses were thus shown to have distinct limitations as 'explanations' of the role of social policy in industrial society (p. 39). Mishra (1981) argues that industrialization theories are deterministic and pitched at a high level of generality. In sum:

> There are no good grounds to suppose that advanced industrial society spells the end of ideology . . . Nor does the evidence bear out the thesis of increasing similarity of social policy to any great extent . . . True, a 'weak' thesis of convergence can be sustained; thus in all Western industrial countries the state has assumed greater responsibility for meeting needs . . . But this still leaves scope for a great deal of diversity in welfare patterns.
>
> (Mishra 1981: 46)

The Keynesian welfare state

Some commentators have linked the classic welfare state with the period of economic growth and full employment after the Second World War. The period from the 1940s to the 1970s is often regarded as the 'golden age' of the welfare state (Pierson 1998a, 2001). More specifically, the economic settlement of the classic welfare state is often identified with the Keynesian welfare state or Keynesian social democracy (Hughes and Lewis 1998). Governments accepted a duty to secure a high and stable level of employment. The means to achieve this were linked with Keynesian demand management (see Marquand 1988; Hennessy 1992; Lowe 1999a; Dell 2000; Glyn 2001). To oversimplify the complex theories of Keynes, market forces do not necessarily produce full employment. Governments should therefore intervene in the economy by managing demand. Rather than cutting public expenditure in a recession as governments had done before the war, post-war governments would increase spending to maintain a high level of demand. The main focus was, therefore, on demand management and macroeconomic policy. In short, governments could and should control unemployment by pulling the appropriate policy levers. Ideally, governments would spend money on useful work such as building houses. However, Keynes once remarked that, if necessary, governments could employ people to dig holes and then fill them in, as there would be multiplier effects in aggregate demand as their wages worked their way around the economy to create a virtuous circle. However, the shorthand of the Keynesian welfare state can confuse more than it can illuminate. Different countries applied 'Keynesianism' in different ways in different degrees at different times. To simply equate Keynesianism with the classic welfare state, or a Keynesian welfare state, is problematic. For example, the USA and Japan have used Keynesian techniques, but would not normally be described as Keynesian welfare states. It was not always the 'most' social democratic governments that ran the largest budget deficits. Conversely, Nordic welfare states have used Keynesian techniques in different ways from the UK (see, for example, Garrett 1998; Thomson 2000; Glyn 2001; C. Pierson 2001).

Moreover, the link or 'fit' between Keynesianism and economic growth and full male employment is unclear. In general, the post-war period was *associated* with prolonged economic growth and low unemployment. Social democrats *believed* that Keynesianism had and would continue to produce the economic goods. For Crosland (1964), continued economic growth would sustain the increased public spending necessary to fund the welfare state. Social welfare would rise with economic growth (see Dell 2000; C. Pierson 2001). However, it is much more difficult to show that Keynesianism *caused* economic growth. Indeed, it has been claimed that Keynesianism was used when it was not needed, but not used when it was most needed (see Marquand 1988; Dell 2000).

It can be argued that too much attention has been directed at Keynesianism as a means and full male employment as an end, while economic growth *per se* has been overlooked. As Castles (2001b: 37) puts it, 'Two decades of extensive comparative research on the determinants of social spending have had little to say concerning the relationship between economic development and the size of the postwar welfare state'. Castles examines this 'dog that didn't bark mystery', concluding that economic growth is still important even in recent times of limited growth, and that 'in every period, the wealth of nations has had a significant role in shaping the trajectory of welfare state development' (p. 53).

The Keynesian consensus came increasingly under challenge in the 1970s. The most immediate challenge came with the increase in world oil prices in the early 1970s. Economic activity ground to a halt. Unemployment increased, leaving governments attempting to balance an increasing welfare bill without the economic growth that had been taken for granted. There was a linked intellectual challenge to Keynesianism. Critics argued that Keynesian policy led to increased inflation at best and 'stagflation' – the existence of both unemployment and inflation – at worst. Instead of controlling employment with demand management, governments should control inflation by controlling the money supply (Dell 2000). This anti-Keynesian or monetarist policy, associated with neo-liberal economists, was taken up in various degrees by Conservative governments (Chapter 3).

While not subscribing to monetarism, new social democrats have recently argued that there is a limited role for demand management in a globalized world. Rather than concentrating on demand, macro-economic policy and old-style 'full employment', governments should focus more on supply, micro-economic policy and employability (Giddens 1998, 2000; Blair and Schroder 1999; Glyn 2001).

Post-industrialism

While industrialization theories account for the growth of the welfare state, another broad set of explanations argue that more recent changes have profound implications for changes in welfare (Esping-Andersen 1999; P. Pierson 2001). The two main strands focus on 'post-industrialism', 'de-industrialisation' and the service sector, and 'the information society'. In some ways, the second label can be seen as a chronological second phase of the first. As Kumar (1995) explains, post-industrialism is associated with the work of the American sociologist Daniel Bell in the 1960s and 1970s. Bell (1973: 467) is clear that 'the post-industrial society is an information society'. However, the basic idea of the post-industrial society was the movement to a service society, while the idea of information itself remained relatively undeveloped'. In later work, Bell argues that just as energy, resources and machine technology were the transforming agencies of industrial society, knowledge and information are the transforming agents of the post-industrial society. These twin themes have led to a proliferation of labels and titles as commentators fought for the defining soundbite of the new era: 'the third wave', 'future shock', 'megatrends', 'the global village', 'computopia', 'information capitalism', 'the home-centred society' and the 'electronic cottage' (see Kumar 1995). According to Fitzpatrick (2001), the post-industrialism literature is replete with a lot of starry-eyed futurism, wishful thinking, hyperbolic claims and non-verifiable hypotheses. As Kumar (1995) points out, different commentators argue both optimistic and pessimistic versions, and there are clear links with disorganized capitalism (above), globalization (below), post-Fordism (below) and post-modernism (Chapter 8). However, reduced to its core, the argument claims that there have been trends in Western economies from a manufacturing to a service base. This is associated with the development of a core workforce in relatively secure employment and a growing peripheral workforce of low-paid, casualized, socially segmented labour (O'Brien and Penna 1998).

These changes are sometimes termed a second industrial revolution, linked with brain rather than brawn. The industrialization thesis (above) argues that the industrial revolution was associated with moves from an agricultural to an industrial society, and led to profound implications for the rise of the welfare state. Similarly, the post-industrialization thesis argues that moves from a manufacturing/industrial economy to a service/ post-industrial economy also leads to far-reaching changes. According to Iversen (2001), it defies credibility and the empirical record if the decline of agriculture and the rise of industrialism is of major importance for the welfare state, while the massive transformation implied by de-industrialization is irrelevant. On the other hand, Fitzpatrick (2001: 159) claims that the service sector is 'too flimsy a peg on which to hang a social revolution'.

In terms of its implications for welfare, post-industrialization is arguably the most neglected of the 'posts-'. For example, Rodger (2000) gives it just three brief mentions. However, the future of welfare in the post-industrial economy is a major theme of Esping-Andersen

(1990, 1999; see O'Brien and Penna 1998) and P. Pierson (2001). Perhaps the clearest treatment is that by Giddens (2000: 69), who claims that the 'knowledge economy' is 'well on the way' to being all-conquering: 'In combination with the broader aspects of globalization, it marks a major transition in the nature of economic activity'. The value of firms cannot be assessed by the 'old' factors of land, plant and raw materials, but by the human capital of their 'knowledge' or 'wired' workers. The implications for government are clear. Social policy must be seen as the other side of the coin of economic policy (e.g. Commission on Social Justice 1994).

> Old-style social democracy concentrated on industrial policy and Keynesian demand measures, while the neoliberals focused on deregulation and market liberalization. Third way economic policy needs to concern itself with different priorities – with education, incentives, entrepreneurial culture, flexibility, devolution and the cultivation of social capital.
>
> (Giddens 2000: 73)

This links with his previous guideline of investment in human capital wherever possible, rather than the direct provision of economic maintenance. In place of the welfare state, we should put the social investment state, operating in the context of a positive welfare society (Giddens 1998). Similarly, Ferrera *et al.* (2001) emphasize the importance of education, training, skills, and employability in a 'learning society'. With the change from an energy-intensive to an information-intensive production and service system, there is a decline in demand for unskilled manufacturing workers. They differentiate between the protected or sheltered and the exposed sectors of employment (cf. Scharpf and Schmidt 2000a; Schwartz 2001). Many manufacturing jobs and some service jobs are vulnerable to international competition in a globalized world (see below). However, other service jobs are protected. To give a simple illustration, banking and insurance jobs are exposed, while restaurant jobs are not. While international financial companies can switch operations from London to Frankfurt, you cannot pop out to Hong Kong for lunch. In short, these accounts stress the current implications for employment and send some warning signals: there may be major problems unless education and training systems adapt. On the other hand, Iversen (2001) takes a longer term view and a more optimistic line, arguing that since the 1960s de-industrialization has driven a significant expansion in welfare expenditure.

Post-Fordism

Post-Fordism is a complex and multifaceted theory. We deal with it as an economic explanation following Kumar (1995), who regards it as a post-industrial theory that stresses the relations of production, and O'Brien and Penna (1998), who discuss it together with globalization, post-industrialism and disorganized capitalism in their chapter on political economy. Similarly, Fitzpatrick (2001) examines it in a chapter on recent economic developments. In simple terms, Fordism is seen as mass production, mass consumption, modernist cultural forms and the mass public provision of welfare. On the other hand, post-Fordism is characterized by an emerging coalition between flexible production, differentiated and segmented consumption patterns, post-modernist cultural forms and a restructured welfare state (Loader and Burrows 1994).

In his discussion of post-Fordism, Kumar (1995) examines the industrial districts of small workshops and factories in the 'Third Italy', 'flexible specialization' and the 'second industrial divide', disorganized capitalism and the 'new times' of British Marxists. Probably the most relevant account for welfare is given by Jessop (1994), who describes four aspects of Fordism: a labour process (the mass production of complex consumer durables), a macro-economic system (mass production and consumption in a largely national economy), a social mode of economic regulation (institutionalized collective bargaining and a Keynesian welfare state) and its general implications for social organization and cohesion (an urban-industrial, 'middle-mass', wage-earning society). Jessop (1994: 15) admits that 'real difficulties remain in operationalising the concept of Fordism', but it seems to make most sense to ground it as a social mode of economic regulation. It follows, using the same four dimensions, that post-Fordism can be seen as a flexible production process based on flexible machines or systems and an appropriately flexible workforce; the dominance of a flexible and permanently innovative pattern of accumulation; supply-side innovation and flexibility in each of the main areas of regulation; but 'it is too soon to anticipate what a post-Fordist mode of socialisation would be like' (Jessop 1994: 19–21). Jessop argues that the Fordist Keynesian welfare state (KWS) has transformed into a 'Schumpeterian workfare state' (SWS). Subsequently, Jessop (1999) develops this work to view a change from the Keynesian welfare national state (KWNS) to the Schumpeterian workfare postnational regime (SWPR). The clear break occurs as domestic full employment is de-prioritized in favour of international competitiveness and redistributive welfare rights take second place to a productivist re-ordering of social policy. The national state is subject to a series of changes, which results in its 'hollowing out': upwards to supranational levels, downwards to local or regional levels of governance; and outward to horizontal networks of power which bypass central states. The four changes that have created pressures for the development of this new state form are the rise of new technologies, growing internationalization, the paradigm shift from Fordism to post-Fordism and the regionalization of global and national economies.

There appear to be three major implications for the welfare state (cf. Fitzpatrick 2001). The first, the move from Keynesianism in the national economy to internationalization, has been widely noted (above). The second is the move to a more productivist regime. According to Jessop, who has provided 'the most influential application of post-Fordism' (Fitzpatrick 2001: 161), this more work-oriented welfare regime – the SWR (Schumpeterian workfare regime) – aims to 'subordinate social policy to the needs of labour market flexibility and/or international competition' (Jessop 1994: 24). Rodger (2000) notes the move from welfare to workfare. Cerny (1997: 179) identifies a general move 'from the welfare state to the competition state', with a shift from the general maximization of welfare within a nation to the promotion of enterprise, innovation and profitability in both private and public sectors. This is linked with the third point of the development of a dual or segmented labour market of core and periphery workers, or 'insiders' and 'outsiders' (Kumar 1995; Mullard and Spicker 1998), and the possibility of a two-tier welfare system (Hoggett 1994) or a 'two nations' strategy (Mishra 1990).

Clarke and Newman (1997) point out that post-Fordism is influential, though much criticized. Pitched at this general level, the post-Fordist explanation of change looks relatively plausible. However, the pattern of change is not as simple as the post-Fordist argument suggests (Clarke and Newman 1997) As Chris Pierson (1998a: 60) points out, 'The watchword of post-Fordism is flexibility'. However, Clarke and Newman (1997) argue that its key concepts, such as 'flexibility' and 'fragmentation', are a little imprecise. As Kumar (1995) puts it, flexibility is too flexible for its own good. It is highly arguable whether the welfare state was ever Fordist. Certainly, many of its organizational structures and labour processes remained resolutely pre- or non-Fordist. Clarke and Newman (1997) are not persuaded that the delivery of universalist services can be constructed as an equivalent to mass consumption. Post-Fordist analyses have tended to be relatively selective in the welfare policy examples that they use. Moreover, the novelty of these points is not clear. Marxist critics have long noted that the welfare state values workers rather than citizens. The work ethic has been vital to British social policy since 1834 and can be seen clearly in the Beveridge Report (Hewitt and Powell 1998; King 1999). The chronology is also unclear. According to Fitzpatrick (2001), Fordism began to break down in the 1970s. If post-Fordism is linked with quasi-markets (Hoggett 1994) or 'Thatcherism' (Jessop 1994), then it dates from the Conservative period of office. On the other hand, if it is linked to the end of Keynesianism (also Jessop 1994), then it predates the Conservatives. Rodger (2000) writes that theories of Fordism and post-Fordism have been developed from within political economy and, on the whole, appear to be rather economically and technologically deterministic when applied to the welfare state. Post-Fordism is the 'economic theory of post-modern welfare', but its relevance must be demonstrated rather than assumed. Loader and Burrows (1994) write that while most of the contributors in their edited collection accept the usefulness of some variant of post-Fordism at a fairly high level of abstraction, most have doubts concerning its more concrete applicability to an analysis of contemporary patterns of division and change in welfare provision. In other words, the question mark in the title of their collection, *Towards a Post-Fordist Welfare State?* (Burrows and Loader 1994), remains significant.

Economic globalization

While the older explanations emerged during the expansion of welfare states, the newer perspective of globalization has emerged during times of limited growth or retrenchment. According to Fitzpatrick (2001: 163), globalization has 'generated a body of literature which has dwarfed that of post-industrialisation and post-Fordism put together'. Yeates (2001) backs up her claim of a 'great deal of work' on globalization and social policy by citing 37 references taking up eight lines of text. However, Mishra (1999) claims that very little of the vast globalization literature is about its impact on the welfare state.

Moreover, there is little agreement on the meaning of 'globalization' and its impacts on social policy (e.g. Hirst and Thompson 1996; Rhodes 1996; Taylor-Gooby 1997; Hay 1998; Jordan 1998; C. Pierson 1998a, 2001; Mishra 1999; Yeates 1999, 2001; Fitzpatrick 2001; Sykes *et al.* 2001). Hirst and Thompson (1996) differentiate between internationalization and globalization. They claim that internationalization refers to increased openness of national economies and a growth in international trade. However, they argue that significant international trade has been present for 500 years and that the level of exchange between different nations is only slightly higher than it was at the end of the nineteenth century. Furthermore, the pattern of international trade is confined to the triad of Europe, the USA and the Far East, who are likely to remain the leading regional centres of exchange.

Globalization, on the other hand, refers to production becoming truly global as transnational corporations, without national identity and with an international management, replace multinational corporations, which still retain a clear national base and are amenable to regulation by the home country. In other words, transnational corporations are the mark of the global. Large flows of capital, labour, finance and information move between countries linking together private corporations, banks and other institutions, including governmental agencies, involved in production and trade. New global forms of business are lubricated by two main factors. First, an open international financial system has seen the abandonment of fixed currency exchange rates and of capital controls. Second, travel and communication systems have reduced the 'friction of distance'; Harvey (1989) writes of 'time–space compression', while Giddens (1994: 4) points to the 'transformation of space and time' and 'action at a distance'.

There are two broad dimensions of views on globalization (cf. Fitzpatrick 2001). The first concerns the strength or inevitability of globalization, while the second is concerned with its desirability. The 'hard' or 'strong' version of globalization asserts that globalization is imposing a uniform set of consequences, one of which is the weakening of nation states. From this perspective, globalization represents a new version of the convergence or end of ideology thesis. Ohmae (1990) argues that, in the context of the global economy, nation states no longer have the power to determine policy in their own national interests, which is neatly summed up in his phrase of 'Sony not soil'. External constraints mean that it is not meaningful to talk about policy choices. Irrespective of domestic politics, a single model of development is being imposed on countries that will all be driven in the same direction by the imperatives of international competition (Yeates 1999). The 'soft' version of globalization argues that the new external environment constrains, but does not determine, the limits of domestic policy (Garrett 1998; Yeates 2001). Jessop (1994, 1999) argues that there has been some 'hollowing out' of the nation state, with power transferred outwards to the supranational level and inwards to the regional and local levels. However, nation states can – and do – make policy choices (Castles and Pierson 1996). Navarro (1999a,b, 2000) claims that social democratic politics is still possible in an era of globalization. Hirst and Thompson (1996: 2–4) point to inter-nationalization rather than globalization as a world economic system 'that still gives a major role to national-level policies and actors'. They conclude that 'whilst the state's capacities for governance have changed and in many respects (especially national macroeconomic management) have weakened considerably, it remains a pivotal institution, especially in terms of creating conditions for effective international governance' (p. 170).

However, a more pessimistic view is given by Mishra (1999), who claims that although responses differ at the moment, globalization appears to be a strong levelling force that, in the long run, threatens to transform the discrete social economies of nation states.

Some commentators, such as Ohmae (1990) and Fukuyama (1992), regard globalization as the welcome triumph of liberal democracy (see Bonoli *et al.* 2000; Rodger 2000; Shin 2000). Most writers regard global-ization as undesirable because it reduces if not eliminates left-of-centre approaches. From this perspective, globalization is seen as a mask for neo-liberal ideology (Hutton 1999; Mishra 1999).

Bonoli *et al.* (2000) outline three types of welfare state response to globalization (cf. Fitzpatrick 2001; Sykes *et al.* 2001). First, globalization requires welfare retrenchment to reduce public expenditure and taxes. Second, globalization requires more rather than less government provision of public services. Third, a middle course emphasizes the compromises between welfare and competitiveness.

The first position is 'globalization against welfare'. It is based on the neo-liberal argument that the welfare state causes economic problems for governments (in addition to social and moral problems). Social wel-fare undermines incentives to work and save for individuals. High tax rates persuade firms not to invest and, in the global economy, they may decide to 'exit' to a better location. This threat is sometimes termed 'social dumping', where countries adjust their wages and working condi-tions downwards in a beauty contest to attract footloose capital (Mishra 1999; Rodger 2000). For several decades, producers have readily laid off surplus labour and, in the case of transnational corporations, resorted to transplanting firms to countries where labour is less costly – in effect, 'exporting unemployment'. Recent accounts argue that this pessimistic thesis is overstated and there is no 'race to the bottom' (Garrett 1998; Leibfried 2001; C. Pierson 2001; P. Pierson 2001). However, Bonoli *et al.* (2000) claim that while the evidence for these views are limited, they are persuasive to governments in that they provide ideological ammunition for welfare retrenchment.

The second position argues that competitiveness requires state welfare. It is claimed that a country such as Britain cannot undercut the low wages in areas such as Asia and Eastern Europe. It must therefore stress areas in which it has a comparative advantage. This means focusing on 'high-technology', 'brain rather than brawn' work. It follows that great stress must be put on a skilled labour force and on education and training. More importantly, it suggests a selective approach to social policy (see below). Sectors with relevance for competitiveness such as education take priority over sectors such as personal social services. 'Core' workers are more important than 'peripheral' workers.

The third approach focuses on compromises between welfare and competitiveness. This differentiates between 'good' and 'bad' spending. Investing in an active welfare state is contrasted with paying people to be inactive. It stresses investment in 'mass' services such as health care and education, emphasizes paid work rather than welfare and views economic and social policy as different sides of the same coin. Shin (2000) emphasizes the importance of policy linkage between economic and social policy. He argues that globalization demands not a welfare state characterized by a hands-off, mimimalist race to the bottom, but rather a 'business friendly social policy'. He detects some common trends in most welfare states towards: a market-conforming policy on business taxation, a reduction in the share of employers' contributions to social protection revenues, more limited income security programmes, an increased allocation of resources for active labour market programmes and less state intervention in the labour market.

Mullard and Spicker (1998) state that the implications of globalization for welfare systems are not immediately clear. Yeates (2001) points out that globalization is a problematic variable, and the causal links between globalization and social policy are difficult to establish. There is little consensus beyond that 'something' has happened to the global economy in recent decades. Chris Pierson (1998a: 64) claims that 'Few serious commentators on social policy accept the globalization story in its simplest and most draconian form' (see Yeates 2001). However, if the 'hard' version of globalization is rejected, that still leaves a large range of 'softer' accounts, stressing varying degrees of influence. According to Bonoli *et al.* (2000), 'the sovereignty of national governments in advanced industrial societies has suffered *to a greater or lesser extent*' (p. 70, emphasis added). Yeates (1999) claims that many globalization narratives exaggerate the structural dependence of the state on capital; they heighten the perceived threat that international capital will abandon a country for a more profitable climate; they encourage national states to abandon expansionary policies that cushion unemployment in favour of financial austerity; they sever the link between domestic economic growth and full employment in the developed nations; and they encourage the transnational diffusion of neo-liberal ideology that supports pro-market policies and national economic retrenchment. According to Schwartz (2001), external accounts such as globalization often simply point out functional necessities for welfare state change and typically lack a causal mechanism. Hay (1998) makes the obvious point that the issue is not whether the parameters of the politically possible are circumscribed by the 'harsh economic realities' and 'inexorable logics' of competitiveness and globalization, but by perceptions of such logics and realities and by what they are held to entail. Bonoli *et al.* (2000) emphasize the importance of 'globalization as ideology'. The notion of globalization sits very comfortably with neo-liberal, anti-welfare state thinking. The effects of globalization on welfare retrenchment may have been far greater than they would have been had the research evidence been used as a guide to policy. It is the political interpretation of the evidence, rather than the evidence itself, that is the crucial factor in influencing government policy. Mishra (1999) makes similar points. Globalization serves as a convenient rationalization for neo-liberal policies. Nevertheless, he adds that this does not make globalization a 'myth'. The obvious problem remains to separate the 'objective' elements of constraint from the 'subjective' or ideological elements.

Economic explanations and welfare change

This section compares the explanations, particularly whether they suggest continuity or change and how they relate to our three-fold working division between the classic, restructured and modern welfare states. We compare the accounts to examine common elements and periodization. In general, industrial theories tend to stress continuity in the rise of the welfare state, but clearly cannot explain changes associated with de-industrialization or post-industrialism. There are some dichotomous accounts, such as post-industrialism, disorganized capitalism and post-Fordism, but their chronology is far from clear. Some Marxist accounts view a series of crises largely in the 1970s. Globalization is problematic as its chronology and even its existence is subject to debate. Some explanations share common elements (Kumar 1995). There are also some common elements between quite different accounts. For example, the stress on investment in human capital in the information society has parallels with the Marxist view on accumulation.

Many accounts link the classic welfare state with the full employment and economic growth of the Keynesian welfare state. For example, Fitzpatrick (2001) claims that the economic justification of the classic welfare state was essentially Keynesian. It follows that the break came in the 1970s. The rise of world oil prices occurred during the Conservative government of 1970–74, but the end of the classic welfare state is sometimes dated to the Labour government of 1974–79 with the end of Keynesianism, rising unemployment and the end of economic growth. Labour *de facto* abandoned Keynesianism in 1975 when they cut spending in a recession. According to Dell (2000: 462), Chancellor Healey's Budget of 1975 had 'for the first time since the war given the battle against inflation priority over full employment. It was a turning point in Britain's post-war economic history'. However, the formal end of Keynesianism is often dated from Prime Minister James Callaghan's speech to the 1976 Labour Party Conference: 'We used to think that you could spend your way out of recession . . . I will tell you in all candour that that option no longer exists' (Timmins 1996: 315). Sullivan (1996) points out that Labour's economic strategy was partially based on monetarist principles that included attempts to control the money supply and to reduce, or at least halt, the rise in public expenditure. However, he continues that some have argued that this should be seen as a politically expedient response to external pressures rather than as a principled abandonment of Keynesianism. Timmins (1996: 316) writes that Healey was 'a virgin chancellor in economically uncharted waters' and that Labour was a minority government. According to Shaw (1996: 158), 'the Government gave an impression of struggling to do its best in extremely bleak conditions, where the familiar landmarks were vanishing, and where few of the levers used in the past to control events any longer worked'. Labour was granted a loan from the International Monetary Fund with conditions of cutting expenditure. In Tony Crosland's famous words, 'The party's over'. All of this appears very different from the reappraisal of Conservatives such as Sir Keith Joseph and Margaret Thatcher in opposition. Joseph made a speech in 1974 that embraced monetarism, regarding inflation rather than unemployment as the major aim of economic policy. With the opening line that 'Inflation is threatening to destroy society', Joseph was 'abandoning post-war Keynesianism two years ahead of Callaghan's Labour Party conference speech' (Timmins 1996: 357).

Marxist accounts of the period stress the contradictions of the welfare state and crisis (Pierson 1998a). There was a fiscal crisis of the state

(O'Connor 1973), a legitimation crisis (Habermas 1976) and fiscal and legitimation 'crisis management' (Offe 1982). According to Klein (1993), O'Goffe's view is that crisis and contradiction is inherent in capitalist welfare states. However, Klein argues that O'Goffe over-predicted the crisis in Western welfare states and under-predicted the turmoil in the communist states of Eastern Europe. Lash and Urry (1987) see the moves from organized to disorganized capitalism occurring from the 1960s in Britain. It is difficult to see any obvious rupture of the welfare state in the 1960s and subsequent problems have been associated with other explanations, such as exogenous shocks and the end of Keynesianism rather than disorganized capitalism *per se*.

Economic explanations appear to be very relevant for the restructured welfare state. In some ways, in the early years of the 1979 Conservative government, there was a clear economic policy but no coherent social policy. Mrs Thatcher's priorities were on industry, taxation and the trade unions: 'the supply side must come first' (in Timmins 1996: 372). There are major departures from the classic welfare state for both means and ends of policy. Although unemployment had risen significantly under the previous Labour government, it was to increase more sharply under the Conservatives. It can be argued that the rise under Labour reflected desperation of government beset by economic and political difficulties and by external constraints where the old policy levers did not work. On the other hand, the Conservatives set a new economic course and relied on very different policy levers. The Conservatives saw inflation rather than employment as the key economic goal. While Labour regretted the loss of their old friend Keynesianism, the Conservatives happily embraced its intellectual adversary of monetarism. Put bluntly, unemployment was seen as a weapon to fight inflation (Sullivan 1996). The labour force was regarded like any other economic commodity. When supply exceeded demand, as in times of high unemployment, labour simply had to reduce its price. The labour market had to be deregulated and made more flexible. Bodies to regulate wages were abolished. The power of the trade unions was challenged. The gap between benefits and earnings was increased to address the problem of work incentives or the 'why work' syndrome. Markets, rather than governments, determine the unemployment rate. Although the term 'globalization' was not generally used, it was stressed that Britain was part of a global economy and must face international competition. External constraints limited increases in wages, taxes and public expenditure. Mrs Thatcher often used the analogy of a 'good housewife' running the household economy. Like a family, the country could not spend more than it earned. Keynesian deficit financing was seen as an irresponsible use of the national credit card. In contrast to the classic welfare state, it was argued that public expenditure as a proportion of national wealth should decrease. Higher and basic rates of income tax were reduced. Neo-liberals argued that this has two beneficial aims. First, it means that citizens rather than governments decide how to spend their own money. Second, low taxes encourage greater enterprise. Critics pointed out the paradox that enterprise at the top meant large pay increases for 'fat cat' executives of privatized utilities, while enterprise at the bottom required 'realistic' (i.e. lower) wages. While not going as far as the New Poor Law that essentially starved the unemployed into work, the Conservatives attempted to make life on benefits far less comfortable. Post-Fordist accounts explain this in terms of a productivist approach to welfare, pointing to significant inequalities between favoured and less favoured elements of the labour force. In short, the restructured welfare state, liberal market approach of deregulation and minimal welfare was characterized by small carrots and large sticks.

The economic explanation of the modern welfare state draws on globalization and post-industrialism. New Labour has accepted that the world has changed and 'takes globalization as a given' (Marquand 1998: 20). Blair has argued that the embrace of globalization is inevitable and desirable, but this acceptance of globalization – 'hook, line and sinker' – has been criticized (e.g. Hutton 1999). In a negative sense, this has parallels with the end of Keynesianism. The global economic environment means that Keynesianism in one country has been rejected (but see Hutton 1999) and one of the central goals of the post-war welfare state, full employment, is no longer viewed as a realistic policy option. Chancellor Gordon Brown's speech to the Labour Party Conference of 1997 echoed Callaghan: 'just as you cannot spend your way out of a recession, you cannot, in a global economy, simply spend your way through a recovery either' (Riddell 1997). Shaw (1996: 201) claims that this is essentially the same economic framework as that of the right. Blair's view that the ability of national governments to fine-tune the economy to secure growth and jobs has been exaggerated (Blair and Schroder 1999) may be compared with that of Denis Healey, that 'in the end markets decide' (Shaw 1996). However, there is a more positive agenda. Although governments cannot ensure 'Keynesian full [male] employment', they wish to promote full employment for all through employability. In a world of ever more rapid globalization and scientific changes, there is a need to create the conditions in which existing businesses can prosper and adapt and new businesses can be set up and grow. The most important task of modernization is to invest in human capital: to make the individual and businesses fit for the knowledge-based economy of the future (Blair and Schroder 1999; Giddens 2000). Blair and Schroder (1999) continue that having the same job for life is a thing of the past. Social democrats must accommodate the growing demands for flexibility. Discussing a 'new supply-side agenda for the left', they argue that both 'micro-economic flexibility and macro-economic stability' – supply and demand sides – are important, but there must not be a renaissance of 1970s-style reliance on deficit spending and heavy-handed state intervention. Sound public finance should be a badge of pride for social democrats. They do not rule out government deficits completely, but in general high levels of government borrowing must decrease. Modern social democrats are not *laissez-faire* neo-liberals. Flexible markets must be combined with a newly defined role for the active state. The main priority must be investment in human and social capital, particularly education, including life-long learning. According to Giddens (2000), a tenet of third way politics – 'wherever possible invest in human capital' – is a guiding theme of welfare reform. The references to flexibility and productivist elements fit with post-Fordist accounts. Holliday (2000) writes that productivist welfare capitalism could be something of an international standard in the twenty-first century.

Conclusions

Few explanations appear to offer an accurate and unambiguous account of welfare change. Industrial and Marxist accounts are pitched at broad and abstract levels. Disorganized capitalism and post-industrial explanations see ruptures from the 1960s that bear no obvious relation to welfare change. The end of Keynesianism and economic growth gives a general break between the classic welfare state and restructured welfare state in the 1970s, although we tend to view the combination with political change in 1979 as more important (see Chapter 6). The chronology of globalization is less clear, but the perception and rhetoric of globalization and the information society is the only plausible economic rationale for the modern welfare state. Economic determinism, one of the main criticisms of industrial theories, can obviously be levelled at all the accounts considered here (cf. Schwartz 2001). While the economic environment provides a powerful broad constraint on welfare policy, economic explanations are unlikely to account for the many complex elements of detail.

Further reading

Ramesh Mishra (1999) *Globalisation and the Welfare State*. Cheltenham: Edward Elgar.
Examines economic and political globalization, linking conceptual and empirical perspectives. It tends to present a pessimistic case, viewing globalization as having a strong and negative impact on the welfare state.

Martin O'Brien and Sue Penna (1998) *Theorising Welfare*. London: Sage.
Offers a more theoretical account with fewer links to policy developments. It provides a range of explanatory perspectives, but is strong on our economic explanations such as Marxism, disorganized capitalism, post-industrialism, post-Fordism and globalization.

Christopher Pierson (1998) *Beyond the Welfare State?*, 2nd edn. Cambridge: Polity Press.
Excellent historical account of welfare change from the nineteenth century combined with a range of explanatory perspectives. Useful for our other explanatory chapters, but perhaps strongest on economic explanations such as industrialization, political economy, Keynesianism, Marxism and globalization.

Rob Sykes, Bruno Palier and Pauline Prior (eds) (2001) *Globalization and European Welfare States*. Basingstoke: Palgrave.
This offers a broad discussion of globalization and relates it to different types of European welfare states, including the 'liberal' regime of the UK.

6 POLITICAL EXPLANATIONS

Introduction

Discussion of the political settlement of the welfare state is generally linked with the social democratic consensus (Hughes and Lewis 1998). However, simply examining changes from social democracy to neo-liberalism provides a limited perspective on political explanation. We take a wider perspective and discuss states, governments and parties. We explore the explanations of citizenship, institutionalism and 'politics matters', before examining the 'new convergence' or whether politics *still* matters.

Citizenship

It is unclear where it is best to place citizenship explanations. We follow the lead of Chris Pierson (1998a), who discusses it as an example of the modernization thesis, which is regarded as a politicized version of the industrialism thesis. In this view, the welfare state is a product of successful political mobilization to attain full citizenship, in the context of industrialism.

According to Flora and Alber (1981), the concept of modernization, linking the economy with the polity, has largely superseded more specific concepts such as industrialization and democratization. They present a complex model that draws on Rokkan's theory of European political development. Rokkan (see Flora *et al.* 1999) sets out four stages of political development: state formation, nation building, participation and redistribution. In simple terms, the last two stages relate to the development of mass democracies and of welfare states, respectively. Flora and Alber (1981) hypothesize that mass democracies are more likely to develop welfare systems based on social rights.

This has clear links with the citizenship account of Marshall (1963), who saw citizenship as composed of three elements of civil, political and social rights. The civil element is composed of the rights necessary for individual freedom, such as equality before the law and freedom of speech. The political element concerns the right to participate in the exercise of political power as a member of a body invested with political authority or as an elector of the members of such a body. The social element was more vague: 'the whole range from the right to a modicum of economic welfare and security to the right to share to the full in the social heritage and to live the life of a civilized being according to the standards prevailing in the society' (Marshall 1963: 74). Marshall links these rights to the institutions of the law, parliament and local councils, and the educational system and social services, respectively. He claims that these rights developed in the eighteenth, nineteenth and twentieth centuries, respectively, in Britain. Citizenship is a status bestowed on those who are full members of a community. All who possess the status are equal with respect to the rights and duties with which that status is endowed. Marshall (1963) is clear that the equality of status of citizenship is compatible with certain inequalities, providing 'the foundation of equality on which the structure of inequality could be built' (p. 91). He writes that the extension of the social services is not primarily a means of equalizing incomes. Equality of status is more important than equality of income. Citizenship contributes towards class fusion and class-abatement, resulting in a progressive divorce between real and money incomes. Critics point out that the definition of social citizenship is unclear (see, for example, Drake 2001; Fitzpatrick 2001), but Marshall (1963) makes it plain that there is no universal principle that determines what the rights and duties of citizenship shall be. Mishra (1981) points out that it is clear that the nature and content of social rights are neither self-evident nor given. They cannot be determined in advance by some *a priori* notion. However, according to Marshall, social rights are influenced by conflicts within a democratic capitalist state. As Mishra (1981) himself puts it, civil and political rights set the rules of the game: social rights represent the outcome of the game. It should not be possible to know the final score in advance, although commentators have made many informed speculations. Flora and Alber (1981) claim that government intervention has probably been shaped predominantly by two basic developmental processes: the creation of state bureaucracies and the creation of mass democracies. We now turn to an examination of these two broad political explanations.

Institutional accounts

Several writers have claimed that 'social institutions matter' (e.g. Bonoli *et al.* 2000). However, Peters (1999: 1) begins his account by pointing out that 'the roots of political science are in the study of institutions'. He claims that Aristotle recognized the importance of institutions to government. This 'old institutionalism' declined in the 1950s and 1960s. Since the 1980s, a number of versions of 'new institutionalism' have appeared. The most relevant for our purposes is 'historical institutionalism' (Thelen and Steinmo 1992; Peters 1999: ch. 4). At its broadest, historical institutionalism represents an attempt to illuminate how political struggles are mediated by the institutional setting in which they take place. Institutions shape the rules of the game of political struggle and government capacities. A whole range of formal organizations, such as state and societal institutions, and informal rules and procedures influence conduct (Leibfried 2001; P. Pierson 2001). Political institutions of different countries vary along crucial dimensions, such as the rules of electoral competition, the relationship between the legislature and executive, the role of the courts and the place of subnational governments in politics (Bonoli 2001; Swank 2001).

Much of the literature focuses on the institution of the state and is termed a 'state-centred approach' or 'bringing the state back in'. As Chris Pierson (1998a) writes, state-centred approaches recognize the importance of industrialization, urbanization, democratization and class interests, but they insist that these influences are mediated by the independent effects of state organization. Writers such as Ashford (1986) and de Swann (1988) stress the importance of political leaders and administrative officials. Much of this approach focuses on the USA and is associated with the work of Skocpol and colleagues (see, for example, C. Pierson 1998a: 95–8, 114–17). According to Paul Pierson (1996), institutionalists make two broad claims. First, strong states are likely to produce strong welfare states. For example, it is easier to launch welfare programmes in countries with 'first-past-the-post', 'winner-takes-all' electoral systems than in those with proportional representation. A similar point can be made for unitary rather than federal states and unilateral rather than bi-cameral assemblies. Second, a degree of path dependency exists. Policy feedbacks or legacies are important: existing programmes constrain future policy options.

Many criticisms have been made of this approach. Peters (1999) claims that it suffers from 'severe problems'. The definition of an institution is not clear and the existence of an institution is largely a given. Similarly, the size and direction of steps away from the path is not clear. There is a functionalist element in that things happened the way they did because they had to, given the historical and institutional forces at work. There is little or no capacity to predict change. There are problems of falsification and tautology: 'if institutional norms are not followed it can be argued either that it was not a fully developed institution or that any institution is permitted to have some deviations from established norms' (Peters 1999: 150). In short, there are no clear criteria for distinguishing between 'path dependent' and 'path shifting' reforms: it is not clear how, why and when path change may occur. Crouch (1999) argues that path dependency procedures lead to exaggeration and even reification of core characteristics. As social institutions are incoherent, the result is partial and deceptive. Followers of these methodologies are likely to miss much of what is going on. Ross (2000) writes that the literature omits any explicit discussion of partisan politics. At best the 'old' conceptualizations of the left and right remain implicit, with greater welfare effort associated with the left. Ross continues that parties do matter under conditions of constraint, but not necessarily in a neat or linear fashion. Party effects are sometimes contingent and sometimes counterintuitive.

Much of the approach may simply be old wine in new bottles. Although not termed 'institutionalist', Wilensky (1975: xiv) suggested that 'differences between the welfare state leaders and laggards can be explained by specific differences in political, social and economic organization including the degree of centralization of government'. He continues that it is also necessary to take into account 'the length of time a country has been in the welfare business' (p. 9). Similarly, Higgins (1981) points to the role of the state, and discusses reasons why the USA is a welfare laggard, including its decentralized state structure. Finally, Flora and Alber (1981) discuss bureaucracy, claiming that an early and strong bureaucratization and centralization may have promoted welfare state development.

'Politics matters'

Democracy, a much used and abused term, is central to political science and cuts deep into language. The common terminological link between 'social democracy', 'liberal democracy' and 'democratic socialism' is clear. The Constitution of the USA begins with the evocative phrase, 'We the people . . .', and is paralleled by President Lincoln's term, 'government of the people, by the people, for the people' (e.g. Freedland 1998: 19). Robson (1976: 16) claims that 'a Welfare State must be democratic'.

Chris Pierson (1998a) claims citizenship approaches share very similar assumptions with traditional social democratic thinking on the development of the welfare state. In particular, there are clear links between social rights and political rights. In some cases, social rights are necessary to maintain political rights. For example, it is often argued that one reason behind the 1870 Education Act was the need to educate the urban working class that had been enfranchised in the 1867 Reform Act. As Robert Lowe, Vice-President of the Education Department, put it, 'I believe it will be absolutely necessary to compel our future masters to learn their letters', or as it became in the more popular version, 'We must educate our masters' (in Fraser 1984: 86). However, the more usual argument is that political rights lead to social rights. The links between democracy and welfare have been stressed by a number of writers from various times and perspectives, which Fraser (1984: xxix) terms the 'democratic perspective'. Marx claimed that universal suffrage would have its 'inevitable result . . . the political supremacy of the working class' (in Marquand 1992: 10). A similar thesis from a rather different perspective was given by the nineteenth-century politician, Lord Salisbury, who is reported to have stated that giving the working class the vote would be like leaving the cat in charge of the cream. According to Sidney Webb, collectivism is the obverse of democracy. If the working man is given the vote,

> he will not forever be satisfied with exercising that vote over such matters as the appointment of the Ambassador to Paris ... he will more and more seek to convert his political democracy into what one may roughly term an industrial democracy, so that he may obtain some kind of control as a voter over the conditions under which he lives.
>
> (in C. Pierson 1998a: 24, fn)

Tawney (1964: 201) argues that if the public, and particularly the working-class public, 'is confronted with the choice between capitalist democracy, with all its nauseous insincerities, and undemocratic socialism, it will choose the former every time'. Bevan (1978: 23–4) writes that 'A free people will always refuse to put up with preventable poverty ... Political democracy brings the welfare of ordinary men and women on to the agenda of political discussion and demands its consideration'. In a famous phrase, Sir Hartley Shawcross, a member of the first majority Labour government in 1945, claimed that 'We are the masters now'. This great faith in parliamentary democracy may be understandable when memories of Fascist and authoritarian forms of government in other countries in the 1930s were fresh.

Chris Pierson (1998a: 27) claims that the power resources model offers a distinctive variant of the social democratic approach. Modelled on Scandinavia in general and Sweden in particular (Korpi 1979), it points to a struggle between the economic and political sphere, or between markets and politics. As Stephens (1979: 72) puts it, 'the welfare state is a product of labour organisation and political rule by labour parties'. Paul Pierson (1996: 150) considers that the power resources model 'has been the leading approach in comparative politics in explaining patterns of welfare state expansion'.

Many studies have examined statistically the links between the dependent variable of welfare effort and independent economic and political variables. We saw in Chapter 5 that 'industrialism' accounts (e.g. Wilensky 1975) tended to downplay the effects of politics. This generated a response from writers who argued that 'politics matters'. This 'reverse side of the coin' argument tends to downplay economic effects and stress the role of politics. Put another way, this argument dismisses the 'end of ideology thesis' (Bell 1960). An early account of Rys (1964) suggests that political factors are the most important 'environmental' element in the evolution of social security. The 'politics matters' position is associated with the work of Francis Castles: 'Contrary to the convergence thesis, politics did matter' (Castles and Pierson 1996: 234). Esping-Andersen (1990, 1999) argues that there are 'three worlds of welfare capitalism' of social democratic, Christian democratic and liberal regimes (see Abrahamson 1999). As Esping-Andersen (1990: 4) puts it, 'politics not only matters, it is decisive'.

Chris Pierson (1998a: 31) concludes that there is some contested evidence that 'politics makes a difference', but we need to consider *how* it makes a difference. A major issue in political science is 'do parties make a difference?' (Rose 1984). There are three broad accounts linking political parties with welfare. First, some political science literature focuses on mandate theory (Hofferbert and Budge 1993) or the 'manifesto model of party government' (Rose 1984). Rose explains that when two parties alternate in office, then, for a given party, opposition intention (t1) is equal to government practice (t2). In opposition, a party will set out its policy intentions and then put these into practice upon entering office. It starts from the assumption that elections should offer voters a choice between alternative ways of governing the country. For an election to be meaningful in policy terms, the parties must not only pledge different policies but also practise what they preach. Some writers have argued that writing manifestos is a waste of paper and examining manifestos is a waste of time: politics does not matter, either because there are no differences between 'bourgeois' parties or that external events shape policies. However, Hofferbert and Budge (1993) conclude that parties appear to perform broadly as called for by the mandate theory of democracy. Moreover, irrespective of whether mandate theory is valid, many voters believe that it should be valid. In a democratic society, the ultimate test of political success is election. In short, there is an assumption of a contract between electors and elected. Different parties have different views of welfare and propose different policies. George and Wilding (1985: 136) claim that it can matter a great deal whether the government is of a Conservative or a Socialist or Social Democratic ideology as far as the type of policies that are pursued. It follows that elections that involve changes of government may mean turning points for policy. For example, a number of social policy texts (e.g. Hill 1993) examine the welfare state by government such as Labour 1945–51 followed by Conservative 1951–64.

The second account focuses on the median voter. Downs (1957: 295) states that 'parties in democratic politics are analogous to entrepreneurs in a profit-seeking economy'. Downs sets out a 'spatial theory of electoral competition' that can be illustrated by the example of selling ice creams (Hay 1999; Heffernan 2000). It can be shown that, on a beach with two sellers, the rational position for each to locate is back-to-back at the centre that gives them a market share of half the beach. Moves away from this equilibrium will enable their rival to capture sales. Similarly, Downs claims there is a tendency towards bipartisan convergence in a two-party polity, with each party trying to resemble its opponent as closely as possible. Downs (1957) states that political parties tend to maintain ideological positions that are consistent over time unless they suffer drastic defeats, in which case they change their ideologies to resemble that of the party that defeated them. Heffernan (2000) claims that to some extent the Conservatives moved to the left after their defeat in 1945, while Labour moved to the right after its defeat in 1983.

The third account applies public choice theories to adversary politics. Chris Pierson (1998a: 44) points out that, under circumstances of adversary politics, parties 'bid up' the electorate's expectations, promising 'more for less' in an attempt to unseat the existing government. Broad examples are manipulating economic variables in the prelude to an election and setting a 'giveaway Budget'. Put more crudely, governments effectively 'bribe' the electorate. An alternative version of this general thesis attempts to undermine the opposing party by 'buying' support. Fraser (1984) points to two examples. In 1895, the Conservative Arthur Balfour stated that 'Social legislation . . . is not merely to be distinguished from Socialist legislation but it is its most direct opposite and its most effective antidote' (Fraser 1984: 139). The Liberals David Lloyd George and Winston Churchill, more than 10 years later, copied this strategy of using social policy to head off socialism. The last two accounts argue that it is the contest for votes rather than the number of votes *per se* that is important in influencing policy.

Most of these accounts assume that the working class unambiguously supported more state welfare. However, the earliest welfare state measures were generally introduced by liberal and/or conservative elites and not by the representatives of organized labour, and there was some organized labour opposition to early welfare state measures (C. Pierson 1998a). It must be stressed that statistical accounts tell us about association rather than cause.

'Politics matters' accounts assume pluralist rather than elitist forms of power; that the 'government' is different from 'state'. However, Pierson (1998a: 33) points out that the historical record shows that the state may have its own interests in the promotion of social policy, not least in the securing of a citizenry fit and able to staff its armies. He gives examples of the concern with 'national efficiency' and the policy reforms such as school meals and the school health service that emerged after the Boer War of 1899–1902, and Prime Minister David Lloyd George's argument that 'you can not maintain an A-1 empire with a C-3 population'. This has some parallels with our discussion in Chapter 8 of war as an agent of social change. Other accounts argue that social policy may result for reasons other than benevolence, such as 'social control' (e.g. Squires 1990) and industrial competition (e.g. Gough 1979). Marxist approaches claim that the state is not a neutral instrument and inevitably serves the long-term interests of capital (see Chapter 5).

A new convergence? Does politics still matter?

Even if politics mattered, it is unclear whether politics *still* matters. Some commentators claim that political and economic globalization have resulted in a new convergence or a new end of ideology thesis. Under political globalization, power is hollowed out from the nation state upwards to supranational agencies. Economic globalization constrains policy choices to the point at which politics and ideology are virtually meaningless, producing 'the end of history' (Fukuyama 1992).

Political globalization has parallels with the 'hollowing out' concept of post-Fordism and governance (Jessop 1994, 1999; R. Rhodes 1997, 2000; see Chapter 7). It is claimed that there have been some moves of power upwards from the national to post-national or supranational level. The two main areas of interest have been on international agencies such as the International Monetary Fund (IMF), World Bank, International Labour Office (ILO), Organization for Economic Cooperation and Development (OECD) and the European Union (EU).

In the first area, the path-breaking work is Deacon's (1997) account of 'global social policy'. He claims that the social policy of a country or locality is increasingly shaped by the implicit and explicit social policies of numerous supranational agencies. These organizations have different agendas and degrees of influence. For example, the OECD promotes investment in human capital (Shin 2000), while the World Bank has been championing the Chilean pension scheme (Deacon 1997). However, the general point is that 'global governance' may be associated with 'semi-sovereign' states (Yeates 1999, 2001).

There remains much uncertainty about the influence of EU social policy over national welfare states. On the one hand, writers such as de Swann

(1992) argue that welfare states are national states. However, Leibfried (2000) challenges the 'minimalist interpretation of EU involvement'. He claims that national welfare states remain the primary institutions of European social policy, but they do so in the context of an increasingly constraining multi-tiered polity, or a European federalism. National social policy is ever more strongly determined by the European level (Leibfried 2000). On the other hand, Geyer (2000) points out that while there have been some moves towards 'Social Europe', the pace of these moves varies in areas such as labour policy, gender policy and anti-poverty policy. He concludes that EU social policy is not significantly replacing or undermining national level social policy and that there is no clear convergence. There appear to be no clear answers to the question of the level of convergence.

There has been much debate about the indirect influence of the EU on convergence in the form of the Maastrict convergence criteria for European monetary union (EMU) (Geyer 2000; Hantrais 2000). In broad terms, this is an agreement by EU states to converge their economies in terms of criteria such as national debt. It follows that this pledge to control public expenditure will have implications for welfare spending. Hirst (1999) writes that European welfare states may not be threatened by an abstract process of globalization, but by the successful creation within the EU of a single market and the advent of monetary union, by 'globalisation in one trade bloc'. He continues that 'French voters may have deliberately chosen to preserve their welfare entitlements, but the socialist government may be unable to secure them and at the same time meet the conditions for EMU' (p. 94).

We reviewed economic globalization in Chapter 5. We focus here on its implications for political choice. Some commentators claim that economic globalization has reduced political choice in a new end of ideology thesis. It has forced a new convergence to the right of the old consensus by eclipsing left-of-centre alternatives. Geyer (1998) summarizes this view:

> The welfare states of advanced industrial countries should become increasingly similar as the forces of globalization squeeze them into a market-orientated, welfare-state model. In essence, it does not matter whether the national institutional contexts are conservative or social democratic, if the welfare state is conservative, liberal or social democratic, or if a leftish or rightist party is in power; the constraints have become so extreme that only market-conforming, welfare-state structures will be allowed.

Some commentators argue that partisan effects have declined over time. Paul Pierson (1996: 151) writes that there are good reasons to believe that the centrality of left party and union strength to welfare state outcomes has declined. Mishra (1999) argues that whether there is a conservative, liberal or social democratic government in office matters, but globalization has meant a narrowing of the choices available to parties of the left, resulting in convergence on a right-of-centre position. According to Esping-Andersen (1999: 256), 'Keynesianism, let alone social democracy, in one country is accordingly no more an option. It may even be that government's freedom to design discrete social policies has eroded'. Stephens *et al.* (1999) claim that while there were strong partisan effects on welfare effort, the 1980s saw a sharp narrowing of political differences. Even Castles (2001b) concludes that the evidence on the irrelevance of partisanship to the present trajectory of welfare state development is quite incontrovertible.

On the other hand, as we saw in Chapter 5, this 'strong' globalization thesis has been criticized (Yeates 2001). Hirst (1999) argues that globalization has not killed social democracy. The welfare state can survive in a globalized world and there is no inevitable 'race to the bottom'. Castles and Pierson (1996) examine the UK, Australia and New Zealand, concluding that the new convergence theory fails to capture the reality of social policy developments in these countries in the 1980s. They continued to follow three quite distinct trajectories of social policy development. Swank (2000) argues against 'the theory of diminished democracy'. He uses case studies and statistical evidence to claim that there is limited support for convergence. Scandinavian welfare states remain resilient and distinctive. Institutional features of welfare states and political systems suggest that government responses to globalization will be quite different in nations such as the Nordic countries. Castles (2001a) finds positive but non-statistically significant correlations between changes in spending between 1984 and 1997 and party complexion, but warns that this should not be interpreted as contradicting the previous evidence. The cross-national evidence for a link between the partisan complexion of government and levels of public spending in the mid-1990s is quite decisive: the finding simply means that there was no systematic tendency towards the relationship becoming stronger in these years. The tentative conclusion from these studies appears to be that politics, in the form of political parties, still matters – but matters less, and perhaps in different ways (Ross 2000) – in determining welfare effort. However, as we have stressed, the character of the welfare state may not be captured by crude measures of welfare effort.

Writers such as Hay (1998) stress that the influence of globalization is subjective more than objective. In other words, what is important is how politicians *perceive* its constraints. In this sense, its impact is primarily ideological (Mishra 1999; Yeates 1999, 2001), providing a convenient rationale, legitimation or excuse for political action or inaction.

Putting political and economic globalization together, the general consensus seems to be that there are new pressures, but that there is little clear evidence of convergence. Hirst (1999) claims that there is still a clear choice in national and EU social policy between the goals of social democracy and neo-liberalism. This is most obvious in the Nordic countries, where there is still a vigorous advocacy of social democratic policies. Moses *et al.* (2000) discuss the multifaceted impact of globalization and Europeanization, concluding that 'the rumours of the end of the Scandinavian social democracy have been exaggerated. Globalization and Europeanization subjected it to new pressures, but its main elements, including the universal welfare state remain more or less intact' (p. 18). More generally, Scharpf and Schmidt (2000b) point to diverse responses to common challenges, with no convergence in the welfare state and no single solution or formula for successful adaption. Each country must find its own way, which depends on a variety of nationally specific factors (P. Pierson 2001; Sykes *et al.* 2001).

Political explanations and welfare change

We have reviewed a diverse set of explanations linked with states, institutions, governments and political parties. Although there appears to be some common ground in that 'politics' still matters, if less than it used to, the question of how it matters is less clear. At times, political explanations seem to consist of a rag-bag of factors varying from electoral systems to union power and from state bureaucracies to voting patterns. Paul Pierson (1996) notes explanations were developed at different times, and based on different countries: 'Just as a focus on Sweden was central to the development of the power resources model, concentration on the United States has underscored the importance of political institutions' (p. 152). There are certain ironies such as calls to 'bring the state back in' at a time when others claim that globalization is pushing the national state back out.

Our starting point in applying these explanations to the changing welfare state begins with continuity over time. Citizenship appears to be

a rather 'apolitical' political explanation. It is not clear why social citizenship might rise and fall. It is reasonable to suppose that citizenship is
linked to politics in some fashion. In a narrow sense, governments may
extend or reduce social rights. In a broad sense, social rights may reflect
the general political and social ethos. However, it is difficult to place
citizenship within a clear political theory of change. This leaves a clear
difference between path dependency and ideological accounts. Path
dependency accounts tend to stress continuity: governments may come
and go, but institutions are more static. The problem is that there clearly
has been welfare change. Path dependency accounts are probably most
useful in comparative analysis, where it can be shown that institutional
features are linked with different degrees of change (e.g. Bonoli and
Palier 2001). A good case can be made that Britain, with its unitary state
and first-past-the-post electoral system, may be more amenable to change
than countries with federalism, strong checks and balances and coalition
governments (cf. P. Pierson 1994). For one country, there is the problem
of the counterfactual: what degree of change would have occurred without the institution?

Ideological accounts suggest change, but are divided between accounts
stressing a division between the Butskellite consensus and Thatcherism,
or a three-fold division into social democracy, neo-liberalism and the
third way. Elections are seen as turning points. The difference between
the accounts revolves around whether the 1997 election of New Labour
is seen as reflecting continuity with Thatcherism, or a 'third way' distinct from both the Old Left and the New Right.

The classic welfare system is generally associated with the social democratic, Butskellite consensus or Keynesian welfare state. However, the
degree of this consensus and its precise nature remain in dispute. It is
difficult to pin down the essence of social democracy (Marquand 1988;
Giddens 1998, 2000; Hirst 1999; Krieger 1999; Thomson 2000; Glyn
2001; C. Pierson 2001). Most commentators regard British social democracy or 'labourism' as an outlier from the Continental European version
(Krieger 1999; Navarro 1999a; Sassoon 1999). The notion of consensus is
equally problematic. At the macro level, the main parties after 1945
agreed about the existence of the mixed economy and the welfare state.
However, on matters of detail there were some disagreements both between and within parties. The degree of consensus varied in different
policy areas, with major divisions in areas such as housing (see Chapter
2). Even if there was a consensus, it is by no means clear that it was
'social democratic'. As Marquand (1988) explains, no-one called themselves a Keynesian social democrat. There was no self-conscious tradition

of Keynesian social democracy with which its adherents could identify, no Keynesian social-democratic myth to stimulate their loyalty. The two major figures representing the consensus, Keynes and Beveridge, were Liberals. George and Wilding (1985) classify them both as 'reluctant collectivists' rather than 'social democrats'. Esping-Andersen (1990) classifies Britain as a 'liberal' rather than 'social democratic' welfare regime. Barry (1999) considers that consensus on welfare did not derive from a coherent social theory. Although there was no coherent design, the Beveridge Report comes closest to a blueprint (Brown 1995). However, it is in the Beveridge Report and the legislation that followed it that we see the 'variety of inchoate welfare principles at work' (Barry 1999: 41). As Hewitt and Powell (1998) point out, there were differences between the Beveridge Report, the Beveridge welfare state and the Beveridge philosophy. Finally, as we saw in Chapter 2, there is a debate about the degree of continuity over time in the classic welfare state. Some see merely incremental changes, while others point to important deviations such as the change from flat-rate to graduated benefits, benefits increasing in line with earnings rather than prices, a state earnings-related pension (SERPS) and greater trends towards equality of outcome and vertical redistribution (Hewitt and Powell 1998).

In some accounts, the restructured welfare state arrives after the 1979 election in the shape of Thatcherism. Near the end of the election campaign, the Labour Prime Minister James Callaghan feared that 'there are times, perhaps once every thirty years, when there is a sea-change in politics . . . I suspect there is now a sea-change – and it is for Mrs Thatcher' (in Timmins 1996: 355). The Conservatives moved to the right in a conscious attempt to break with the post-war consensus. However, it is not clear that Thatcherism represents a coherent political ideology. It certainly contains elements of neo-liberalism and neo-conservatism: 'the free economy and the strong state'. Similarly, there is a debate as to whether Conservative social policy contained a coherent design plan or whether it varied over time. The resilient welfare state thesis argues that Thatcherism's bark was worse than its bite. Other accounts suggest that there was continuity during the first two terms of the Conservative government (1979–87) but that the third term saw change with the introduction of quasi-markets. Some claim that this period may be compared with 1945 in that a wide range of reforms possessed some common ground. Yet other accounts stress essential continuity throughout the Conservative period of office. There was an 'implementation gap' between rhetoric and reality, and it is misleading to 'read off' policies from values. One explanation of this gap is that welfare retrenchment is 'unpopular politics' (P. Pierson 1994, 1996, 2001). The Conservatives certainly considered that electoral realities provided some constraints. Social policy is not traditionally regarded as a natural vote-winning territory for the Conservatives. Mrs Thatcher famously attempted to reassure the electorate with the statement that the NHS is safe with us. The radical marketeer, Sir Keith Joseph, considered that the introduction of tuition fees for university students would incur middle-class electoral wrath (Timmins 1996). Mrs Thatcher fiercely resisted the attempt to reduce tax relief on mortgages (MIRAS) in Cabinet. Timmins' (1996: 426) version of a Cabinet meeting on another issue: 'fifteen ayes and one no, and the no had it' might be accurate. However, electoral and institutional accounts have difficulty in explaining the fiasco of the 'Community Charge' or 'poll tax'.

The debate continues about the existence of the modern welfare state. New Labour claims that its 'third way' is new and distinctive from both the Old Left and the New Right. Supporters argue that the third way is a modernized or renewed social democracy (Blair 1998, 2001; Giddens 1998, 2000, 2001). Critics claim that it represents a new paternalist social service state (MacGregor 1999). For good or ill, this gives a three-fold typology. On the other hand, some commentators claim that there are few differences between the Conservatives' and New Labour's welfare policies (e.g. Hay 1999; Heffernan 2000; Burden *et al.* 2000). On this view, there is a single break in 1979 between the classic welfare state and the restructured welfare state that replaced it. Our view is that while it is possible to point to both policy continuities and discontinuities, it is too simplistic to equate Conservative and New Labour approaches and that there are sufficient differences to use a different term (cf. Driver and Martell 1998, 2000; Marquand 1998; Glennerster 1999, 2001; Powell 1999a, 2000a,b). Whether the modern welfare state is a variant of the restructured welfare state or a completely different type can be subjected to the endless debate that characterizes all such 'cataloguing butterflies' activity (see, for example, Abrahamson 1999). However, the issue of whether the third way represents 'ideology' or the end of ideology is more important.

Some commentators see New Labour as changing its ideology. However, there is little consensus as to the beginning and end-points. There remains considerable disagreement as to what extent Labour was a 'socialist' party. There were a number of versions of 'Old Labour' and the category arguably includes individuals as diverse as Attlee, Bevan, Crosland and Benn. Just as it is difficult to define 'old' social democracy, the versions of 'new' social democracy offered by Gamble and Wright (1999), Thomson (2000) and White (2001) vary. In the space of not many pages, Shaw

(1996) mentions trends towards European-style social democracy, pre-Keynesianism and 'the American vision of an economically and socially mobile society'. Although Blair (1998), Wright (1996) and Sassoon (1999) appear to align Labour with European social democracy, most writers claim that is has more links to New Democrats in the USA (Dolowitz *et al.* 1999; King and Wickham-Jones 1999; Walker 1999b; Deacon 2000). Powell (2000b) argues that the third way has been transported more by transatlantic jumbo jet than by Eurostar.

Blair (1998, 2001) claims that New Labour has fixed values and goals but is pragmatic or flexible about means. Policies flow from values. Blair and Schroder (1999) write that across Europe social democracy has found new acceptance by retaining its traditional values, but is beginning in a credible way to renew its ideas and modernize its programmes, making timeless values relevant to today's world. Modernization is 'the application of enduring lasting principles for a new generation' (Blair, in Hay 1999: 15). This 'permanent revisionism' has some parallels with Croslandite revisionism of the 1950s (see Leonard 1999). Temple (2000; cf. Dell 2000) stresses the importance of pragmatism and expediency to New Labour and argues that its agenda is output-driven rather than being ideologically driven. Policy must be 'evidence-based' rather than being based on ideological dogma: 'what counts is what works' (see Davies *et al.* 2000). New Labour certainly places great stress on targets and objectives and on delivering its pledges (Temple 2000; Powell 2002). However, there is a danger that the welfare debate will be steered from basic principles to secondary technical issues of delivery and efficiency (Powell and Hewitt 1998: 9–10). Moreover, there are examples, such as the Private Finance Initiative and the London Underground, where there appears to be a 'public bad, private good' view that is difficult to reconcile with such an undogmatic, non-ideological vision. In short, we do not know 'what works' or why it 'counts'. In other words, it is unclear whether the parts fit together to form a coherent whole: Powell (2000b) regards the third way as 'jackdaw politics' where New Labour's nest has a variety of shiny policy objects from diverse sources.

Having been out of office for 18 years, New Labour places great stress – some say too much stress – on electoral appeal (Hay 1999; Heffernan 2000). New Labour recognizes that it must respond to a new political landscape. Just as the Conservatives in 1951 could not turn back the clock to the 1930s, Labour in 1997 could not undo the Conservative changes such as the 'right to buy' legislation. More specifically, it was necessary for Labour to appeal to the voters in the marginal constituencies. In particular, Labour had to capture seats in southern, affluent areas: to claim back 'Essex Man' into the Labour fold. At first sight, this appears an apt description of Labour's move to the political middle ground, jettisoning unpopular 'left' policies. However, as noted in Chapter 1, Labour's welfare policies were generally popular. This meant that the electoral explanation may have an indirect impact on welfare. It may explain an emphasis on key pledges limiting taxation and a trend away from redistribution.

Conclusion

Political explanations do not unambiguously favour continuity, a dichotomy or a trichotomy. Institutional or path-dependent accounts tend to stress resilience. While the emphasis placed on historical context by historical institutionalism is welcome, such accounts are rarely clear on which of their dependent variables (i.e. welfare changes) or independent variables (i.e. institutions) are central. In our terms, how many steps from the path mean a change from the classic to the restructured welfare system? Electoral explanations are clearly as important to politicians as they are disdained by academics not acquainted with Marquand's (1992) argument that, for nearly 100 years, the 'progressive dilemma' has been to reconcile principles with electoral appeal. The great success of the 1945 Labour government in Britain and of the Democrats in the 1930s and 1960s in the USA was that they were able to form a broad alliance that was popular and credible.

It is relatively simple to form either a two- or three-fold division of principles that indicate either one or two turning points (cf. Hay 1999 with Powell 1999a). While such crude juxtapositions (e.g. universalism versus selectivity; equality of outcome versus equality of opportunity; rights versus responsibilities versus rights *and* responsibilities) are useful as first-order, ideal-type approximations, they obscure many important nuances and caveats. Again, the link to the dependent variable is not clear. It is probably not particularly reassuring to live in a 'social democratic welfare state' when daily welfare realities are of long queues, crumbling buildings and perfunctory treatment (cf. Marquand 1992). We tend towards a three-fold division, but are aware that this broad-brush approach leaves much of importance out of the picture. If political parties matter, on a pluralist view it follows that we get the governments and the welfare states that we deserve – and this is not necessarily an optimistic thesis.

Further reading

Giuliano Bonoli, Vic George and Peter Taylor-Gooby (2000) *European Welfare Futures: Towards a Theory of Welfare Retrenchment*. Cambridge: Polity Press.
Provides a range of explanations, including political and institutional perspectives, arguing that old explanations of growth are not sufficient to explain retrenchment. It integrates conceptual and empirical material on Europe.

Frank Castles (1998) *Comparative Public Policy*. Aldershot: Edward Elgar.
An excellent comparative account of post-1945 public policy. It emphasizes a quantitative approach, presenting much rich data and many tables and diagrams.

Bob Deacon (1997) *Global Social Policy*. London: Sage.
Provides an important perspective on 'political globalization', arguing that it is necessary to look beyond the nation state towards international organizations and agencies such as the European Union, the International Monetary Fund and the World Bank.

Paul Pierson (ed.) (2001) *The New Politics of the Welfare State*. Oxford: Oxford University Press.
Diverse and wide-ranging accounts by leading authorities. It tends to emphasize the importance of political institutions and endogenous rather than exogenous factors of change. Contains a number of largely quantitative chapters and is not, in general, an easy read.

7 ORGANIZATIONAL EXPLANATIONS

Introduction

The organizational settlement has tended to be largely neglected and has come to attention relatively recently (e.g. Clarke *et al.* 1994; Clarke and Newman 1997; Hughes and Lewis 1998; Clarke *et al.* 2000). Much of this work focuses on the growth of managerialism in recent years, but also acts as a prism to throw light on the organizational settlement of the classic welfare state. It can be argued that organizational explanations are of a different explanatory type to our other explanatory chapters, in that it is a 'second-order' explanation as organizational changes result from economic, political and social changes. Nevertheless, it is a useful device to examine a diverse set of literatures covering new public management, hierarchies, markets and networks, the mixed economy of welfare, governance and governmentality, neo-Taylorism and McDonaldization.

New public management

'New public management' is a useful overarching term to introduce a number of diverse ideas. Much of this 'new management' draws on two sacred texts (Peters and Waterman 1982; Osborne and Gaebler 1992) that together provided the possibilities of large-scale transformations from unresponsive, paternalistic and leaden bureaucracies to the customer-driven, flexible, quality-orientated and responsive organizations of the future (Clarke and Newman 1997).

Peters and Waterman (1982) is reputed to be the best selling management text of all time. Together with later work by Tom Peters, it established the 'excellence' school (Newman and Clarke 1994; Ferlie *et al.* 1996). This focuses not on short-term competitiveness, but on building long-term capacity through transforming relations with customers and staff empowering staff. It is concerned with transforming the values and culture of the workforce and strengthening the commitment to organizations through partnership and the flattening of hierarchies (Clarke and Newman 1997). If social capital is vital for outcomes in civil society, this 'competitive capital' ensures success in the public and business spheres.

According to the authors of the other sacred text, entrepreneurial governance consists of 10 essential principles that link together to 'reinvent' public sector organizations:

> Entrepreneurial governments promote competition between service providers. They empower citizens by pushing control out of the bureaucracy, into the community. They measure the performance of their agencies, focusing not on inputs but on outcomes. They are driven by their goals – their missions – not by their rules and regulations. They redefine their clients as customers and offer them choices

– between schools, between training programs, between housing options. They prevent problems before they emerge, rather than simply offering services afterward. They put their energies into earning money, not simply spending it. They decentralise authority, enhancing participatory management. They prefer market mechanisms to bureaucratic mechanisms. And they focus not simply on providing public services but on catalysing all sectors – public, private and voluntary – into action to solve their community's problems.

(Osborne and Gaebler 1992: 19–20)

Such an avalanche of diverse ideas illustrates the difficulty of defining 'new public management' (Ferlie *et al.* 1996; Flynn 1997). Ferlie *et al.* (1996) outline the key changes, of which some, as they point out, are contradictory: privatization; quasi-markets; hierarchies to contracts; the creation of devolved and quasi-autonomous agencies; market testing; new forms of regulation; performance management; 'doing more with less' and 'value-for-money'. Flynn (1997) sets out six general themes: from equality of treatment to the promotion of different treatment for different people; from universal eligibility towards targeting; from public provision to the mixed economy of welfare; choice; from local policy autonomy to central control, combined with an opposite move towards more local managerial and financial autonomy; and funding based on some measure of performance or volume of work. Different strands of new public management have been noted (e.g. Pollitt 1993; Walsh 1995). For example, Ferlie *et al.* (1996: 10) outline four different models of new public management: efficiency drive; downsizing and decentralization; 'in search of excellence'; and the public sector orientation. Lowndes' (1999) survey of local authorities revealed three key orientations centred on efficiency, market and user and/or community. In short, new public management is a multi-coloured tapestry.

Many accounts contrast the old (bad) with the good (new) position (see, for example, Clarke and Newman 1997; Flynn 1997). Clarke and Newman (1997) criticize such dualisms. They oversimplify complex changes, presenting them as inevitable, unidirectional, linear and homogeneous. They detract attention from the process of change. They present change as discrete moves and disguise the complexity of the 'from' and 'to' positions, viewing them as 'a stereotyped and demonized past' and 'a visionary and idealized future'. As Lowndes (1999) points out, there is no one 'new management' but different, and potentially contradictory, streams of ideas and practices. Dualities impose an artificial coherence on both 'old' and 'new' management and overemphasize the discontinuity between old and new. Management change is non-linear, involving continuities between old and new approaches, movements forwards and backwards, and change at different levels.

In the next sections, we set out a number of linked narratives. Some topics and themes (e.g. hollowing out) recur in different sections. Like Clarke and Newman (1997), we stress the interconnectedness of different analyses, and will return later to the question of to what extent some of the explanations fit with each other.

Hierarchies, markets and networks

Some accounts take as their starting points the different modes of coordination of hierarchies, markets and networks (e.g. Thompson *et al.* 1991). It is claimed that there have been moves from hierarchy to market to network (see Exworthy *et al.* 1999).

Clarke and Newman (1997) argue that the organizational construction of the classic welfare state was structured by a commitment to two modes of coordination: bureaucratic administration and professionalism. The first element is based on Weber's classic account of bureaucracy, begun during the First World War when he superintended several hospitals. It consists of a hierarchy and a division of labour. Each employee holds an office whose tasks are fixed according to rational principles governing the division of labour and the allocation of authority within a hierarchical structure of accountability. Orders are transmitted down the hierarchy, enabling its apex to command and control. This produces routinized or predictable outcomes, where trained staff apply a body of rules and regulations to produce equitable treatment.

The second mode of coordination is professionalism. Unlike the impersonal administrator, the professional provided a personal service for the client. Professionals share a body of expert knowledge that gives them control over issues such as entry, standards and resource allocation. They have a large degree of autonomy over work and power over their clients (Wilding 1982; Gladstone 1999: ch. 6; Foster and Wilding 2000). One distinctive feature of public sector organizations is that they are highly professionalized (Ferlie *et al.* 1996). Perkin (1989) claims that, from 1945 to the mid-1970s, professional expertise was largely accepted and that the professions played an important part in the development of the welfare state. According to Foster and Wilding (2000), the 1950s and 1960s were the 'golden age' for welfare professionalism. The significant degree of autonomy enjoyed by professions and semi-professionals led Lipsky (1980) to term them 'Street Level Bureaucrats'.

Hoggett (1994) argues that the welfare state was a 'mongrel' organization, based on an uneasy marriage between a pre-Fordist craft (professional) productive system and a Taylorized (rational bureaucratic administrative) system. It is this distinctive mix that Clarke and Newman (1997) term 'bureau-professionalism'.

Both elements came under attack from the New Right. Bureaucracies were seen as inefficient, inflexible and unresponsive to consumers (see Clarke and Newman 1997: ch. 6). Peters and Waterman (1982: 157) state that 'in observing excellent companies, and specifically the way they interact with customers, what we found most striking was the consistent presence of obsession. This characteristically occurred as a seemingly unjustified over-commitment to some form of quality, reliability or service'. Similarly, Osborne and Gaebler (1992: 194) claim that, 'In a world in which cable television systems have fifty channels, banks let their customers do business by phone, and even department stores have begun to customize their services for the individual, bureaucratic, unresponsive, one-size-fits-all government cannot last'.

There were also criticisms of welfare professionals. The government was concerned about cost. One analogy stated that health service managers were like general managers in a factory who had no control over their production managers. Professionals were exhorted to become more cost-conscious and to stay within budgets. There was an attempt to incorporate professionals into management as a 'hybrid manager-professional' (Clarke and Newman 1997). Although there were changes in professional-management boundaries, the perspective that managers and professionals were necessarily in conflict and that professionals have lost out to managers is too simplistic (Ferlie *et al.* 1996). On the other hand, the public was concerned about the quality of service. According to Clarke and Newman (1997), there has been a decline in trust of experts such as welfare professionals. The other side of the coin of care is control: definitions of 'normality' also define 'deviance' (Gladstone 1999). Wider social control perspectives point to the disciplinary state (Jones and Novak 1999) and to 'anti-social policy' (Squires 1990). Beresford (1997) argues that the relationship between producers and consumers remains social policy's 'last social division'. He points to the recognition of the contribution made by organizations of disabled people and survivors of psychiatric care. This signals the importance of user voices in shaping services (Beresford *et al.* 1999) and of 'new' social movements from below (Drake 2001; Fitzpatrick 2001).

Shakespeare (2000) and Fitzpatrick (2001) present an example of the social relations of care from the disability movement. This movement challenges the discourse of dependency and advocates a change of emphasis from the dominant medical model towards a social model of disability. The medical model treats disability simply as a physical or mental impairment of the individual in reference to physiological and psychological 'norms'. The social model, on the other hand, argues that it is not the individual who is disabled, but that he or she is made disabled by society that does not accommodate varying levels of ability. For example, if someone in a wheelchair cannot gain access to a building, that is not due to any inadequacy on his or her part, but rather on the part of those who designed and administer the building. Like other groups, such as older people, children and people with HIV/AIDS, disabled people are often 'othered' and subordinated in the social relations of welfare. Broad structural relations are reconceptualized in terms of the notion of dependence, based on models of infantilization and incapacity, leaving the 'victim' in a state of dependence. Issues of 'voice' and rights are not considered necessary for those treated as a 'burden' or as 'charity cases'. At best, a benign paternalism or clientism replaces the 'normal' rights of citizenship.

Marquand (1992) brings both elements of bureaucracies and welfare professionals together in his thesis on the failure of social citizenship. The institutions of social citizenship were not effectively subject to popular control in a fashion in which the citizens themselves – the patients in the doctor's waiting room, the parents outside the school playground, the crowd waiting to approach the DHSS counter – considered satisfactory. At the point where the shoe pinched, at the point where ordinary members of the public brushed up against the institutions that were supposed to act in their names, the social citizenship state did not feel like a citizenship state at all. All too often, it felt more like a rather ramshackle, on the whole benevolent, but often remote and high-handed despotism. Top-down statism had failed. The case for non-statist, decentralist, participatory forms of public intervention was rarely made, and still more rarely heard. Exit won the argument, because the culture provided too little space for Voice.

The 'exit' argument was provided by the New Right and included new public management (NPM) perspectives. According to Clarke and Newman (1997), the application of market mechanisms became the dominant strand of reform. Walsh (1995) claims that a major feature of new public management is the marketization of public services. However, this term includes a variety of mechanisms. It includes outright privatization, but more usually means the introduction of managerial techniques from the private sector and the development of market mechanisms within public services. Ferlie *et al.* (1996) argue that 'NPM Model 1: the efficiency drive' can be seen as the earliest model to emerge. It was dominant throughout the early and mid-1980s and represented an attempt to make the public sector more business-like. This was led by crude notions of efficiency, value for money and getting more from less, and delivered by stress on greater customer-orientation, a strong hierarchy and perform-ance indicators (Carter *et al.* 1992; Cutler and Waine 1998). This tended to be followed by 'NPM 2: downsizing and decentralization', which con-centrated on contracts, quasi-markets and contracting out (Le Grand and Bartlett 1993). The main rationale is that customers should have choice. For example, parents should choose schools for their children, rather than being allocated to the nearest school by a catchment area indicated on a map on the wall of the LEA. Forcing the producers to compete for the custom of consumers would lead to a welfare state that empowered people rather than treating them as supplicants (Marsland 1996).

Markets, in turn, have been subject to criticism. Critiques of quasi-markets have claimed that while there may have been some increases in efficiency, these may have been combined with problems of inequity and fragmentation (Le Grand and Bartlett 1993). Some see the solution in terms of networks and partnerships, which aim to address problems of coordination. However, for many years governments have exhorted greater coordination to solve the 'wicked' or 'interconnected and intractable problems' (Challis *et al.* 1988). Following the success of network forms in some industries, it has been suggested that relational, long-term con-tracts are more appropriate in some circumstances than adversarial, short-term or 'spot' contracts (e.g. Sako 1992; Walsh 1995; Ferlie *et al.* 1996). For example, Flynn *et al.* (1996) claim that networks are particularly appropriate for sectors such as community health services.

Although there is some validity to these accounts, there are a number of problems (Exworthy *et al.* 1999). First, the forms were far from ideal types. Just as it has been claimed that it is best to term markets in the public sector 'quasi-markets' (Le Grand and Bartlett 1993), it may be more accurate to speak of 'quasi-hierachies' and 'quasi-networks'. Sec-ond, a clear chronology of linear change is problematic. At best, there has been a move from a situation where elements of hierarchy were prominent to more plural forms.

Mixed economy of welfare

As with hierarchies, markets and networks, this perspective also views a trend to the greater use of markets, but also points to moves towards the voluntary and informal sectors. The state is viewed not as the only actor in welfare, but as part of a wider mix that also includes the market, voluntary and informal sectors. As Chapters 2–4 showed, there has always been a mixed economy of welfare, but this perspective points towards changes in the mix or a greater welfare pluralism. The term 'welfare pluralism' can be used in both a descriptive and prescriptive sense. Authors such as Brenton (1985), Mishra (1990) and Johnson (1999) describe trends towards greater pluralism that they generally regret. On the other hand, writers such as Hadley and Hatch (1981) focus on the 'failure of the state' and argue in favour of pluralist, decentralized and participative services.

The sometimes neglected distinction between production, finance and regulation (Burchardt 1997; Burchardt *et al.* 1999) is vital. For example, the term 'privatization' may be used promiscuously to include the very different phenomena of a transfer of assets from the public to the private sector, increased charging, or a transfer of provider where the recipient still has access to the good or service at zero cost. All of these strategies have been used in several different sectors (Burchardt 1997; Burchardt *et al.* 1999; Johnson 1999; Drakeford 2000).

Supporters of the voluntary sector also argue for a variety of strategies (see, for example, Brenton 1985; Finlayson 1994; Johnson 1999). At one level, this entails the greater use of voluntary agencies to deliver services at zero or subsidized cost that are largely funded by the state, which is sometimes termed the 'contract culture'. In contrast, writers such as Whelan (1996, 1999) consider that the 'real' voluntary sector is not tainted by state support. There has also been a revival of interest in mutual or civil society solutions. From a broadly left perspective, Hirst (1994) suggests associative democracy. Giddens (1998, 2000) argues for an expansion of welfare rooted in civil society. Field (2000) puts forward stakeholder pensions operated through approved welfare suppliers. From the right, Green (1996) proposes reinventing the old mutual organizations that were destroyed by the state. This fits with an emphasis from commentators in the USA on communitarianism (Etzioni 1996) and 'social capital' (Putnam 2000). These initiatives are often seen as part of a welfare society rather than a welfare state (Freedland 1998; Giddens 1998, 2000). Critics regard them as part of a nostalgic view of a better yesterday, turning the clock back to a golden era of children playing safely in the streets and leaving doors unlocked for neighbours to pop in (Rodger 2000: see Chapter 8).

While supporters of mutual solutions encompass both left and right, in general those favouring informal welfare – family, friends and neighbours – are largely located on the political right. For example, Marsland (1996) argues that state welfare has eroded individual responsibility. Rodger (2000) characterizes this view as 'anti-modernism': welfare was better in a golden past where the community and the family rather than the state were the main providers of welfare. Such views have been criticized by feminists who claim that this view of the 'traditional' family and 'male breadwinner model' reinforces the sexual division of welfare. They point out that, in practice, care in the community means care by the community and that informal care equals family care that equals care by women. Such 'enforced altruism' has clear implications for women's lives (Land 1999).

Governance

The governance narrative (e.g. R. Rhodes 1997, 2000) focuses on networks (cf. HMN) and on hollowing out (cf. post-Fordism). Governance is the 'product of the hollowing-out of the state': upwards to international bodies, downwards to special-purpose bodies and outwards to agencies. For Rod Rhodes (2000), governance refers to self-organizing, interorganizational networks, with the characteristics of interdependence between organizations, continuing interactions between network members, game-like interactions and a significant degree of autonomy from the state. He presents nine aphorisms of the 'governance narrative'. He claims that there has been a change over the past 20 years or so from government or the 'Westminster model' to governance. There has been a shift from line bureaucracies to fragmented service delivery. These networks include private and voluntary sectors. Government privatized the utilities, swapped direct for indirect control, contracted out services and introduced quasi-markets, bypassed local authorities for special-purpose bodies and removed operational management from central departments and vested it in separate agencies. Central departments are no longer either necessarily or invariably the fulcrum, or focal organization, of a network. Government has decentralized services, but introduced a 'massive extension of regulation' with 'more control over less'.

Governance challenges the language of the new public management (R. Rhodes 2000). The language of governance – differentiation, networks, hollowing out, trust and diplomacy – contrasts sharply with that of managerialism, markets and contracts. Under governance, networks rival markets and bureaucracy as a means of delivering services. Trust is a central coordinating mechanism of networks. The limits to markets and hierarchies are well known. The limits to networks are less well known, but networks are likely to be effective in certain contexts such as when actors need reliable, 'thicker' information, and quality cannot be specified or difficult to define and measure (Flynn *et al.* 1996). The governance literature draws on HMN (Stoker 1999), but to a very limited extent on post-Fordism, even though 'hollowing out' is a major feature of both.

Rod Rhodes (2000) views New Labour's desire for joined-up or holistic government in terms of steering networks. It is the 'third way in action'. However, Rhodes goes on to undermine his own thesis. The currency of networks is trust rather than authority or price competition. Thus, if there are significant indications of authority reducing the autonomy of network members, networks blur into hierarchies. He notes the danger of a 'command operating code in a velvet glove' (R. Rhodes 2000: 360). The supporters of networks or governance have yet to demonstrate that such networks have sufficient autonomy from the state to justify their status (Exworthy *et al.* 1999).

Governmentality

The notion of governance captures the weakening of state government and the growing influence of centres of power outside government. The French philosopher Michel Foucault anticipated this trend in the late 1970s with his theory of governmentality (see Foucault 1991; see also Chapter 8). The radical import of this theory is that government since the emergence of capitalism in the seventeenth century has had to address the limits of its political power if market relations are to thrive. Political economists in the eighteenth and nineteenth centuries were acutely aware of the problems of the fragile relations between government and market that politicians on the neo-liberal right and third-way centre-left have had to grapple with more recently. Governments since the seventeenth century have faced a long-term dilemma of, on the one hand, maintaining order among the state's subjects, while, on the other, coming to terms with the limited methods of control that governments could exercise over their subjects. For Foucault, government in the seventeenth century began to abandon its attempts at controlling its subjects by exercising total and constant surveillance in favour of a more subtle and detached method associated with the rise of market capitalism and *laissez-faire*. Foucault coined the term 'governmentality' for this new object of historical inquiry, in which observation switches from the traditional objects of *systems* of government and overarching principles of statehood to the *processes*, methods and conduct of government. Foucault (1991: 97) insists that government was governing 'according to rational principles that are intrinsic to it and which cannot be derived solely from natural or divine laws or the principles of wisdom and prudence; the state like nature has its own proper form of rationality'. Government developed methods for inculcating a greater sense of self-regulation in each individual. These methods were tailored to the needs of each individual while maintaining overall government of every one. The ideal sought in inculcating self-discipline was to give to each subject a sense of self-empowerment over his or her own life. Hence, the disciplines of the market place epitomized the combination of individual freedom to take risks and self-discipline to work for one's personal ends.

During the 1990s, several writers applied Foucault's notion of governmentality to the critical transformations of the state and welfare state in the late twentieth century (e.g. Watson 2000). For example, Ling (2000) argues that the changing nature of health partnerships reflects a wider change in the British state over the last 30 years, which may be described as a shift from government to governance to governmentality. In other words, Ling extends the argument of Rod Rhodes (1997), claiming that while governance was an appropriate term for the 1980s, the new context is one of an emerging governmentality. Ling draws on Foucault, stating that governmentality concerns the colonization of identity through which an obedient population and civil society is secured. Before joining the partnership, groups must demonstrate their capacity to be good partners. For example, voluntary groups must be able to demonstrate measurable outcomes through performance indicators, and have a vision, a mission statement, a business plan and so on. However, this analysis builds on Rhodes' (1997) definition of 'governance' and considers that governmentality has recently arrived. Both of these are problematic. As we point out above, governance with its notion of horizontal partnership may give too little emphasis to vertical lines of authority. As such, Ling's use of governmentality may simply be a corrective to a flawed concept rather than as a new phase in itself. Second, Foucault saw governmentality as the overarching theme of modern statecraft, under which different modes of government come and go. Ling's argument that New Labour's approach to government represents the closest approximation to governmentality so far reached, therefore, is at variance with Foucault's claim that governmentality has been around since the seventeenth century.

Neo-Taylorism

'Taylorism' is a model of 'scientific management' developed by Fredrick Taylor. It leads to a strict division of labour that is based on the breakdown of industrial activity into definable tasks, exemplified by the assembly line in Henry Ford's car plants (Mullard and Spicker 1998). It has clear links with one of Jessop's (1994) four definitions of Fordism, namely as a labour process (cf. Walsh 1995). As Fitzpatrick (2001: 159) puts it, the scientific management of Taylorism is 'at the heart of Fordism'. Although both Fordism and Taylorism were widely practised, neither could be said to have dominated the processes of industrial production, but were important in certain industries, such as the car industry (Mullard and Spicker 1998).

Pollitt (1993) views the initial period of changes in the UK, characterized by cost control and decentralized management, as underpinned by a 'neo-Taylorist' form of managerialism. There is an emphasis on targets and results, where the strengthening and incentivizing of line management is a constant theme. He identifies this 'narrow conception of management' as neo-Taylorism and views the later reforms as a 're-evaluation of neo-Taylorism', leading to the introduction of quasi-markets, a greater emphasis on decentralization, a constant emphasis on the need to improve quality and insistence on greater attention being given to meeting the wishes of the individual service users. Much of this explicitly drew on the work of Peters and Waterman (1982) and Osborne and Gaebler (1992).

McDonaldization

Ritzer (1996) has sought to explain developments in the organization of the labour process in terms of the global proliferation of a particular form of organization found in the fast-food industry and spreading throughout the service industries of the world. He terms this phenomenon 'McDonaldization'. The principal contention is that producers have adapted to the emerging uncertainties of the global economy less by encouraging new skills of flexibility and innovation in their workforce, but more by instilling qualities on the job of robot-like compliance in attitude, demeanour and performance that ensures the product is uniform in quality and delivery around the world.

Within social policy, there is, arguably, a 'McDonaldization of human need' in sectors such as healthcare, nursery provision and higher education. For example, birth and death are highly unpredictable events with equally unpredictable consequences that expose the most basic contingencies of human need. Yet in recent decades birth, for example, has succumbed to increasing rationalization as seen in the development of new medical interventions for male impotence, predictors for ovulation and genetic defects, home pregnancy testing and clear cost-criteria for legally aborting births (Ritzer 1996). The extension of rationalization techniques to these areas of human need constitutes a clear sign of the encroachment of McDonaldization into the sphere of 'McWelfare'.

Ritzer (1996: 9) argues that McDonaldization 'offers consumers, workers and managers efficiency, calculability, predictability and control'. As we saw above, 'efficiency' is a major concern of the new public management and hierarchies, markets and networks perspectives. Calculability refers to the quantitative aspect of production, especially to the process of controlling and speeding up the number of products produced, where 'quantity tends to be surrogate for quality' (Ritzer 1996: 59). In the public sector, it is a matter of continuously keeping costs down at times of cash constraints. Ritzer discusses the effect of calculability in higher education in stressing the number of students who are herded through the system and whose success is judged in terms of grades earned, the 'grade point average' achieved overall, 'value added' to students by the conclusion of their studies and the numerical score on quality measures such as student feedback questionnaires. Predictability ensures that continuity and uniformity of product are sustained in an increasingly competitive and uncertain world. Employers strive to ensure that their products, outlets and employees' behaviour are all predictably uniform across different locations For example, staff–customer interaction is 'ritualised, routinised and scripted'. Even the number of rings of the phone before answering must be carefully calibrated so that staff respond neither too soon (answering too quickly can catch the caller off guard) nor too late. Rationality concerns the increasing application of new technologies of control over the production process, often involving substituting new non-human technologies for skilled human activity. Enhancing control by means of new technology and de-skilling human labour complements the other dimension in helping to sustain profits and keep costs down in an increasingly insecure economic world.

Both neo-Taylorism and McDonaldization, then, are alternatives to post-Fordism: far from increasing flexibility, there are moves to the top-down, inspected, batch production of Fordism/Taylorism. For example, in higher education there are trends towards inspection, modularization and semesterization. This may not quite be (Fredrick) Taylorist, but it is certainly anti-(A.J.P.) Taylorist in that the brilliance of the historian's unscripted and solely aural presentations would certainly have failed any 'quality inspection'.

Organizational explanations and welfare change

Some of the explanations are clearly linked. There are a number of common themes. For example, trust features in hierarchies, markets and networks (HMN) governance. Markets feature in HMN and the mixed economy of welfare. Ferlie *et al.* discuss 'NPM 2' in the context of post-Fordism and HMN, and 'NPM 1' as neo-Taylorism (cf. Pollitt 1993). According to Rodger (2000), the post-Fordist welfare state is a 'hollowed-out state', with the main responsibilities for the welfare state infrastructure increasingly being renegotiated by governments with their citizenry and devolved to voluntary and commercial supply. There are also links to our other chapters. For example, Rodger (2000) states that consumption rather than production is the key feature of the post-Fordist economy, citing Bauman (1998: 132) that 'in a world populated by consumers there is no place for a welfare state'. However, there are a number of problems of consistency and chronology. Some explanations show little overlap, even though they refer to the same concepts. For example, Jessop (1999) writes on the 'changing governance of welfare' without reference to Rhodes. Few post-Fordist accounts show much knowledge of the governance literature or vice versa. More problematic is that McDonaldization shows some contrasts with post-Fordism and the 'Risk Society' (Chapter 8).

Some of the schemas entail dichotomies (e.g. bureau-professionalism to managerialism), whereas others entail trichotomies (e.g. hierarchies, markets and networks). There are therefore questions about the chronological fit between these schemas. Does one phase in a two-fold schema stretch across two phases of a three-fold schema and, if so, which? Or, are all three categories of a three-fold schema emerging simultaneously, although not necessarily evenly, within each stage of a two-fold (or for that matter three-fold) schema?

At the risk of some oversimplification, the ideal type organizational shell for the classic welfare state appears to be bureau-professionalism and state monopoly. Clarke and Newman (1997) link the classic welfare state with bureau-professionalism. Sullivan (1996) writes of Fabianism's faith in the expert administrator. In the 1930s, Douglas Jay, later to become a Labour MP, famously claimed that the 'gentleman in Whitehall' knows best (Gladstone 1999: 113). As Richard Crossman, a Labour Cabinet Minister, reflected, 'In the construction of the new social service state we turned our backs on philanthropy and replaced the do-gooder by highly professional administrators and experts' (in Brenton 1985: 21). Professional expertise was important in sectors such as health and education. Sullivan (1996: 69) claims that the Fabian approach of placing the views of the producers – the professionals – above those of the consumers was 'to make clientism one of the most prominent features of the welfare state'. Hierarchies and bureaucracies were clearly evident in areas such as social security, where administrators enforced complex rules. The classic welfare state treated its citizens as 'pawns' (Le Grand 1997): it did things for people and to people, but rarely considered asking for their views.

The nature of welfare pluralism in the classic welfare state is unclear. Certainly Beveridge saw a role for agencies outside the state (Hewitt and Powell 1998). Many Labour politicians in the era of the classic welfare state stressed the state's role in production, finance and regulation. Even many Conservatives saw only a limited role for agencies outside the state. While the degree of statism varied between sectors such as health care and housing, socialists such as Bevan (1978) saw an ideal of high-quality services in health and housing covering rich and poor (Powell 1995a). Socialists saw private health and education as defects to be reduced or eradicated, but Labour governments generally softened their attitude, particularly in their acceptance of owner-occupation as the normal, preferred tenure of housing. While there was a role for other parts of the mixed economy of welfare, the state's role in both production and finance was dominant, albeit increasingly questioned (Brenton 1985; Finalyson 1994). There were 'partnerships' in the classic welfare state, but non-state partners were clearly junior partners in the welfare firm (Owen 1965).

The ideal type of the restructured welfare state features new public management and the mixed economy of welfare. Certainly, many of the elements of new public management can be seen in the restructured welfare state, most notably marketization in the shape of privatization, contracting out and quasi-markets (Walsh 1995; Ferlie *et al.* 1996; Clarke and Newman 1997; Flynn 1997). Prime Minister John Major's 'big idea', the Citizen's Charter, is essentially a Consumer's Charter. However, a number of caveats must be made. First, the market was never as red in tooth and claw as favoured by its supporters or feared by its critics. For example, the NHS was a 'managed market', with clear limits on 'market forces'. As the Conservative reforms progressed, commentators noted a softening of market language and moves from competition to collaboration (Powell 1997a, 1997b). According to Enthoven (1999), often credited – or blamed – for the ideas behind the purchaser/provider split: on a scale of 0 to 10, where 0 is Soviet-style planning and 10 is the economics textbook free market, the NHS reached about 2.5. As Boyne (1998) puts it, there was marketization at the margins. Second, some of the new public management measures were inconsistent, for example stressing both devolution and central control. Similarly, according to Walsh (1995), the two strands of new public management are quite distinctive. The first, Taylorist strand is based on the acceptance of industrial production engineering techniques within the public sector. It is not a rejection of bureaucracy but its fulfilment. The second strand is based on the primacy of market-based coordination. At best, then, some parts of the restructured welfare state were consistent with some elements of new public management.

The restructured welfare state favoured moves from the state to the other components of the mixed economy of welfare. Private provision was encouraged. In education, places at private schools were bought with public money through the Assisted Places Scheme. Tax relief was given to encourage more private health care and pensions. Local authorities were encouraged, and in some cases forced, to become 'enablers' rather than 'providers'. The 'enabling authority' made contracts with private and voluntary providers for service provision through the 'contract culture'. The Conservatives favoured voluntary and informal provision, stressing the 'active citizen' and the 'politics of contribution' (Finlayson 1994; Lewis 1999; May and Brunsdon 1999). In contrast to the utilities such as gas, electricity and water, relatively little 'full' privatization took place in social policy. The major exception was in housing, where many sitting tenants bought their council houses in the 'sale of the century'. However, in most cases the mixed economy of welfare led to a different mix in provision rather than finance. This new landscape saw a significant role for regulation. On the lines of the regulators of the privatized utilities such as OFGAS, regulatory bodies such as Ofsted were set up for education. However, the Private Finance Initiative (PFI) may significantly change the ownership of facilities in future. Under the PFI, major facilities such as schools and hospitals are owned by private companies and leased to the public sector, rather like photocopiers.

Both post-Fordism (Chapter 5) and governance perspectives stress the importance of hollowing out. We examine the upwards direction elsewhere (Chapter 6). We focus here on hollowing out downwards in the form of devolution to purchasers and providers in a quasi-market and across to agencies. Operational responsibility was certainly devolved to local agencies, but critics argued that this hid managerialist centralization where central control was tightened through line management structures and performance measures. Similarly, parts of central government ministries were set up as independent service providers or 'agencies' such as the Benefits Agency. The rationale was the separation of 'policy' and 'operational' levels. In the classic welfare state, ministers were responsible for everything that happened within the area of their brief. For example, in the classic version of Parliamentary accountability, Bevan argued that he was responsible for every spilled bucket in the NHS (Powell 1997a). However, the 'Howard' doctrine, after Conservative Home Secretary Michael Howard, was that ministers were responsible for policy but agencies were responsible for operational matters. In practice, Bevan's views were largely a constitutional fiction: if ministers resigned for every mistake made in a service, they would hardly have time to open their Red Boxes on their first day in office. However, it marked a significant symbolic change. Critics pointed to a similar lack of accountability and a 'democratic deficit' at local levels where it was claimed that unelected bodies or 'QUANGOs' rather than elected local government increasingly ran local services. This gave rise to terms such as 'the appointed state', 'the quango state' and the 'new magistracy' (see Jenkins 1995; Skelcher 1998), However, this ignores the fact that there has always been unelected bodies in services such as the NHS. In this sense, the democratic deficit was created by Bevan, which was subject to the critique of localists such as Robson, but 'Old Labour' was always committed – at least on paper – to 'democratizing the NHS' (Powell 1997a; Powell and Boyne 2001). Perhaps Herbert Morrison in the 1940s was the last major politician to believe in localism. Many Conservatives made speeches in support of localism and the 'little platoons' (Flynn 1997), but in policy terms strengthened central control, producing in the NHS 'a line management structure that Stalin would have been proud of' (Timmins 1996; cf. Jenkins 1995). There may have been an increase in the democratic deficit since 1979, but to imply that it appeared in 1979 is simply false.

The ideal-type of the modern welfare state is more difficult to discern, partly because it appears to be more of a hybrid and partly because it still represents work in progress. However, it seems to consist of some elements of new public management, networks, governance and regulation. The first issue is whether New Labour subscribes to the new public management. Cutler and Waine (2000) argue that Labour has embraced new public management, but has also sought to establish its own agenda of 'reformed managerialism'. This consists of a more rounded approach to performance management and combining competition with 'partnership'. Newman (2000) claims that despite significant areas of continuity in the focus on performance and efficiency, the discourse of 'modern management' suggests some subtle shifts from that of the 'new public management'. She points to changes at three levels. First, the boundary between policy and management that was central to new public management is being challenged, with organizational fragmentation addressed by 'joined-up government'. Second, there is a stress on collaboration, less adversarial and longer-term contracting, and the need to build relationships with multiple stakeholders. Third, managerialism has become subject to a new set of discourses of citizen and user participation. Although she stresses that it is important not to 'over-read' the changes, it is possible to detect some moves 'beyond NPM' towards 'modern management'.

Most of Newman's (2000) argument is constructed from New Labour's discourse. However, this tells us that New Labour talks a good game on partnership, coordination and 'joined-up government'. Its promise to abolish the market in sectors such as health care has been partially delivered. Newman (2000) points to a softening of the approach to contracting. Market structure has been changed in that there are fewer purchasers and providers. Purchasers and providers are encouraged to jointly form strategy rather than being in a principal–agent relationship. There has been a trend from short-term contracts to long-term agreements. In short, there are some moves towards relational contracting. Some Conservative market mechanisms, such as approved welfare suppliers and nursery vouchers, have been abolished, but the PFI is being extended. Tax relief for elderly people on private health care has been abolished, but New Labour has crossed the Rubicon in signing a 'concordat' with private medicine, making it easier for NHS money to buy health care in private hospitals. Gewirtz (1999) argues that New Labour's Education Action Zones include elements of marketization, managerialization and privatization, concluding that it is difficult to see much difference from the New Right. Glennerster (1999, 2001) points to a pragmatic New Labour conversion to the market, based on using the market where it works, not where it does not. He claims that this explains the view that, 'broadly speaking, providing for your income in old age is to be a personal affair', because the pensions insurance market works reasonably well. It does not in long-term care. However, as we have seen, it is possible to be less optimistic about the performance of public–private partnerships in pensions.

In addition to public–private partnerships, New Labour also seeks partnerships with the voluntary sector through its national 'Compact' and with the community through its Social Exclusion Unit and New Deal for Communities. This is in line with the stress placed on mutualism, communitarianism, civil society, and social capital (Blair 1998; Giddens 1998, 2000; Field 2000; see Rodger 2000).

New Labour has extended the regulatory approach of the Conservatives. It has introduced new institutions such as the National Institute for Clinical Excellence and the Commission for Health Improvement, and has strengthened existing institutions such as Ofsted. This fits with the central control aspect of New Labour that includes stronger line management, replacing failing institutions and 'name and shame'. All this is concerned with national standards and 'command-and-control' hierarchies. However, it eclipses the devolution and local networks approach (Boyne 1998; Glennerster 1999; Powell 1999a, 2000a). There is also the 'double jeopardy' of quantitative (performance indicator) and qualitative (peer inspection) performance review and tensions between different performance indicators. For example, there are possible tensions between higher examination results and lower exclusion rates in schools. Moreover, there is the possibility of a good Ofsted report but poor examination results and vice versa.

However, it is in the area of financial regulation that the outline of a distinctive 'third way' approach may be evolving. According to this view, the public should be encouraged to take greater charge of their financial needs by saving for the future, in return for which the state provides the means to inform individuals about personal financial management, including financial education, regulating financial services and product benchmarking, and even endowing citizens with assets. This approach has been termed financial or economic citizenship (White in press). The government has extended the scope of regulation, starting with naming and shaming life insurance companies for delaying compensating misselling victims; expressed its concern at some bank charging practices and the financial exclusion of poor people in rural and inner-city areas from access to banking services (HM Treasury 1999); and introduced new private or stakeholder pensions limited to 1 per cent charges and new benchmarked individual savings accounts (ISAs); it is also considering extending CAT (charges, access, terms) standards to other financial products such as long-term care insurance and credit cards. Of broader significance, it has established the Financial Services Authority as the sole financial regulatory authority in October 1997. In return, people should take greater responsibility for their finances. New Labour is committed to advancing 'financial literacy', which is defined as the ability to make informed judgements and to take effective decisions regarding the use and management of money. For example, people should save for their retirement, so that a higher proportion of national income devoted to pensions will come from private, funded pensions, and the state's share of pension income will fall from 60 per cent currently to around 40 per cent in 2050 (DSS 1998). A similar slogan for pensions could be said to parallel the government's slogan about work: savings for those who can, security for those who cannot. There are a number of mechanisms to achieve this broad aim. First, the government is developing programmes to educate individuals in financial literacy. Second, it is attempting to reduce 'financial exclusion', such as reducing the number of people without access to bank accounts through working with the commercial sector as well as encouraging organizations such as credit unions. Third, it proposes to give assets in the form of cash dowries to all children at birth and periodically until majority. In addition, a savings gateway is proposed to match pound for pound the savings of low-income adults up to a maximum of £1800 saved (HM Treasury 2001). Building on initiatives in the USA, fiscal welfare in the form of tax credits, childcare tax credits and pension credits help those who help themselves. However, so far you would not be wise to bet your mortgage on the performance of government regulation, although that is precisely what you are meant to do. Despite financial regulation, the 'Equitable Life' failure in particular suggests that the maxim *caveat emptor* (buyer beware!) still needs to be writ large, but often remains buried in the small print. Field (2000) has launched an assault on the government over their failure to follow the plans of his Green Paper (DSS 1998). For example, he claims that the popularity of stakeholder pensions will be limited because, unless a large pension sum is likely, people will be punished for their thrift. This is because most people will be better off not saving and relying on the means-tested pensioners minimum income guarantee (MIG): in his words, the poverty trap will turn into a chasm (Field 2000).

Many critics do not see major differences between the organizational settlement of the restructured welfare state and the modern welfare state. Although there are clear parallels, there are also some differences. First, New Labour claims a more pragmatic or evidence-based view of the market: it will use it not as a matter of ideology, but only when it is deemed to work. Second, it has introduced new organizations in the NHS, such as the National Institute for Clinical Excellence and the Commission for Health Improvement, to ensure more national standards. Third, its performance measures go beyond the narrow efficiency concerns of the Conservatives to include issues such as equity. Fourth, there is the outline of a distinctive approach to financial citizenship.

Conclusions

This chapter has reviewed a series of complex, sometimes abstract and contradictory perspectives. The most important organizational change appears to be marketization of public services, or 'bringing the market to the state' (C. Pierson 1996). This should not be overstated as the degree of marketization appears in different guises and varies between different sectors. However, the rise of quasi-markets and contracts are arguably the most pervasive change. The statist nature of the classic welfare state has also declined as voluntary and civil society elements have increased their share of the welfare mix. The boundaries between the public and private sectors, the hallmark of the classic welfare state, have become blurred (Clarke and Newman 1997). The changing organizational settlement shows a number of contradictory aspects. For example, new public management cannot give a clear and unambiguous explanation of change, as different aspects of it suggest different trajectories. The general trend is away from direct state provision through large, bureaucratic, monolithic command-and-control hierarchies, although there are some indications of clearer central control.

In conclusion, there is no clear agreement on the best explanatory framework or even whether a two- or three-fold schema fits best. While the market emphasis on a mixed economy of welfare and HMN has some relevance, governance and the network element within HMN perhaps overstate the autonomy of network members. Post-Fordist explanations are problematic and need to be set against the opposing perspectives of neo-Taylorism and McDonaldization. A two-fold division appears more accurate, with the break broadly between the classic and restructured welfare states. While there are some differences between the restructured and modern welfare states, the elements of continuity outweigh those of discontinuity.

Further reading

John Clarke and Janet Newman (1997) *The Managerial State*. London: Sage.
One of the first accounts that stressed the importance of the organizational settlement, focusing on managerialism and the welfare state. It relates the many facets of new public management to social policy.

John Clarke, Sharon Gewirtz and Eugene McLauglin (eds) (2000) *New Managerialism, New Welfare?* London: Sage.
Recent account that includes material on the New Labour government. It has chapters on the main policy areas, as well as wider issues such as partnerships and new public management.

Tony Cutler and Barbara Waine (1998) *Managing the Welfare State*, 2nd edn. Oxford: Berg.
Contains good material on performance measurement and quasi-markets, but is light on theory, apart from a discussion on post-Fordism. It includes an extensive section of documents.

Norman Flynn (2001) *Public Services Management*, 4th edn. Hemel Hempstead: Prentice-Hall.
Up-to-date account of the public sector, public expenditure and social policy, together with material on markets, contracts and performance measurement.

8   SOCIAL EXPLANATIONS

Introduction

Our final set of explanations may be termed social. It is clear that British society has changed markedly over the past 50 years or so. Similarly, the ways in which individuals experience the welfare state have changed. Recently, there has been an emphasis on discussing individuals as welfare subjects (e.g. Hughes and Lewis 1998). The subject refers to a person who is *subject* to social, political or economic forces that act on him or her. However, the idea of welfare subjects being constructed by social policies is a strongly deterministic one, a characteristic influenced by the structuralist theories of Althusser and, to a lesser extent, Foucault (see Hewitt 1991, 1992). It gives the unfortunate impression that events shape people and that they cannot shape events. There is little role for individual agency within broad determining structures. Of course, some subjects have more power than others (Hughes and Lewis 1998). Adapting the famous phrase of Marx, welfare subjects make their own history, but not in circumstances of their own choosing. In short, welfare subjects must be seen within the perennial sociological debate about structure and agency. Deacon and Mann (1999) and Hoggett (2001) examine the recent revival of interest in human agency within both sociological and social policy debates. Williams (1999) points to the reconstitution of the welfare subject as an active element in the social relations of welfare, rather than the passive recipient of welfare. For Foucault (1986, 1988), agency is a human experience that tells us more about the historically specific political and social structure shaping society and less about the nature of humankind's capacity to determine the course of social change – which, for him, appears almost illusory. Giddens (1984) develops a theory of 'structuration', which maps the conceptual terrain conjoining agency and structure, but offers less in the way of explanatory import. The nature of the challenge in coming to terms with the notion of agency in politics and social policy can be grasped by turning to philosophers for whom agency is the defining and inescapable feature of humankind. For Sartre (2001) 'man [*sic*] is condemned to be free' (p. 32), in the sense of accepting his or her responsibility for one's action and acting in a way that has implications for all humankind, a 'legislator for the whole of mankind [*sic*]' (p. 30).

We examine two broad levels of change. The micro level examines changes at the individual level or the level of the 'welfare subject' and, in particular, the individual subject's consciousness of the values that spur them to welfare action. The macro level focuses on changes in society, leading to 'welfare under altered circumstances' (Taylor-Gooby 1991). According to Giddens (1994), the welfare state project has foundered, partly because it came to embody what turned out to be the failing aspirations of socialism and partly because of the impact of wider social changes. Of course, the separation is to some extent artificial and there are clear links between the levels. Indeed, these links are at the heart of major debates. For example, Inglehart (1990: 432) claims that 'Culture not only responds to changes in the environment: it also helps shape the social, economic and political world'. The question is whether policies should reflect changing values, or whether policies should be used to mould values and behaviour.

We emphasize changes in values rather than broader changes in society for two main reasons. First, the former has tended to be neglected. Second, societal changes have been covered extensively elsewhere (e.g. Crouch 1999; George and Wilding 1999; Abercrombie and Warde 2000). However, many of these accounts show a faint mark of determinism: policy *has* to change because society has changed (Schwartz 2001).

The social conscience thesis

A traditional explanation of the welfare state is the social conscience thesis. Higgins (1981) points out that it was found in English textbooks of the 1950s. Carrier and Kendall (1973: 212) state that such 'moral determinism' is based on the assumption that a universal, moral force pervades social action, and directs social problem-solving in the one 'right' (morally just) direction. As Higgins (1981) comments, unless it is claimed that these sentiments were peculiarly English, the humanitarian impulse would in time lead to a recognition that all civilized societies had an obligation to provide for their dependent members. The social conscience thesis is summarized by Baker (1979): social policy manifests, through the state, the love that individuals have for each other. It is benevolent and is provided for the benefit of recipients and the community as a whole. Changes in social policy result from two factors – a widening and deepening sense of social obligation and an increase in our knowledge of need. Changes are cumulative and policy evolves constantly, although not evenly, in the direction of greater generosity and wider range. Improvements are irreversible and contemporary services are the highest historical form. Pierson (1998a) states that the intellectual authority of this 'moral' approach has been rapidly eroded over the past 25 years.

The Titmuss thesis ('Titmuss 1')

Although not regarded as part of the social conscience thesis, Titmuss' writing on social policy and the Second World War shares some of its characteristics, in particular those identified by Baker (1979) that changes in social policy result from two factors: a widening and deepening sense of social obligation and an increase in our knowledge of need. Titmuss (1950) argued that the Second World War led to changes in social policy because it demonstrated a greater knowledge about social conditions (e.g. evacuated children were poorly fed and unhealthy; small, rural hospitals were poorly equipped) and a sense of social solidarity (e.g. that equal suffering in wartime should lead to more equal welfare in peacetime) that together led to demands for a more egalitarian social policy.

This thesis may be seen within the wider context of the links between war and social change. It has been claimed that the Boer War and the First World War led to important changes in British social policy (Fraser 1984). In many ways, the 'total war' of the Second World War was associated with more significant changes. Writing in 1941, Orwell (1982) argued that the war had demonstrated that private capitalism did not work. Drawing on his experience from the Spanish Civil War, he pointed to the importance of 'equality of sacrifice': almost certainly the main reason why the Spanish Republic could keep up the fight for two and a half years against impossible odds was that there were no gross contrasts of wealth. The people suffered horribly, but they all suffered alike. When the private soldier didn't have a cigarette, the general didn't have one either. War speeded up the 'English revolution', turning socialism from a textbook word into a realizable policy. 'War is the greatest of all agents of change. It speeds up all processes, wipes out minor distinctions, brings realities to the surface. Above all, war brings it home to the individual that he is not altogether an individual' (Orwell 1982: 102). While the general explanation of war on social policy should not be discarded, Baldwin (1990: 110) writes that the specific features of Titmuss' analysis 'has begun to decay only after a long and distinguished half-life' (see Hennessy 1992; Page 1996).

The gift relationship ('Titmuss 2')

In another famous account, Titmuss (1971) stressed the role of altruism in social policy. He examined the 'gift relationship' of blood donation.

Around 80 per cent of blood donors suggested they gave blood because of 'a high sense of social responsibility towards the needs of other members of society' (p. 236). Practically all the voluntary donors 'employed a moral vocabulary to explain their reasons for giving blood' (p. 237), resulting in the free gift of blood to unnamed strangers that signified Tawney's (1964) notion of fellowship. Titmuss widened his argument 'from human blood to social policy' to criticize the commercialized blood market in countries such as the USA, claiming that while the bilateral exchange is the mark of the economic, the unilateral transfer is the mark of the social. He declared that the NHS, the 'most unsordid act of British social policy in the twentieth century has allowed and encouraged sentiments of altruism, reciprocity and social duty to express themselves' (Titmuss 1971: 225). The evidence of the 'altruistic welfare state' is fully examined by Page (1996). It may be difficult to generalize 'from blood donation to social policy', as blood donation may fall below a 'threshold' of altruism. In other words, conclusions based on the limited degree of altruism associated with blood donation may be extended to much greater acts of sacrifice, such as looking after an elderly relative for many years. Finally, Titmuss' celebration of a voluntary gift sits uneasily with his stress on a taxation-based, coercive funding system for welfare services. Alt (1979: 258) views support for the welfare state to be basically 'altruistic . . . supporting a benefit that will go largely to others'. He claims that people may be prepared to support such 'altruistic policies' in good times, but problems may be associated with less generosity and a preference for spending cuts over taxation. In other words, altruism may vary over time, linked to external forces such as the economy (see C. Pierson 1998a).

The Great Disruption

More recently, Inglehart (1990, 1997) and Fukuyama (1999) have presented two grand narratives. Writing over a period of more than 30 years, Inglehart has argued that society has moved from being based on 'material' to 'postmaterial values. Inglehart (1990) claims that during the past few decades the cultures of advanced industrial societies have been transformed in profoundly important ways. 'One of the key developments of recent years has been a growing scepticism about the desirability and effectiveness of state planning and control, a growing concern for individual autonomy, and a growing respect for market forces' (Inglehart 1990: 8). He continues:

The welfare state has begun to reach a point of diminishing returns. Paradoxically, this does not reflect the failure of the welfare state, but the fact that it has succeeded in alleviating those problems it can most readily solve. . . . Today, in contrast with previous history, the masses do not starve . . . their standard of living has been stabilized at a modest level of economic security.

(Inglehart 1990: 9–10)

He notes broad cultural changes in gender roles and sexual norms, a trend to permissiveness and individual autonomy. Societies with relatively large proportions of postmaterialists have markedly lower rates of economic growth and much higher divorce rates than materialist societies.

Inglehart (1997) presents a revised modernization or industrial theory. He argues that modernization based on economic growth has given way to postmodernization or a 'postmodern value syndrome'. Inglehart states that his revised modernization theory is in agreement on the most central point that economic development, cultural change and political change are linked in coherent and even, to some extent, predictable patterns. However, he presents four essential differences, rejecting linear change, rejecting determinism, whether towards economic determinism in Marx or cultural determinism in Weber, rejecting an ethnocentric perspective equating modernization with Westernization, and finally, he rejects that democracy is not inherent in the modernization phase.

Fukuyama (1999) writes that the consequences of the shift from agricultural to industrial societies on social norms were so large that they gave birth to an entirely new academic discipline, sociology. Virtually all of the great social thinkers at the end of the nineteenth century, including Tonnies, Weber and Durkheim, devoted their careers to examining the nature of this transition. The transition from a predominantly agricultural to a predominantly industrial society produced a shift in norms, 'perhaps the most famous concept in modern sociology' (Fukuyama 1999: 8) that Tonnies (1955) termed *gemeinschaft* (community) to *gesellschaft* (society). Fukuyama (1999) claims that over the past 50 years, the trend of advanced countries moving to an 'information society' or a 'post-industrial era' (see Chapter 5) has been accompanied by seriously deteriorating social conditions that he terms 'the Great Disruption'. He claims that the 'culture of intensive individualism, which in the marketplace and laboratory leads to innovation and growth, spilled over into the realm of social norms, where it corroded virtually all forms of authority and weakened the bonds holding families, neighbourhoods, and nations together' (pp. 5–6). Fukuyama (1999) outlines four arguments that have been advanced to explain the Great Disruption. First, it was caused by poverty and inequality. Second, and conversely, it was caused by greater wealth and security. Third, it was caused by mistaken government policies. Fourth, and 'most plausibly' (p. 72), it was caused by a broad cultural shift. 'The shift away from Victorian values had been occurring gradually for two or three generations by the time the Disruption began; then, all of a sudden, the pace of change sped up enormously' (p. 75).

The demoralization of society

Changing values and morals are central to the 'demoralization of society' thesis (Rodger 2000: ch. 4). Rodger (2000: 76–7) discerns a common 'anti-modernist philosophy' that claims that we need to return to the 'virtues' of a 'welfare society' that were found in the Victorian era. Himmelfarb (1995) claims that Victorian society included a recognition that self-help, self-interest and individualism were inextricably connected to a sense of duty and responsibility for family, community and the general interest. She claims that social indicators of respectability and social cohesion can be linked with crime rates and illegitimacy rates. The latter fell throughout most of the Victorian age. In other words, growing affluence and material progress in some ways has an inverse relationship with moral progress (cf. affluent society, below). Virtues are not a reflection of economic realities as claimed by Marxists, but as often as not, the crucial agent in shaping those realities.

The explanations above all focus to some extent on changing values. However, assuming that changes in values are important influences on social policy leaves the important question of *why* values change (cf. Fukuyama 1999). Green (1996) points out that two approaches have emerged from the American welfare debate: those which explain behaviour as a result of perverse incentives and those which contend that there has been cultural breakdown. Most commentators tend to refer to both explanations, but place greater emphasis on one (Green 1996: ch. 4). For some writers, the demoralization of society is associated with the welfare state. Whelan (1996: 89) argues that the failure of the welfare state is, in its most important aspects, 'a moral one . . . The welfare system encourages and rewards the very types of behaviour which are damaging to society – dishonesty, idleness, irresponsibility in personal relationships – while discouraging and penalising the sort of behaviour which builds up the community, such as industry, thrift and self-restraint'.

Green (1996) writes that the welfare problem is not primarily financial but moral.

Murray (1984, 1996) emphasizes that people tend to respond to incentives. However, perverse incentives mean that what is 'rational' for individuals leads to an irrational outcome for society. Murray (1984) argues that, between 1950 and 1980, American social policy was 'losing ground'. He explains the reverse in social indicators, such as education and crime, by the government changing the 'rules of the game'. More spending led to worsening outcomes: an example of 'doing more, but feeling worse'. In short, 'the system is to blame'. In 1960, the logic of the world of the poor led them to behave in 'traditional working-class ways' such as marriage and employment. Ten years later, the logic of their world had changed and their behaviour changed. Murray (1984) stresses that his argument is not based on the shifting of social norms but adds that 'when economic behaviour incentives are buttressed by social norms, the effects on behaviour are multiplied' (p. 162). Murray (1996) developed his argument in his work on the 'underclass': 'The underclass does not refer to a degree of poverty, but to a type of poverty' (p. 23). The underclass exhibit irresponsible behaviour that is measured in three dimensions: illegitimacy, criminal activity and a lack of employment among able-bodied males.

On the other hand, Dennis (1997) stresses the importance of changing civic and cultural norms and change in public opinion. For example, until the 1950s he argues that there was moral disapproval of illegitimacy. However, 'the growing independence of the individual from cultural controls' (Dennis 1997: 153) has meant a decline in personal responsibility that was a central feature of the 'Old Labour' views of ethical socialism. He claims that his views are regarded as common sense and commonplace by 'ordinary people on housing estates' but 'as recently as three or four years ago they were anathema to the academic and metropolitan Labour intelligentsia' (p. 1). According to Whelan (1996: 70), the exponent *par excellence* of the view that the system is to blame is Bob Holman (1993, 1995), whose unwillingness to confront the moral failings of the poor is remarkable. According to Whelan, Holman (1995) gives a 'depressing tale of fecklessness, selfishness, violence and drug abuse' and describes one family consisting of a lone mother and seven children, which was 'so chronically dysfunctional that it made Crapston Villas look like the Waltons' (Whelan 1996: 70). Murray (1996) refers to the division between the new Victorians and New Rabble. The affluent, well-educated part of society will edge back towards traditional morality, while a large proportion of what used to be the British working class goes the way of the American underclass. Murray points to a 'contagion' effect that operates at the level of neighbourhoods. Areas where there are few fathers, many lone mothers and few workers transmit the wrong cultural norms: 'values are now contaminating the life of entire neighbourhoods' (Murray 1996: 25). More recently, Field (2000) writes of 'a new barbarism' where 'decent families feel that a new kind of warfare is being waged against them' (p. 152). Mullard and Spicker (1998) claim that, like many other popular myths, the perception of moral decline is half-true.

A somewhat less strident tone is given in some communitarian accounts (see Rodger 2000: ch. 5). Communitarianism is a useful label for a number of diverse views. However, at root, they are bound together by the concepts of community and duty. In the USA, Etzioni (1996: 125) claims that people 'have to pay the hired hand for what used to be done by the community'. Freedland (1998) argues that we must break away from the instinct of looking to the state, not ourselves, to solve our problems. In the UK, Selbourne (1994) stresses the importance of duty: notions of egalitarian entitlement to rights which owe nothing to the individual's desert or merit undermine the moral basis of the civic order (p. 60). Finlayson (1994) has contrasted the citizenship of entitlement with the citizenship of contribution.

Consumerism and the affluent society

Marshall (1963) notes that the rival of the welfare state is the affluent society. The welfare state with its philosophy of 'fair shares' was born at a time when the sense of national solidarity created by the war coincided with the enforced restraints on consumption and the regime of sharing imposed by post-war scarcity. 'I cannot escape the conclusion that the Welfare State reigned unchallenged while linked with the Austerity Society and was attacked from all sides as soon as it became associated with the Affluent Society' (Marshall 1963: 282). Following Galbraith (1958), Marshall views the term 'affluent society' as having a 'definitely derogatory flavour'. It does not simply mean a rich society, but denotes a standard of values – worshipping at the shrine of production – rather than a level of living. It is the antithesis of the welfare state, with its emphasis on the satisfaction of genuine needs and fair shares. Linked with the Austerity Society, the welfare state is at a disadvantage in the clash of ideologies. Marshall (1963) concludes that it is necessary to remodel the machinery of the welfare state to fit the conditions of the Affluent Society, but equally essential to change the spirit of the Affluent Society to fit the principles of the welfare state (cf. Robson 1976).

Bauman (1998: 24) notes the transition from the producer to the consumer society in present late-modern, second-modern or post-modern society. In passing (see below), if 'one of the foremost commentators on the postmodern condition' (according to the book cover) is unclear about terminology, there is little hope for rest of us. Bauman claims that choice is the consumer society's meta-value and that the welfare state is starkly out of tune with the climate of consumer society, where a significant majority now prefer to make their own consumer choices rather than the less risky reliance on the guaranteed provision of all basic necessities. People are now content with being left to their own resources, counting on nothing but their own wit and ingenuity. Bauman's concept of the welfare state appears a little thin. He does not refer to the previous discussion of Galbraith or Marshall, or provide any evidence to support his assertion (cf. Taylor-Gooby 2000). His chronology is also unclear. He claims that the welfare state arrived at the beginning of the century, and there is no clear discussion of the beginning of the consumer society.

Risk society

A key feature of life under 'late', 'high' 'post' or 'reflexive' modernity – call it what you will – about which there seems to be at least some consensus among commentators, is that contemporary society is increasingly characterized by risk (Nettleton and Burrows 1998; Fitzpatrick 2001). Sociologists such as Beck (1992), Giddens (1994) and Beck *et al.* (1995) examine the changing nature of risk. According to Culpitt (1999), Beck's theoretical explication of risk society is one of those signal pieces of social analysis that have the capacity to alter the structure of our theoretical thinking about the world. In simple terms, the thesis claims that while modern or industrial society emphasized the distribution of goods along the main axis of social class, risk society is more concerned with the more egalitarian distribution of 'bads'. Safety is the ideal in risk societies, just as equality had been the ideal in class societies. Moreover, while old risks were natural, identifiable and predictable, new risks are manufactured and unexpected. Risk society is atomized: it is the individuals who take the risks (Mullard and Spicker 1998). 'We no longer live in a class society, but in a risk society' (Offe 1996: 33). While the function of the welfare state was amelioration of class, it is now the management of risk (Giddens 1994).

Risk society is linked with the concept of reflexive modernization that refers to the need for individuals in modern societies to reflect on the outcomes of their actions and to adapt their actions accordingly. This enables individuals to develop new abilities for reflexive action, by which they can use the feedback from different situations to regularly reorder and redefine what these situations are about (Giddens 1994). Individuals are more knowledgeable and critical in late modern societies. They filter and act on information, forming 'a world of clever people' (Giddens 1994: 7). However, Beck (1992) recognizes that risk society contains an inherent tendency to become a scapegoat society.

This thesis is potentially of great significance for social policy, but so far its empirical application is limited (Culpitt 1999; Taylor-Gooby 2000) and Beck's view of welfare has been criticized (Turner 1994). Risk in the classic welfare state was characterized by a degree of regularity that affected the entire population, such as the cycle of life from birth to death and economic cycles of growth and recession. Risks were identifiable and predictable and so amenable to scientific study and technological intervention to control their impact and to compensate for their foreseeable consequences. The classic mechanisms were Keynesian demand management and social insurance for risks such as sickness, unemployment and old age. The state socialized risk, creating a common risk pool by forcing citizens to save for a rainy day (Johnson 1996). Risk society points to a number of 'individualization processes' transcending health and housing policy, such as self-reliance, individual responsibility, personal financial planning, entrepreneurship and calculation, privatization of risks and individualization. Several writers have commented on moves towards 'privatization of risk' (O'Malley 1992) or 'DIY welfare' (Klein and Millar 1995).

The concept of risk society has been heavily criticized (Turner 1994; Culpitt 1999: ch. 7). It is claimed that Beck failed to take into account earlier analyses of risk and uncertainty, and his knowledge of the welfare state is particularly problematic. Similarly, Johnson (1996) and, amazingly, Beveridge (1942) are not cited by Culpitt (1999). Beck and Giddens present an optimistic thesis that risk society affords individuals greater freedom in determining their life plans. However, the complexity of the products and the difficulty of estimating the risks that one might face in the future mean that the assessment of the value of money offered by such a policy is in many cases impossible (Burchardt 1997). Taylor-Gooby (2000) concludes that currently influential academic approaches are inadequate to understand the way people perceive and respond to risk.

Postmodernism

The 'postmodern turn' has appeared in areas such as literature, art and architecture, and in many academic disciplines (Kumar 1995). Most commentators stress the difficulty of defining postmodernism and differentiating it from the other 'posts' (e.g. Kumar 1995; Carter 1998). Inglehart (1997) writes that the literature is complex, contradictory, full of hyperbole and sometimes reads like gibberish. It is loaded with so many meanings that it is in danger of conveying everything and nothing. He cannot resist contributing to the 'playfulness' of postmodernism by pointing out that a 'spoof' article (Sokal 1996) containing nonsense satisfied a 'panel of PhDs' to get accepted for a journal. Certainly, eighteen-line sentences and the proclivity of forming words unknown to the dictionary by adding '-ivity' to existing words do not make kathakalic recensivity (see what we mean!).

There is a significant debate about whether postmodernism represents progress or regress for social policy (Taylor-Gooby 1994; Fitzpatrick 1996, 2001; Hillyard and Watson 1996; Penna and O'Brien 1996; Carter 1998; O'Brien and Penna 1998; Rodger 2000). There are a number of implications for welfare. One of the central tenets of postmodernism is its radical scepticism or, in the words of Lyotard (1984: xxiv), its 'incredulity towards metanarratives' (see Kumar 1995). In crude terms, postmodernism rejects 'grand narratives' such as liberalism or Marxism, as well as the advance of reason associated with the progress of modern science, rational administration and rigorous scientific analysis of social problems. As Kumar (1995) points out, it follows that post-modernity is expressed in the language of 'discourses' and 'voices' rather than of falsifiable propositions. Critics claim that it does not offer itself as a theory to be tested and assessed in the usual fashion. It has to be assessed not from the detached viewpoint of the external observer, but from within, from inside its own discourse. The question of whether postmodernity is 'true' cannot be answered literally. In place of universal criteria claimed by modernists, postmodernists argue that values and truth criteria have at best local applicability, limited scope and a shortened life.

A focus on the 'politics of difference' emphasizes moves from national, collective identities and cultures to local, more pluralized and privatized forms of identity and minority cultures (Kumar 1995). According to Carter (1998), postmodernism's Holy Trinity is ambivalence, eclecticism and diversity. Similarly, Rodger (2000) claims that its guiding principle is particularism. Selectivity and particularism replace the old, false universalism (Williams 1989; Thompson and Hoggett 1996; Hoggett and Thompson 1998; Ellison 1999; Drake 2001; Fitzpatrick 2001). However, Taylor-Gooby (1994) regards these moves away from class and universalism as an ideological smokescreen for a 'great leap backwards'. Mann (1998) criticizes postmodern accounts for their narrow definition of welfare: 'the concern here is not what social policy might glean from postmodernism . . . but what critics of modernity can learn from social policy' (p. 85). He goes on to claim that 'acknowledging difference and diversity within the confines of a universalistic welfare state, have been part of the welfare agenda for a considerable period' (p. 99). In other words, it is possible to examine issues of gender, race, and disability without postmodernism.

The turn from universal to particularist values chimes with the emerging salience of new social identities such as gender, race and sexual orientation, whose interests have replaced the traditional solidarities of class, family and nation. These new identities have given rise to so-called 'new' social movements with their particular interests that tend to be associated more with cultural resources rather than solely with material resources as with social class (C. Pierson 1998a: ch. 3). As Fitzpatrick (2001) puts it, they are not new in the sense that there always have been divisions based on criteria such as race and gender. What is new is the acknowledgement that we now give to the importance of these divisions in terms both of personal identity and social relations (Williams 1989; Hughes and Lewis 1998). However, Kumar (1995) stresses that identity is not unitary or essential, it is fluid and shifting, fed by multiple meanings and taking multiple forms.

Post-structuralist theory: Foucault's account of welfare

In the previous section, we addressed the postmodern trinity of ambivalence, eclecticism and diversity seen in the rise of a new politics of difference and new social movements, each driven by their own particularistic concerns. One of the leading influences on postmodern accounts of welfare was the post-structuralist philosopher Michel Foucault. Fitzpatrick (2001: 56) claims that Foucault is 'probably the most influential theorist of the last 30 years'. Several writers have signalled the relevance – and limitations – of Foucault's insights for social policy (Hewitt 1991, 1992; Hillyard and Watson 1996; O'Brien and Penna 1998; Watson

2000; Fitzpatrick 2001). One aspect of his work is its capacity to address both processes of micro change affecting individual welfare subjects and the broader macro structures of power and knowledge shaping welfare apparatuses. This ability to bridge the micro and macro partly accounts for his appeal to postmodern writers in the 1980s and 1990s, who became critical of the universal aspirations of much social, economic and political theory in seeking to explain everything in sight.

One of Foucault's contributions was in the discussion of power (Watson 2000). He charts the shift from what he terms the 'sovereign power' of premodern societies, where the king exercises absolute and unmitigated power over the mass of his subjects, to the 'disciplinary' power of modernity. Here the relationship between the sovereign and his subjects is reversed. In the modern liberal polity, each subject is endowed with individual qualities and powers and is subject not to a supreme head, but a multitude of different experts, each plying their skills and technologies on the individual. For Foucault, the formation of the individual's identity, and its assumed freedoms, is not so much an aspect of liberal freedom and human rights, as the result of proliferating bodies of knowledge and technologies of control. This challenges the notion of power as necessarily repressive, negative and possessed by the few. For Foucault, power is exercised, not possessed, and where there is power there is also resistance. Power is fluid and present in all encounters. The metaphor for disciplinary power is Jeremy Bentham's notion of the 'panopticon' (Watson 2000; Fitzpatrick 2001). To illustrate this in terms of the application to a prison, it enables as few as possible prison officers to survey as many as possible prisoners, without the latter being certain that they were being observed. The prisoners must therefore behave as though they were being observed. Foucault wrote largely in terms of institutions with an obvious link to social policy, such as prisons, asylums, clinics and workhouses. However, modern applications of the all-pervasive 'gaze' give examples such as CCTV and speeding cameras. The welfare state plays an important role in the emergence of 'disciplinary' society because it involves a host of specialists in medicine, education, social work, administration and crime-control and punishment, each with their specific interventions, technologies and disciplines. Foucault (1979a) refers to these 'micro-technologies' of discipline as power/knowledge.

Foucault's other pole of power is 'bio-power' (e.g. Foucault 1979b; see Watson 2000; Fitzpatrick 2001). Foucault claims that, in the late eighteenth century, the human body became the target for a particular form of discipline. The body was endowed by these new experts with a range of properties that were amenable to control. Bodies were placed in prisons and subject to the controlling gaze of prison staff, placed into order behind classroom desks and supervised by school teachers exercising pedagogic discipline, treated in hospitals under the medical gaze of doctors and nurses, cared for in communities, and counselled by social workers and therapists (Foucault 1979a). In each of these examples, the body was placed in a particular order of space and subject to a specific type of expert discipline. However, the disciplines were not just new technologies of control that secured conformity to specific norms of conduct. Rather, they defined degrees of acceptable compliance around the norm. Individuals became 'free' to exercise autonomy. A central issue for liberal discipline in the modern welfare state is the question of defining the degrees of deviation permitted from a strict notion of the norm, what Foucault (1979b: 144) termed the problem of 'normalization'. Normalizing disciplines are relativizing rather than absolute – unlike the discipline of the premodern sovereign – and so contribute towards the making of liberal freedom.

Towards the end of his life, Foucault began to extend his account of modern discipline, which focused on what he termed the objectification of the body, to a study of the construction of human subjects, a process of 'subjectification'. In this way, he was moving from a deterministic account of the individualization of the welfare subject provided by his explanation of the micro-disciplines of power, to an account that sought to explain how individual subjects experience their specific identity. This is one of the reasons why his approach to social theory bridges the divide between micro and macro. It is also the part of his work that ventures beyond a history of modernity to anticipate postmodernism. This is seen especially in his aesthetic conception of personal morality, which he saw as the cultivation of the self and the uses of pleasure in the 'care of the self'. Hadot (1992) has described this as a post-conventional morality based on an ethics of 'chance and contingency and not tradition', in a way that anticipates later themes we have explored about risk society and postmodernity. Foucault's account of subjectification applies mainly to accounts of the experiences of sexuality in Ancient Greek (Foucault 1986) and Roman (Foucault 1988) societies. However, the perspective can be applied more broadly to specific ways in which the modern self is shaped, expressed and experienced by subjects themselves at particular moments in recent history. For example, how do welfare subjects come to experience themselves as having particular types of need requiring specific forms of intervention that are specific to the present time and place? By what means are governments today attempting to change these experiences of neediness at the turn of the new century? Such questions point to the new discourses of citizenship that readjust the balance between rights and duties, and the new policies and disciplines associated with new, more conditional forms of welfare that seek to bring about these readjustments.

Petersen (1997) refers to the shift in policy towards a government of the self in the 'new public health', the principal aim of which is to encourage the self-management of risk and the 'care of the self'. The multitude of situations where environmental risks exist – at home, work, in the car, in the community – is seen as a challenge for the individual to address with the support of self-applied programmes of health maintenance devised by public health experts. Keep-fit regimes, stress reduction measures at work, assertiveness training courses for relationships at work and home, all are examples of this burgeoning repertoire. Petersen (1997) argues that disciplinary self-improvement in pursuit of health and fitness has become a 'key means by which individuals can express their agency and constitute themselves in conformity with the demands of a competitive world' (p. 198). It constitutes a moral signifier that delineates the difference between normality and abnormality (see also Petersen *et al.* 1999).

However, Foucault's contention that one gains one's experiential bearings from the contemporary discourses and practices, including disciplinary practices, that make up a particular culture, suggests that he remained caught in a relatively deterministic, discursive and (post-) structural cast of mind from which he was unable to delve much further into the nature of human agency, other than as the internalization of self-discipline.

Macro changes

This set of explanations is pitched above the level of the individual at the welfare system and society. Society has changed (Crouch 1999; George and Wilding 1999; Abercrombie and Warde 2000; Esping-Andersen 2000) and it is necessary to focus on social policy in a changing world (Mullard and Spicker 1998). These accounts are broadly based on the idea of system disequilibrium, where the old welfare state cannot cope with new demands. Current policies do not live up to the demands created by the massive changes – economic, social, political and demographic – that have transformed British society during the post-war era. Many of these

changes, such as rising standards of living and health, have been positive. Other changes, such as crime rates, have made individual and public life more difficult. Still other changes, such as marriage instability,
have had effects that are open to more than one interpretation (George
and Wilding 1999). Esping-Andersen (1999, 2000) claims that the roots
of the current welfare crisis are three 'shocks' that emanate from economic and societal transformation: economic internationalization, population ageing, and family change and women's new economic role. He
claims that these have led to a growing disjuncture between the emerging need structure and welfare state organization. We have a 'Fordist'
welfare state in a 'post-industrial' society. Similarly, Ferrera *et al.* (2001)
argue that the 'goodness of fit' between the welfare state and the
evolving socio-economic reality has been eroded. Writers such as Paul
Pierson (1996, 2001) differentiate between endogeneous/domestic and
exogeneous/international influences or, as Schwartz (2001) puts it,
between the 'external intruder' and the 'insider job' (see also Scharpf and
Schmidt 2000a,b; Ferrera *et al.* 2001; Sykes *et al.* 2001). These profound
transformations are often examined in terms of the relatively fluid
categories of economic, demographic and household changes.

We examined economic influences such as post-industrialism, de-
industrialism, the information society and economic globalization in
Chapter 5. While most writers regard globalization as an external influence, the other factors are generally seen as internal factors, although
there are clearly links between both sets of factors (Iversen 2001). As we
saw, changes in the new post-industrial labour market have implications
for the welfare state. The old welfare state was based on the assumption
of insuring against relatively predictable and relatively short-term risks.
However, there have been changes from a 'male breadwinner model' in
which men worked for 40 hours a week for 40 years towards a more
flexible, part-time, temporary and casual pattern of working. As 'full
employment' can no longer be guaranteed by old-style solutions of
Keynesian demand management, it is necessary to concentrate on the
supply side of 'employability' by investing in human and social capital.
Education and training must provide new generic, transferable skills.
While people can no longer expect a job for life, they must acquire the
skills and knowledge to enable them to respond to this world of change
(Ferrera *et al.* 2001). Similarly, the social insurance of the welfare state
that was designed to respond to old risks is no longer suitable for a new
set of social risks. Neo-liberals welcome this increasing flexibility in the
labour market, but Ferrera *et al.* (2001) argue that this must be balanced
by greater security to produce 'flexicurity'.

Second, there is the ageing or greying of the population and the 'demographic time bomb' (C. Pierson 2001). There have been changes in the 'dependency ratio' that essentially mean that there are fewer workers to support more pensioners and children. This will result in a demographic crisis of the welfare state that will be most obvious in terms of health care and pensions. It is generally considered that demography is an important pressure on health care spending. In general, older people require most health and social care. As people live longer, pessimists warn that health care spending may spiral out of control. Similarly, longer periods of retirement will put strains on pension systems. Most pension systems operate on a 'pay as you go' method, where today's workers pay for today's pensions in the expectation that a new generation of workers will support them in the future. In other words, in public pension systems, individuals do not tend to contribute to their own retirement fund. Pensions are based on an implicit inter-generational contract rather than an individual actuarial contract. There may be a disruption in the 'steady-state' balance between the income of workers and the expenditure on pensions, as in future there will be fewer workers to pay for more people and more years of pension. There have been a number of responses, such as calls to raise the compulsory and/or voluntary age of retirement, greater selectivity of benefits, and to persuade more people to save privately for their own pension. However, despite alarms from the World Bank and OECD, it has been shown that the implications for the UK have been overstated (C. Pierson 1998a). For example, Hills (1997) shows that if pensioners' benefits in the UK were to be uprated in line with the increase in earnings over the next 50 years, it would add roughly 4 per cent to gross domestic product, the same increase as was experienced in the welfare budget in 3 years of recession in the early 1990s.

Third, there has been change in household structures. There have been shifts towards more female employment and a polarization in terms of earnings and 'work-rich' and 'work-poor' households. There have been changes in the family, as seen by a decline in marriage and in fertility, and increases in divorce, cohabitation, family break-up, lone parenthood, step-families and in births outside marriage (George and Wilding 1999). In other words, the male breadwinner model of the old welfare state, in which the role of married women was seen to be primarily in terms of unpaid care of the family, has largely disappeared. However, it is less clear that a new settlement has replaced it. On the one hand, there are moves towards the 'citizen-worker'. This means that on one level men and women will be treated equally in the labour market in that all are expected to work. However, this ignores the fact that on the whole women tend to suffer lower pay and conditions in the labour market. On the other hand, some commentators stress the importance of the 'Beveridge' role of care. In short, it is not clear whether women are expected to be workers, carers, or – as many fear – take on the double burden of being workers and carers (see, for example, Land 1999; Daly 2000).

Social change and the welfare state

We have outlined many explanations in this chapter. Many are complex and the subject of extensive debate. Their application to welfare is far from clear. A major contribution to the study of values and social policy can be found in the work of Taylor-Gooby (1985, 1991, 2000). It has been claimed that different groups have different views on the welfare state and that these may be increasing. There are some differences between mass services that meet the common needs of the majority of the population such as the NHS, and the services directed at minorities such as means-tested benefits. Similarly, there are differences between the 'deserving and undeserving poor': old people and disabled people have more public support than single parents and the unemployed. Support for the 'middle class welfare state' can be understood in terms of self-interest rather than altruism (Pierson 1998a). Bonoli *et al.* (2000) argue that the pattern of attitudes does not fit the idea that general cultural values or those of particular groups have shifted sharply against state welfare.

With the above notable exception, there has been relatively little work on values and welfare change. The social conscience thesis is largely concerned with continuity and has difficulty with explaining change (Higgins 1981). Titmuss' argument of the effect of war on social policy ('Titmuss 1') was widely believed to be important in the formation of the classic welfare state. However, his thesis on the gift relationship ('Titmuss 2') had more lasting impact. This saw altruism as the driving force behind welfare. More generally, Titmuss saw poverty in structural rather than behavioural terms, with unconditional welfare seen as the solution. The denial of agency was central to the Titmuss paradigm (Deacon and Mann 1999). Field (in Deacon and Mann 1999: 424) considers that the Titmuss paradigm was 'built on sand' and was 'as dangerous as it was futile'. It 'lingered about the political debate with such force that I, for one, felt that it covered me with a form of intellectual treacle which made movement difficult' (cf. Field 2000).

This neglect means that basic questions remain about the degree, direction and chronology of value change. For example, it is difficult to reconcile postmaterial values with greater consumerism. Marshall and Galbraith view the rise of the 'affluent' or 'consumer' society earlier than Bauman. More importantly, it is unclear how any value change is linked with welfare change (but see Higgins 1981). For example, do politicians follow or initiate change? Should policies reflect or attempt to mould values? Only Foucault went so far as to suggest that politicians, welfare providers and welfare subjects alike are subject to a deeper and longer-term process of change that shapes the values reflected in emerging forms of power/knowledge.

A number of accounts point to the classic welfare state having a clear relationship to the Second World War and the 1945 Labour government. Titmuss (1950: 507) writes that, 'the pooling of national resources and the sharing of risks were not always practicable nor always applied; but they were the guiding principles'. Mass observation reported that the 'selfish' set of attitudes revealed in pre-war studies was changed by experience of total war, giving way to a sense of purpose which went beyond self and immediate convenience (Hennessy 1992). Harris (1977) argues that the Beveridge Report fitted the prevailing popular mood. It suited the feelings of national solidarity that seems to have been engendered in all sections of the community by the Second World War. Britain suffered austerity in fuel and bread crises: it had to 'Shiver with Shinwell and Starve with Strachey' (Hennessy 1992: 100). Britain trusted its leaders, who in return regarded them as 'our people' or, for the Foreign Secretary and former Trade Union leader, Ernie Bevin, 'my people' (Hennessy 1992: 68). According to the journalist, Anthony Howard, 'Far from introducing a "social revolution" the overwhelming Labour victory of 1945 brought about the greatest restoration of traditional values since 1660' (Marwick 1990: 107). Hennessy (1992) sums up that post-war Britain cannot be understood at all without a proper appreciation of the great formative experience which shaped it and dominated its economics, its politics and its ethos for at least three decades – the war itself. Similarly, according to George and Wilding (1999: 4), 'War helped to create a social capital on which postwar governments drew for a generation'.

There are some different views about subsequent changes in values. Marwick (1990: ch. 9) terms the cultural changes of the 1960s 'the end of Victorianism'. A significant relaxation of the Victorian moral guide was seen in liberal legislation in divorce, abortion and homosexuality.

Glennerster (1995: ch. 7) writes of morality, family and the state, viewing the 1960s as the decade in which the intrusiveness of the state was reduced in the field of morals and personal life. According to Marwick (1990: 10), 'the upheavals of the 1960s were at least as great as those from the Second World War and have had, I believe, an irreversible influence on British society'. In 1982, Mrs Thatcher's diagnosis was that: 'We are reaping what was sown in the sixties ... fashionable theories and permissive clap-trap set the scene for a society in which the old virtues of discipline and restraint were denigrated' (in Marwick 1990: 10). On the other hand, George and Wilding (1999) emphasize the relative stability of British society in the period from the Second World War to the mid-1970s. As Morgan (1985) puts it, there endured after 1945 a powerful civic culture, a commitment to hierarchical and organic values, to Crown and Parliament, to law and order, to authority however it manifested itself.

The restructured welfare state of the Conservatives had to face a potential tension. They desired a free economy and a strong state, or liberal economic policy with an illiberal or 'anti-modernist' social policy. There are no clear, unambiguous links between the two, but it is at least arguable that the celebration of the egoism and greed of the entrepreneurial (or 'yuppie') culture may have spilled over into social relationships. For example, Beck (1992: 87) writes of a 'social surge of individualism', a growth of normlessness and moral relativism. Nettleton and Burrows (1998) point out that, since the late 1970s, housing policy has rested on the notion that individuals or households are able and should be encouraged to take responsibility for their own homes. The restructured welfare state saw a privatization of risk in areas such as private insurance to cover mortgage repayments and in long-term care. John Major's wish was that wealth should cascade down the generations. Instead, many elderly homeowners were puzzled that the 'cradle to grave' welfare state that they had contributed towards was not there, and that their thrift was penalized with their wealth cascading to pay for their residential care. Individualism and consumerism were celebrated in areas such as the Citizen's Charter, quasi-markets and private provision. 'I'm All Right, Jack', the title of the 1959 film satire of relations between capital and labour unions, could have been remade about social policy in the 1980s.

The Conservatives attempted, with limited success, to reconcile the economic tide flowing in a different direction from the social tide. Glennerster (1995) points out that, in the 1990s, the Conservatives reasserted the state's duty to set a moral climate and support the 'traditional family'. Prime Minister, John Major's 'Back to Basics' campaign dissolved into farce as it became clear that there was a gulf between what was preached and what was practised by some Conservative MPs. However, 'morality' was on the policy agenda, even if it was missing from some personal lives of the policy makers. Influenced by the new moralism of writers in the USA such as Murray and Mead, and in the UK by Green, Dennis and Patricia Morgan, they pointed to the moral failure of the welfare state. Duty, responsibility, independence and contribution permeated political speeches. People were exhorted to become 'active citizens' and contribute to their community in the shape of voluntary work, governing boards and magistrates. Conservative Minister Lord Young read a battered copy of Beveridge: 'there should ideally be no unconditional benefit at all' for young people (Timmins 1996: 449–50). Unemployment benefit became rebadged as the jobseeker's allowance, suggesting that benefit was no longer unconditional and paid only to those willing to help themselves. To this end, the unemployed were urged, in the words of one government minister, to get on their bike and look for work. The Child Support Agency was set up, showing that men had a financial responsibility to their children. Dean (2000) terms the period 1990–97 'the new moral agenda'.

The Conservatives also argued that changing conditions meant changing welfare. They were particularly concerned at the rising cost of the 'demand-led' social security budget. In Mrs Thatcher's words, social security was a 'time bomb' whose consequences needed to be addressed 'before it is too late' (Timmins 1996: 400).

Responsibility is a key strand in the third way of New Labour's modern welfare state. According to Giddens (1998: 65), 'One might suggest as a prime motto for the new politics, no rights without responsibilities'. The prime focus is on the obligation to work. New Labour wishes to rebuild the welfare state around the work ethic: 'our ambition is nothing less than a change of culture among benefit claimants, employers and public servants – with rights and responsibilities on all sides' (DSS 1998: 1, 24). Dwyer (2000) points to obligations in other areas such as probationary tenancy periods and mutual aid clauses in housing, and community safety orders and curfews in crime policy. It is important to note that there is some popular support for this more conditional regime. Dwyer (2000) noted some resentment against 'scroungers' and some support for a more conditional housing regime, for excluding or reducing entitlements of immigrants and excluding sex offenders from local communities. A majority of informants in his focus groups supported the jobseeker's allowance, but almost two-thirds opposed individual financing of long-term care. Citizens must be encouraged or forced to accept their obligations (Lund 1999; Dwyer 2000). Barlow and Duncan (2000) give an example from the 'Supporting Families' White Paper. They claim that 'Supporting Families', like the Conservatives' Child Support Agency, is built on assumptions of 'rational economic man' and suffers from the 'rationality mistake': impose change and assume that people will change behaviour in response to carrots and sticks. This is followed by the 'morality mistake': if policy does not work, assume policy is correct and make it compulsory. People are not behaving 'rationally' because of lack of information or ignorance. If more information does not work, policy moves to the second more authoritarian stage, which justifies compulsion as people are not behaving 'rationally' because of their own moral or cultural deviancy. Labour places great stress on concepts such as the 'deal' and the 'contract'. One reading of this is the importance of entitlement grounded in bilateral transfers rather than unilateral gifts (cf. Pinker 1979; van Oorschot 2000). This suggests a distribution based on process rather than pattern and leads to a tension between responsibility and security: the 'irresponsible' must be excluded. 'Work for those who can, security for those who cannot' implies no security for those 'who can' but who do not (Powell 2000a). New Labour in many areas attempts to present a populist line (Powell 2000a). For example, Mandelson and Liddle (1996) claim that New Labour stands for the ordinary families who work hard and play by the rules. New Labour's enemies include the 'irresponsible who fall down on their obligations to their families and therefore their community' (p. 20). It is claimed that, particularly on matters such as crime, the politicians, professionals and 'do-gooders' of the 'liberal elite' are out of touch with 'ordinary' people (cf. Dennis 1997; Gould 1998).

Labour claims that its third way is not based on either individual victim-blaming or the nanny state, but information for choice (Department of Health 1998, 1999). This fits with the 'risk society' (Mullard and Spicker 1998), but does not fit with compulsion in the wearing of car seat belts and banning beef on the bone where individuals are *not* allowed to choose. Moreover, it is possible to argue that the government has fallen down on *its* obligations. Before the 1997 election, Blair accepted that elderly people should not have to sell their homes to finance long-term care. Labour set up a Royal Commission to examine this problem, only to reject its main recommendation. Risk continues to be privatized. In the case of cash benefits, the risk society is associated with 'financial citizenship' (Chapter 7). However, continuing fears over the possible shortfall in endowment mortgages and the Equitable Life fiasco suggest that financial market regulation is not yet equipped to protect the rights of financial citizenship implied by asset-based welfare. Dean (2000) terms the period since 1997 'New Labour Welfarism', but the difference from his earlier period is not fully clear.

Field (2000) is clear that character and behaviour are linked with welfare. When he was Minister of Welfare Reform, he seemed intent on remoralizing welfare (Dwyer 2000). With Field's departure from office, the cutting edge of the 'new moral agenda' (Rodger 2000) has probably been blunted. Field (2000) argues that, in going down the road of greater means testing, the government is undermining 'the very behaviour that was central to the building of strong communities and the existence of a vibrant and honest society' (pp. 41–4).

Labour has argued that the welfare state has to change because of changing social and economic pressures. In his introduction to the Welfare Green Paper (DSS 1998: iv), Blair states that 'the system must change because the world has changed, beyond the recognition of Beveridge's generation. We need a system designed not for yesterday, but for today'. Later it is claimed (DSS 1998: ch. 1) that the welfare system has failed to keep pace with profound economic, social and political changes. The machinery of welfare has the air of yesteryear and has failed to take account of changing work, working women, changing families, an ageing society and rising expectations. On one level, it is reasonable to argue that changing values and expectations might lead to contacting government agencies by e-mail, moves to individual appointment times and longer opening times for NHS 'walk-in' centres. However, claiming that the world 'must change' in more profound ways parallels some of the more deterministic arguments associated with the 'functional imperatives' of some Marxist and industrial accounts (Chapter 5).

Conclusion

Of all our four explanatory chapters, social explanations perhaps show the least clear links with welfare change. Many of these explanations are complex. They are also pitched at high levels of abstraction and have only a limited engagement with empirical data. Moreover, from some of the limited evidence that is available, there appear to be some inconsistent trends with little clear fit to time periods. We have emphasized changes in values rather than broader changes in society for two main reasons. First, it is clear that the former is important, but until recently relatively underemphasized. Taylor-Gooby (1991) was one of the first writers to point to a new moral debate. Subsequently, Rodger (2000) focuses on the new moral economy of welfare. Similarly, according to Le Grand (1997: 153), 'assumptions concerning human motivation and behaviour are the key to the design of social policy'. Hewitt (2000: 163, 2001) claims that 'Human nature is a central concern of social policy'. Second, societal changes have a faint mark of determinism – policy *has* to change because society has changed. Such changes must be examined within the context of agency. The question of agency in the context of imposing social structure has challenged several writers during the last three decades, including Foucault and Giddens, and has recently begun to exercise the minds of social policy writers. However, relatively little is known about the relationships between values and policies, particularly whether policies reflect or shape values or behaviour.

It is clear that social values and social structures have changed since 1945. The chronology and the links between them are less clear. The impact of war ('Titmuss 1') is an essential ingredient of the classic welfare state. It is possible that the role of altruism ('Titmuss 2') exerted more effect on social policy analysts than social policy itself. The consumer or affluent society and risk society theses appear to fit with a very general trend from collective towards individual experiences of welfare. Whether the disruption was great in terms of significance is not clear. Whether it was great in terms of desirability depends on your view of the demoralization of society thesis. Welfare needs have clearly changed, but to argue that the welfare state must adapt accordingly seems to come close to resurrecting the discredited social conscience or industrialization theses. The phrase 'intelligent welfare state' does not mean that welfare structures have the power to change themselves with no input from agency.

Further reading

N. Abercrombie and A. Warde (2000) *Contemporary British Society*, 3rd end. Cambridge: Polity Press.
Standard sociological text that provides an accessible account of social change in Britain.

Tony Fitzpatrick (2001) *Welfare Theory*. Basingstoke: Palgrave.
Many of the theories examined have relevance for our explanations, notably postmodernism. Use of the index may be necessary, as treatments of the same author sometimes appear in different parts of the book.

Vic George and Paul Wilding (1999) *British Society and Social Welfare*. Basingstoke: Macmillan.
Examines social change in Britain in a series of chapters with a common structure that deal with issues including work, the family and social divisions.

Richard Rodger (2000) *From a Welfare State to a Welfare Society*. Basingstoke: Macmillan.
Focuses on the 'postmodern era' and covers a wide range of perspectives, but is strongest on our social explanations, including postmodernism and changing values such as the demoralization of society thesis.

9 WELFARE CHANGE

Introduction
Summary of main arguments
What?
When?
Why?
The British welfare state in context
Twenty-first century welfare
Conclusions

Introduction

We began our account in Chapter 1 focusing on Clarke and co-workers' (1994: 1) claim that 'something happened'. In similar fashion, Clarke and Newman (1997: ix) emphasize the degree of welfare change over the last two decades:

> For those working in public services, the experience has been one of 'permanent revolution'. At times, it has seemed that not a week has gone by without another reform, a new White paper, a further

initiative. There has always been a next step to be taken. The depth and breadth of change has led to a proliferation of terms intended to capture and explain these changes: globalisation, post-Fordism, modernisation, the post-bureaucratic organisation, the 'new' public management, the mixed economy of welfare, plus a whole host of terms identifying change in the nature of the state itself: the contract state, the hollow state, the enabling state, the surveillance state, the evaluative state, the minimal state, the skeleton state, the strong state and more.

In this text, we have attempted to place these changes in a wider context. Our aim has been to describe, analyse and explain welfare change in Britain. Put another way, we have drawn attention to the basic but relatively neglected issues of the 'what?, when? and why?' of welfare change. It is clearly a preliminary and ambitious task. However, at least we have drawn together a range of diverse material and placed it within a coherent framework. It will be obvious that we have sacrificed depth for breadth and that at times our arguments may be oversimplified. We have posed more questions than we have supplied answers and our answers are clearly provisional. Nevertheless, we hope that we have provided the foundations for important debates in social policy.

In this final chapter, we provide a brief overview of our main arguments from earlier chapters. We then draw them together to address the 'what?, when? and why?' issues of welfare change. After placing the British welfare state in its historical and comparative context, we speculate on the shape of twenty-first century welfare.

Summary of main arguments

In this section, we restate some of our main conclusions from the individual chapters. Chapter 1 raised some of the main issues to be addressed and provided some of the basic building blocks or raw material for our argument. Our starting point was to show that the term 'welfare state' itself is problematic. We reviewed the terms of welfare state, welfare society and welfare regime, and concepts such as the mixed economy of welfare and the social division of welfare. Next, we examined inductive and deductive approaches to the welfare state. We found inductive approaches to be of limited value, as 'welfare states' were composed of a wide variety of circumstances over time and place, and gave little purchase to defining the British welfare state. We considered that deductive approaches held greater promise. Their value was that they focused attention on basic questions such as how to conceptualize and measure welfare states and welfare change. In particular, we presented the useful broad framework of the production of welfare model. Drawing on this model, we argued that aims are more important than means, and the structure or character of a welfare state are more important than input measures of expenditure or welfare effort. The main rationale of this chapter was to illuminate the problems of defining the main dependent variables of welfare state and welfare change.

Chapters 2–4 provided descriptive and analytical perspectives, or the 'what' of welfare change. Chapter 2 examined the emergence of the classic welfare state. We discussed 'pre-classic welfare states' associated with the Poor Law and Liberal social reforms, giving greater attention than some accounts to non-state and local forms of welfare. We argued that the classic welfare state derived from the 1940s with the Second World War and the 1945–51 Labour government. The classic welfare state was less coherent than often considered, with no clear design plan. The closest to a blueprint can be found in the Beveridge Report of 1942. However, while this provided a great deal of detail for cash benefits, it was less specific on other services and on how all services fitted together into the welfare state and wider society. Moreover, the Report is often considered inconsistent and Labour's implemented scheme showed some deviations from the Report (Glennerster 1995; Hewitt and Powell 1998; Lowe 1999a). At a very broad level, the classic welfare state was part of the Butskellite consensus, although there were sharp differences between the main political parties on sectors such as housing and over issues such as universalism versus selectivity. The classic welfare state saw a number of changes over its 30 or so years. Some of these saw important changes of principle, such as moves from flat-rate to graduated benefits and from universalism to greater means testing. However, they were probably of insufficient significance to challenge the concept of the classic welfare state itself. In our search for the classic welfare state, we favoured a soft or minimalist rather than a hard or maximalist interpretation. This consists of a more limited form of citizenship based on status rather than outcome, with limited rich-to-poor redistribution, and stressing the importance of a state base and a non-state superstructure. It follows that assumptions based on hard accounts overemphasize the significance of the classic welfare state in terms of criteria such as equality of outcome. In contrast, we argue that some limited moves towards equality of outcome and vertical redistribution began later with Labour governments of the 1960s and 1970s (cf. Glennerster 1995). However, accounts often underemphasize the importance of the break with the Poor Law. In this sense, the main features of the classic welfare state that were stressed by contemporaries were that it provided a national, state base of universal provision beyond the Poor Law. In other words, it nationalized and dignified rather than de-commodified (cf. Esping-Andersen 1990). With hindsight, and through modern eyes, it is easy to dismiss the significance of these measures (e.g. Hay 1996), but to contemporaries and historians they are unmistakeable (e.g. Hennessy 1992).

Chapter 3 examined social policy during the 1974–79 Labour governments and 1979–97 Conservative governments. This focus is necessary because a debate remains on whether a move from the classic welfare state to a restructured welfare state took place at some time in this period. We have given a more positive account of the 1974–79 Labour government than is generally offered. Some of its positive features in social policy, such as a desire for greater equality in service delivery, are often neglected. In general, Labour's social ambitions were only partially delivered. Beset by economic and political difficulties, it staggered from crisis to crisis. It struggled to pull the correct policy levers, resulting in an image of high unemployment and cuts in public expenditure. The Conservative government of 1979 continued this image. However, social policy took a back seat in the Conservatives' first term. Although there was much rhetoric about moving from the dependency culture towards the enterprise culture, the basic shape of the welfare state continued. In spite of promising cuts in public expenditure, social expenditure increased in most sectors, with the exception of public housing, which saw a sharp decrease. The main result of the first term can be seen as an indirect result of economic policy as the Conservatives sought to concentrate on the economy and the supply side, particularly on trade unions, taxation and unemployment. Similarly, apart from social security and pensions, the second term from 1983 to 1987 was marked largely by continuity. A clearer direction may be seen in the third term after 1987 with the introduction of the purchaser/provider split and quasi-markets in many sectors. Choice was to be increased for consumers by enforcing competition among providers. The state would largely continue to finance, but not necessarily provide, services. After the resignation of Mrs Thatcher in 1990, John Major gave a few contradictory signals before finally settling on his big idea of the Citizen's Charter. We tend to view the transition from the classic to the restructured welfare state as occurring later rather than sooner in the Conservative period of office. The Conservatives clearly had different aims from Labour, even if the image of cuts and unemployment characterized both governments. While Labour regretted their relatively minor cuts, some in the Conservative government regretted that their cuts were not deep enough. The governments clearly had different attitudes to equality and redistribution. Turning to mechanisms, Labour drifted as their traditional policy levers no longer worked. The Conservatives turned to new levers. They considered that high unemployment was a price worth paying to squeeze inflation from the economic system. Also that there should be a greater role for non-state elements in the mixed economy of welfare, largely in terms of provision, but partly also in terms of finance. In short, the Conservatives desired a more limited welfare state, with some advocating a welfare society. There were a number of clear moves away from the classic welfare state in the shape of greater means testing. The Conservatives moved away from the Beveridge national minimum towards a series of residual means-tested minima. However, there were also some moves back to Beveridge, such as an emphasis on the national minimum rather than equality and an extension ladder rising above the state base (Hewitt and Powell 1998).

Our discussion of New Labour in Chapter 4 is more provisional. If we date the classic welfare state from 1945 to 1979, its historical era lasted for some 34 years, compared to the 18 years for the restructured welfare state. At the time of writing, the modern welfare state accounts for only 4 years and work is clearly still in progress. Nevertheless, we argue that there are some clear evolving trends. The modern welfare state is based on a third way that is new and distinctive from both the Old Left and the New Right (Powell 1999a, 2000a). It is generally argued that continuities outweigh discontinuities (Hay 1999; Burden *et al.* 2000), but there are also some notable differences (cf. Driver and Martell 1998). From the point of view of analysis or classification, the main problem is that the third way appears to be largely pragmatic and unlike the 'big ideas' or 'grand narratives' of the Old Left and New Right. It is argued that it represented 'jackdaw politics' (Powell 2000b). Again, there are some signs of a more limited 'back to Beveridge' shift (cf. Glennerster 1999).

Chapters 5–8 introduced the main explanatory perspectives. Chapter 5 examines economic explanations in the form of Marxism, industrialism, post-industrialism, the Keynesian welfare state, post-Fordism and economic globalization. There appears to be some loose fit between some explanations and our framework of three welfare states. The classic welfare state is often linked with economic growth and the demand management and full employment of the Keynesian welfare state. The restructured welfare state was marked by monetarism and the proto-globalization of household economics. The modern welfare state stresses economic globalization and post-industrialism or the knowledge economy, with the importance of the supply side and investment in human capital.

Chapter 6 focused on political explanations, including the apolitical citizenship/modernization theory, institutional accounts and 'politics matters'. We also examined whether 'politics still matters' in a global era. The classic welfare state is generally linked with consensus, Butskellism or Keynesian social democracy. Similarly, the restructured welfare state is often associated with neo-liberalism, while the third way of the modern welfare state is claimed to be a renewed social democracy. We argue that in terms of ends and means, discontinuity outweighs continuity between the classic and reconstructed welfare states. Although this is a more difficult exercise, it appears that the same can be said between the restructured and the embryonic modern welfare state. Moreover, it is likely that, over time, the differences will become clearer. Just as you cannot build Rome in a day, you cannot construct a modern welfare state in 4 years.

In Chapter 7, we considered the relatively neglected organizational explanations. These included hierarchies, markets and networks (HMN), the mixed economy of welfare, governance, governmentality, neo-Taylorism, and McDonaldization. New public management may be seen as an overarching theme, binding some of the other explanations together. The classic welfare state is often linked with bureau-professionalism. The restructured welfare state may be characterized by elements of new public management, notably markets, but also with central control. A simple emphasis on a mixed economy of welfare or privatization does not capture the control dimension. So far, it seems more accurate to speak in terms of two rather than three organizational settlements. Although there are some differences, the organizational settlement of New Labour's modern welfare state is sufficiently similar to the Conservatives' restructured welfare state. However, over time, a distinct variant of new public management, 'modern management', and clearer directions in regulation and financial citizenship may arise. However, an emphasis on networks and hollowing out as seen by HMN and governance (and post-Fordism) may overstate the horizontal dimension of 'self-regulating networks' and flat organizational forms and understate the vertical dimension of central control and hierarchy.

Chapter 8 explored social explanations of the social conscience thesis, the Titmuss thesis on war and social policy (Titmuss 1), the gift relationship of altruism (Titmuss 2), the great disruption, the demoralization of society, consumerism and the affluent society, risk society, post-modernism, post-structuralism and macro or exogeneous changes. These explanations are very diverse and their relevance for welfare is not completely clear. We concentrated on the generally neglected area of values. The classic welfare state was built on the memories of the 1930s – 'Never Again' (Hennessy 1992) – and the Second World War. Commentators vary on whether the major period of value change occurred in the 1960s or the 1970s. The restructured welfare state attempted to reconcile the values of the free economy and the strong state, but tended to send out mixed messages of 'greed is good' and 'look after neighbours'. The modern welfare state aims to send out a strong moral agenda, based on a mix of ethical or Christian socialism and communitarianism. However, as yet, the message is not very clear. For example, at different times and from different parts of government, it is claimed that family forms are becoming more diverse and that no form is superior to any other, but also that the traditional two-parent nuclear family is best.

What?

Recent years have seen some reappraisal of the extent of welfare change. The stress on 'crisis' and the 'end of the welfare state' has given way to accounts based on resilience and survival (e.g. Le Grand 1991; P. Pierson 1994; Kuhnle 2000; Castles 2001a). According to Ferrara and Rhodes (2000), European welfare states are undergoing a process of recasting and redefinition rather than retrenchment. However, it is difficult to assess these claims, as concepts and measures remain problematic. For example, there does not appear to be a generally agreed definition for terms such as retrenchment. Similarly, there is little consensus on the main dependent variables of welfare change. The 'resilient welfare state thesis' rests largely on measures of welfare effort (Mishra 1990). Martin Rhodes (2000) argues that Mrs Thatcher's Conservative reforms were much less radical in practice than in rhetoric, and the limits of retrenchment and continuity in welfare policy have often been emphasized. However, he continues that a focus on spending ignores wider changes. One of the most significant is that Thatcherism effectively destroyed social democracy as a political force and made its bearers, the British Labour Party, reinvent itself in her image (M. Rhodes 2000; see also Wilding 1992). In short, there are both continuities and discontinuities. There are inevitably different answers to different questions. More confusingly, there appear to be different answers to similar questions, as commentators present different interpretations of the evidence (cf. Gough 1991; Le Grand 1991). Progress remains limited as analysts tend to talk past rather than to each other. Put another way, a non-debate is taking place, consisting of a series of monologues rather than a dialogue. There is little sign as yet that thesis and antithesis are moving closer to any synthesis. To move forward, we need to set up a vocabulary and grammar of welfare change, converting the different languages into an analytical Esperanto.

Welfare is changing constantly. Analysing welfare change clearly requires some consensus on the important measures and the magnitude of change. For example, claims that the classic welfare state changed into the restructured welfare state need to show that important measures moved sufficiently to warrant the new term. Neither significant change in more trivial measures nor limited change in important measures will suffice. We have argued that the main dependent variables are concerned with ends rather than means (cf. Crosland 1964). For example, the choice of equality rather than minimum standards as an aim is of fundamental importance, and of greater significance than choice of welfare instruments. Of course, it is difficult to separate means and ends. For example, social democrats tend to favour equality that is linked with the state and universalism. However, Field (2000), 'thinking the unthinkable', argues that the only way of preserving universalism is through the private sector. Glennerster (2001) points to the importance of 'selective universalism', where greater emphasis is being placed on the mass, universal services such as health care and education, while the limits to social security spending and eligibility are being investigated. Similarly, the 'character' of a welfare state is more important than the level of spending or welfare effort. Clearly, the same sum of money can be used in different ways for different ends (cf. Esping-Andersen 1990; Bonoli 1997). In practice, welfare effort is often correlated with other important measures, but again our view is that it is necessary to separate the primary from the secondary measure.

Analysing the structure or mechanisms of a welfare state is problematic. Some quantitative measures, such as the percentage of benefits delivered via means testing, are useful. However, we consider that the question is best approached through historical analysis. It is important to examine the debates in terms of the understanding of contemporary actors rather than impose modern interpretations with excessive hindsight (cf. Hennessy 1992). Analyses through a modern lens have sometimes resulted in 'whiggish' interpretations that have both overemphasized and under-emphasized the significance of the classic welfare state. Viewed historically, the classic welfare state stressed minimum standards and weak universalism rather than strong equality and redistribution (Powell 1995a; Tomlinson 1998). As Martin Rhodes (2000) argues, the British welfare state was always a rather lean and mean, much less than a 24-carat 'golden age'. On the other hand, for contemporary observers, the break from the Poor Law had a significance that modern writers often fail to appreciate. For example, the reluctance of elderly people to go into hospital – not wanting to 'go to the workhouse' – illustrates the power of a law that was formally abolished over 50 years ago.

When?

As there is little agreement on the 'what?' issue, it follows that there is a similar lack of agreement on the 'when?' question. It is easy to periodize the reigns of monarchs, but more difficult to do so for welfare states. This is because a coronation is a discrete event that can be dated precisely. On the other hand, as we saw above, welfare change is more continuous. Politicians make many speeches. Governments pass many Acts. A large number of implementation decisions are made by 'street level bureaucrats'. It is difficult to draw a line in the sand, indicating the start of the classic, restructured or modern welfare state. Sometimes a single Act, such as the 1834 Poor Law Amendment Act, is given great significance in welfare change. More often, attention is drawn to a series of Acts in a relatively short period, such as the Liberal government of 1906–11 or the Labour government of 1945–51. Pinpointing the watershed is probably easiest in the case of the classic welfare state. As we saw in Chapter 2, some very precise dates have been offered, most often 5 July 1948 when the provisions of a number of Acts came into force. For example, if a woman was having twins on the night of 4 July 1948, a baby born before midnight may have cost money, while the twin born after midnight would be born into the 'cradle to grave' NHS. However, this degree of precision is unusual. Sometimes events may have great symbolic importance, but may be subject to reassessment. For example, Callaghan's 1976 speech is sometimes regarded as the end of Keynesianism, but it is difficult to speculate on what might have happened if Labour had won an election called in 1978. For example, Jefferys (1999: ch. 24) presents a reappraisal of the IMF crisis of 1976. The IMF required cuts in the public sector borrowing requirement (PSBR) as a condition of its loan. Those who regard the crisis as the 'last nail in the coffin of

Croslandism' generally depict the events of 1976 as a great watershed in British politics. However, this arguably succumbs to retrospective judgements coloured by Labour's collapse after the 'winter of discontent' in 1979. There was some economic recovery in 1977: interest rates fell, sterling recovered and Chancellor Healey never had to draw on more than half the available loan. Earlier than anticipated, he was celebrating 'Sod off day' – the moment when Britain became free of IMF control. Healey sought to restore many of the cuts when it seemed safe to do so and allowed the PSBR to rise above the level that generated such alarm in 1976. Economic policy in the last years of the Labour government differed little from what it had been before the arrival of the IMF. Labour was temporarily blown off course, but wished to restore spending and achieve greater equality. Leonard (1999) stresses the importance of the counterfactual. The issue is not to compare 'Croslandism' with events in the 1990s, but to speculate on what Crosland may have done when confronted with the new times. To simply point out that Brown is different to many previous Labour Chancellors is only part of the argument. Moreover, the importance of an Act may be linked with its subsequent implementation. This is particularly the case with permissive legislation. For example, the 1929 Local Government Act had a great potential to 'break up the Poor Law', but it was unevenly implemented across the country (Powell 1997b). Marsh and Rhodes (1992) point to an 'implementation gap' or deficit associated with Thatcherism. Measures such as quasi-markets had great potential impact on paper, but the experience on the ground may have been more limited. Many analysts in 1979 conflated intention with outcome, which assumes no implementation deficit. However, it is generally agreed that, in a number of areas, Thatcherism's bark was worse than its bite. The impact of some measures may be cumulative, with their major impact only apparent in the longer term. For example, the decision to uprate benefits in line with prices rather than earnings would not have a great effect in the short term, but over a number of years the gap would become increasingly obvious.

All of this makes for a large number of suggested turning points and the proliferation of labels. As we saw in Chapter 1, there are different suggested start times for the welfare state itself, let alone changes in types of welfare states. For example, some writers see the beginnings of modern welfare states in the late nineteenth century (Flora and Alber 1981; Heclo 1981; C. Pierson 1998a). In contrast, we have argued for the 1940s. Heclo (1981: 383) quotes Briggs from end of 1950s: 'recent writings from all sides make it abundantly clear that the ideals which inspired the achievement of a "welfare state" are now no longer universally shared' – a time many observers now identify as marking the onset of a new and enthusiastic burst of welfare spending and programming.

There is a proliferation of labels, often with a 'post-' prefix signifying a binary division. These include post-traditional, post-scarcity, post-structuralism, post-emotional, post-Fordism, postmodern and so on (e.g. Kumar 1995; Rodger 2000). We have noted different views about whether the 'post' or even the 'pre-post' existed. For example, some claim that we never had Fordism, others claim that we are still in Fordism, yet more that we are in post-Fordism. Accepting for the moment that these transformations exist, there is the difficulty of identifying their chronology. For example, is it possible to detect a single historical moment when Fordism became post-Fordism, or it is more reasonable to indicate a vague period of transition?

We are in a period of bold claims. President Clinton promised to 'end welfare as we know it'. According to the *Guardian* newspaper, the welfare state ended on 7 May 1996 (Powell and Hewitt 1998). More recently, according to the *Daily Telegraph* (27 April 2001), 'Blair signals break with welfare state'. Giddens (1994) suggests that there will not be a welfare state in a post-scarcity society (see C. Pierson 1998a; 2001). Some claim that we are moving 'beyond the welfare state', but Pierson (1998a) considers that the evidence for this is rather mixed. Heclo (1981: 383) suggests that 'Perhaps it is natural vanity for every writer to see himself [*sic*] as standing on the edge of a decisive historical moment'. He goes on to write: 'My answer to the question of whether or not there is a movement toward a new welfare state is yes and no' (p. 384). Similarly, our verdict is a definite 'maybe'. Like historical assessments of the French Revolution, it is too early to tell.

The organization of welfare is changing in ways that can be described as more 'imbricated' than linear. For example, it is difficult to see the development of welfare organizations as a movement from post-war hierarchies through Tory quasi-markets to New Labour networks. It is more realistic to see changes as more of a process whereby organizations have responded to changing social, political and economic circumstances by developing new structures that are overlaid on old ones and which, in turn, affect the overall structure of the organization. The imbrication of networks and markets on top of hierarchies suggests a process of growing organizational complexity and metamorphosis, where some aspects of organizational development can be determined but much else is indeterminate and unforeseen, resulting in unexpected problems and difficulties. In other words, governments cannot start from a blank piece of paper or turn the political clock back. It is unlikely that there has been a neat transition from hierarchies to markets to networks. It is more realistic to talk in terms of quasi-hierachies and so on, and to stress the changing mix between the elements (Exworthy *et al.* 1999).

Why?

We have covered many potential explanations for welfare change. Some (e.g. Saunders 1981) would consider many of these not to be 'explantions' in a technical sense. For example, the theory of gravity explains why objects fall to earth, and this theory can be tested in a variety of conditions. Based on the classic ideas of Popper (1968), Mullard and Spicker (1998) point out that the central requirement is that a theory has to be capable of falsification, which means that it needs to be in a form that can be tested and shown to be wrong. They add that many of the theories that they examined in their book are not falsifiable (but see O'Brien and Penna 1998). Most of the explanations that we have reviewed suggest change over time, but most simply suggest a change in label such as from 'Fordism' to 'post-Fordism'. The forces that cause this change are less clear, particularly when attempting to isolate these forces from other forces that are not considered part of the explanation. Explanations are often deficient on issues such as specificity, falsification and the counterfactual (what would have occurred without the force in question). For example, Saunders (1981) rejects some Marxist theories as being essentially tautologous and effectively immune from any empirical evaluation. Postmodernism claims that it cannot be assessed in the 'normal' scientific fashion. However, while explanations may fall short of a 'scientific' 'gold standard', they may still be useful in providing clues and insights into welfare change.

We have considered economic, political, organizational and social explanations in separate chapters. Our classification is inevitably somewhat arbitrary in places. It would have been possible to deal with some explanations in different chapters. There is clearly some overlap between explanations such as postmodernism and post-Fordism (e.g. Kumar 1995). Our way around these problems is to present the main material within one chapter, but to point out the links to other chapters. As O'Brien and Penna (1998) point out, there cannot be a single, total or complete theory of welfare. Similarly, Carrier and Kendall (1973) argue against mono-causal accounts, while Esping-Andersen (1990: 29) states that 'The hope of finding one single powerful causal factor must be abandoned'.

According to Castles and Pierson (1996), all the accounts of the forces pushing contemporary welfare state development have some merit and explanatory power. Those who tell any story to the exclusion of the others does serious violence to reality. Focusing on the decline in social democracy, Thomson (2000) writes that there can be no mono-causal explanation, making it necessary to bring together economic, political, sociological and institutional explanations. The approach that sets up a contest between explanations is less helpful than one that focuses on factors lying behind them: not functionalism, structuralism, societal and statist explanations, but economic base, external factors, social base and political superstructure. In essence, what we are attempting to do is to establish the correct balance within a matrix of factors, many of which have already been debated in the literature and all of which differ by time and place. 'It would be artificial and unnecessary to try and choose one dominant motive among all the forces at work – class interests versus reformers' moral zeal, economic versus political forces' (Heclo 1981: 388).

It is clear that many of the explanations are linked. For example, according to Gribbins (1998), many of the practices and preconditions of politics in the modern world are being undermined by technological, informational, organizational, social and above all cultural changes, which create discontinuities, incongruity, dissonance, fragmentation and dis-sensus. He continues that, like most postmodernists, we see these as being associated with (although not causally determined by) the transition to a post-industrial, information and consumer society; the disorganization of capitalism, socialism and bureaucracy; traditionalism and globalization processes; the decline of an international order brokered by the USA; the restructuring of employment, unemployment and leisure discussed in the post-Fordist debate; the restructuring of the social categories 'classes', 'gender', 'race' and 'sexuality'; and the dissolution of old and the emergence of new knowledges and discourses. However, this appears to raise more questions than supply answers. One can be forgiven by being overwhelmed by this torrent of ideas. Some progress on how these changes are linked seems desirable. As we have pointed out, there seem to be some inconsistencies between, say, post-Fordism and McDonaldization. It is not clear whether the links are similar across space and time. The chronology of change is not clear; for example, which changes appeared first? (see below). In short, it is difficult to know how to put the pieces of the jigsaw together.

Some progress can be made in two main directions. First, the explanations may be multi-layered. In other words, 'grand' theories such as

Marxism operate on a general level. They may provide broad constraints such as the necessity for profit. However, they may not have much to say about whether waiting at the local surgery operates on an individual or block appointment or a 'first come, first served' basis. Conversely, postmodern explanations argue that there are no superior truths and focus on local narratives.

Second, there is some linear development of explanations. For example, Higgins (1981) writes that the social conscience theories of the late 1950s, which argued that humanitarianism was the main spur to the development of social policy, were overtaken in the early 1960s by convergence or end-of-ideology theories, which claimed that welfare states necessarily and inevitably developed as part of the logic of industrialism. More generally, Mullard and Spicker (1998) divide their book into 'old paradigms: how we used to think of society' and 'new paradigms: interpretations of a changing society'. P. Pierson (1996, 2001) presents the new politics of welfare. Crudely, old theories explained the rise of the welfare state, while new theories explain retrenchment (cf. Bonoli et al. 2000). However, this 'out with the old and in with the new' may be too sharp (see Scarborough 2000). First, the rise and fall of welfare may be overstated. Second, many of the newer explanations remain problematic and their implications for welfare are not fully clear. As Mullard and Spicker (1998) put it, there has been an explosion of literature covering new theoretical approaches, but most of it says little about how it relates to social policy.

In a series of largely forgotten articles, Carrier and Kendall (1973, 1977, 1986) make some valuable points on the explanations of welfare states. They criticize the 'positivist', structural and deterministic elements. They point out that explanations need to be located in terms of the actors' views rather than with hindsight. They list four 'acounting problems' of the fetish of the single cause: history as hagiography and biography; periodization and the search for turning points; grand; and *a priori* theorizing. They argue against definitive accounts and suggest a range of plausible accounts.

The various explanations are shown in Fig. 1. We have examined the literature to identify ruptures or breaks over time. Some either suggest continuity or do not identify the chronology of change. Some of these timings are very vague. These breaks are compared in Fig. 1. Most explanations suggest a dichotomy, but there is no clear temporal fit between them. For example, in terms of economic explanations, the change from organized to disorganized capitalism occurs earlier than changes from industrialism to post-industrialism, Keynesianism to post-Keynesianism

	1950	1960	1970	1980	1990	2000

Economic

Organized capitalism   ---------Organized----//////////////////////-------Disorganized-----

Industrial   ----------------Industrial----///////////////////-Post-industrial-----

Keynesian welfare state ------------KWS---------------------///////////-----Post-KWS----

Post-Fordism   ---------------Fordism------------///////////////////////-Post-Fordism--

Globalization ???????????

Political

Citizenship ???????????

Institutional ???????????

'Politics matters' --------------old left--------------/////------new right--/////---third way--

Organizational

New public management -----bureau-professionalism----------////////////////----NPM--

Hierarchies, markets and   -----hierarchies-------////////-----markets-----/////-networks-
networks

Mixed economy of welfare -------------statist-------------//////////----pluralist-------------

Governance ??????????

Neo-Taylorism ??????????

McDonaldization ???????????

Social

Social conscience thesis ???????????

Titmuss 1   ---------------------) end

Titmuss 2   ---------------------) end

Great disruption/   moral--------------------//////////////----------amoral/immoral-------
Demoralization of
society

Consumerism/ ---------------austerity--------/////////////////////---------affluent--------
affluent society

Risk society -------------modern society--------------------////////----------risk society-----

Post-modernism ??????????

Macro/exogeneous ???????????

Figure 1 Explanations of welfare change. ////// = break/rupture;
?????? = no clear chronology.

and from Fordism to post-Fordism. The only trichotomies are concerned with the political explanation of Old Left, New Right and third way, and the organizational change from hierarchies to markets to networks. It is notable that very generally social changes tend to point towards the 1960s, organizational changes are clustered in the period since the 1980s, while economic explanations vary from the 1960s to the 1980s. In short, putting the explanations together – albeit very crudely – seems to confuse rather than inform.

The British welfare state in context

We have concentrated on the British welfare state. We now turn to two broad contextual perspectives. First, it is illuminating to examine welfare change over the *longue duree*. Like other writers, we have tended to adopt a marginal or incremental perspective. For example, we have asked whether the classic welfare state turned into the restructured welfare state. How different was, say, 1976 from 1979? It is possible, however, to stand back and take a longer-term perspective. From this view, the 'welfare state' occupies a rather minor piece of history, so far roughly 50 of the 2000 A.D. years. In historical time, it is clearly the exception rather than the norm. Economic liberals have always maintained that the true object of the welfare state is to teach people how to do without it (see Digby 1989). In 1960, a Conservative MP considered that applying the Beveridge Report 'is to swallow the drug after the disease has gone'. The end of primary poverty and full employment meant that the Beveridge welfare state was no longer necessary. A year later, another writer suggested that 'the whole Welfare State apparatus must be regarded as a passing phenomenon' (in Marshall 1963: 276). A modern optimistic view is that, in a post-industrial knowledge economy, all can afford to meet basic needs through the market. In this perspective, the state is the odd one out in the mixed economy of welfare. The welfare state is a brief historical interlude between the Poor Law and a future welfare society (see below). A further implication of the long-term perspective is that short-term changes that appear of great significance fade into insignificance over the long term. In the grand scheme of things, minor losses in eligibility can be set against huge long-term gains. Predictions of a new Poor Law or a residual welfare state appear as a massive overstatement. They may be correct in their specification of direction, but hopelessly inaccurate on magnitude. Recent changes may have meant a few steps backwards, but these are small when compared with the distance travelled.

Second, changes in the British welfare state may be compared to those in other countries (Krieger 1999; Scharpf and Schmidt 2000a,b; Thomson 2000; Alcock and Craig 2001; Giddens 2001; Kennett 2001; C. Pierson 2001; Sykes *et al.* 2001; White 2001). In his path-breaking account, Esping-Andersen (1990) argued that there were three worlds of welfare capitalism of liberal, social democratic and conservative welfare regimes. Britain has generally been regarded as a liberal welfare state. However, on closer inspection, it may be seen as more of a mixture or hybrid. In crude terms, it is liberal with respect to cash benefits and social democratic with respect to services. However, underlying both these dimensions is an emphasis on austerity. There is a large debate about whether these three worlds are converging. Thomson (2000) suggests convergence on a single new model of social democracy. Similarly, Giddens (2001) claims that, across the world, left-of-centre governments are attempting to institute third way programmes. However, the general consensus appears to be that while there may be some convergence, there remain distinctive paths (Scharpf and Schmidt 2000a,b; P. Pierson 2001). As Martin Rhodes (2000: 19) put it, 'Britain has always been exceptional among European welfare states, and it continues to be so at the dawn of a new century'.

A related debate is concerned with Europeanization versus Americanization. The British welfare state has seen some European influences (Geyer 2000; Hantrais 2000; Rodger 2000). A generally neglected element of Europeanization is that in moving away from direct state provision in areas such as health and housing, the UK is coming more into line with much of Europe. In Continental Europe, very broadly governments achieve their objectives more in terms of finance and regulation, and less in terms of owning the houses and hospitals. However, most commentators suggest that Americanization has the greater impact. Discourse from the USA influenced Conservative thinking and policies from the USA have shaped New Labour. The most striking parallels may be found in the centrality of work; moves to more conditional welfare; flexible labour markets and 'zero tolerance' on crime and failing schools; a new contract between citizens and the state; tax credits, 'workfare' (e.g. Driver and Martell 1998; Marquand 1998; Dolowitz *et al.* 1999; King and Wickham-Jones 1999; Walker 1999a; Deacon 2000). It is said that Gordon Brown's officials joke that the best way to persuade him of a policy's merit is to tell him 'it is how they do things in Wisconsin' (*Sunday Telegraph*, 4 June 2000). However, while there are parallels with the USA, it is an oversimplification to regard the whole welfare programme as a US import. First, New Labour is influenced by policies from other countries such as Australia. Second, while welfare to work is arguably the centrepiece of welfare reform, it is not the whole story for 'welfare' (or social security) in the narrow (US) sense, nor for the wider welfare state where services such as the NHS still bear some of the democratic socialist touches of founder Aneurin Bevan. Third, much of recent Republican and Democratic social policy involves devolution from Federal to State level. Arguably, despite the rhetoric, New Labour is concerned with increasing central control. Nevertheless, it is undeniable that New Labour has borrowed heavily in terms of both style and substance from the New Democrats. Policy borrowing has arrived on a transatlantic Jumbo Jet rather than on Eurostar. Indeed, rather than borrowing from Europe, there have been some attempts to export Blairism. On a number of occasions, Blair has urged the EU socialist leaders that they must follow the US economic model; but the economic success of America must be combined with social justice. In some ways, Blair wants to lead the European social democrats via his third way to the promised land of the New Democrats in the USA. Giddens (1998: ix) claims that 'rather than merely appropriating American trends and notions, Britain could be a sparking point for creative interaction between the US and Continental Europe'.

Twenty-first century welfare

The Green Paper on welfare reform (DSS 1998) set out the framework for welfare reform over a 10–20 year time horizon. By 2020, when the reform process is complete, we will step into the 'Fourth Age of the welfare state'. Welfare 2020 will be built on three core values of work, security and opportunity. At the heart of the modern welfare state will be a new contract between the citizen and the government based on responsibilities and rights. Welfare will be delivered through three channels: a modern service, a greater emphasis on high-quality services and less on social security payments, and with mutuals and private providers delivering a substantial share of welfare provision, particularly pensions. The 2001 election manifesto (Labour Party 2001) sets out directions for the next 5 years. The main aims are prosperity for all, world-class public services, a modern welfare state and strong and safe communities. 'Investment and reform' in public services are at the heart of the manifesto. It confirms earlier promises for more money and more staff. However, in return, the public services must accept new ways of working, including a greater, but vaguely specified, role for the private sector. It has been claimed that public–private partnerships (PPPs) are the 'big idea' for the second term (Institute for Public Policy Research 2001). The emphasis on work remains: 'employment is not just the foundation of affordable welfare, it is the best anti-poverty, anti-crime and pro-family policy yet invented'. In general, the manifesto claims that a lot has been done, but there is a lot yet to do. It provides some new targets for old policies and stresses the importance of the long term, such as 'ten year plans' and the 'ten year vision for an active welfare state'. These general lines of policy development were stressed in the Queen's Speech (Hansard 2001). The main priorities will be reform in education, health, crime and welfare. An Education Bill will promote diversity and higher standards, provide new opportunities for sponsorship, more policies for tackling failing schools, and increase freedom for successful headteachers and governors. A National Health Service Bill will decentralize power to staff, give patients greater influence in the running of the NHS and strengthen the regulation of the professions. A Welfare Bill will help more people back to work, set up new tax credits and introduce a new pension credit for pensioners. The latter will mean 'that for the first time in the history of the social welfare system pensioners will be rewarded and not penalised for having worked and saved to provide for themselves' (col. 54). Tony Blair (cols 49–55) stated that the Queen's Speech launches the most fundamental programme of reform in the public services for many years: 'The individual citizen is the focus of all the reforms – the pupil first, the patient first, the victim of crime first'. There are three specific goals: universally high standards, services built around choice with sufficient diversity to achieve it, and devolution to the front line, thus empowering staff who deliver on the ground. This is not the place for a detailed critique of plans for Labour's second term, but two points can be made. First, the rhetoric could be (has been?) said by many Conservatives. Second, it is difficult to see how more power can be given to both producers and consumers, without taking some away from the (unmentioned) Secretaries of State who generally saw their control increased during the first term of government.

We are clearly in a transitional period of 'work in progress', with the route to Welfare 2020 not fully mapped out. There are, however, some clear directions for this route (e.g. Blair 1998, 2001; Giddens 1998, 2000, 2001; Blair and Schroder 1999; Green-Pedersen *et al.* 2001). The core of the modern welfare state will be:

- active rather than passive
- redistributing opportunities rather than income
- pluralist rather than statist
- enabling rather than providing
- conditional rather than unconditional
- process- rather than pattern-driven
- inclusive rather than egalitarian

Rodger (2000: 2) sees the formation of a new 'moral' framework for social policy in the twenty-first century. Its axial principle is the privatization of responsibility in a welfare society based on individualist assumptions rooted in markets, family and community. Pitched at this general level, there is some agreement between right and left on some of the main principles. According to Freedland (1998: 219):

We need to curb the instinct which makes us look to the state, not ourselves to solve our problems . . . The paternalists and socialists who built [the welfare state] were people of the noblest intentions, but their creation turned too many of us into passive recipients – as grateful for a state handout as subjects on a Maundy Thursday, bowing their heads to receive a purse from a kindly king . . . We need to make the move from passive to active, from subject to citizen.

Freedland continues that 'we have spent a century equating the state with compassion . . . Any retreat from public provision is immediately condemned as a betrayal of a government's sacred obligation to protect the weak . . . The goal is a smaller welfare state – embedded in a welfare nation' (p. 219). For some on the left, this translates into socialist traditions predating the state socialism of 1945 (Freedland 1998; cf. Hirst 1994; Field 2000). For some on the right, it has resonances of self-help and Friendly Societies (e.g. Green 1993, 1996, 1998; Whelan 1996). Whether expressed in terms of communitarianism, stakeholding, associative welfare, social capital, capacity building, community without politics or civil society, the common strand is that we have focused on the wrong dependent variable and concentrated on the state rather than the welfare element of the welfare state. The solution is seen in terms of a welfare society (see Rodger 2000).

However, it is more difficult to translate these broad and often vague principles into policies. We have noted the importance of pragmatism for New Labour. The third way is a composite model rather than a coherent whole. Searching for its pedigree is illusory, as the third way is a mongrel. New Labour's policy learning resembles a jackdaw's search for shiny objects, with pieces from Old Labour and the Conservatives in Britain, Continental Europe and the USA. The third way is an eclectic and evolving pick and mix rather than a coherent whole; a cafeteria stocked with old and new, domestic and overseas dishes rather than the set meals of right and left. It is not yet clear whether the flavours will blend (Powell 2000b). Many voters are quite happy with policies that are 'right' on crime but 'left' on the NHS (Gould 1998), but commentators are more concerned with the lack of a template. The jackdaw politics of the third way leaves New Labour adrift in uncharted waters without a political compass. Unlike Old Labour, there is no clear credo or instinct; no political soul. It has neither doctrine nor ethos.

This makes it difficult to predict policy developments. First, the political vocabulary is more flexible. Terms such as 'full employment' and 'equality' have changed their meaning. Discourse and 'winning the welfare debate' become important. In many ways, a good description of current developments is a 'redefined welfare state' (Powell and Hewitt 1998). Second, debates tend to concentrate on technical criteria and delivery of results rather than on principles. It is more difficult to predict policy on the basis of principle. For example, a similar principle of subsidizing access for poorer students appears to underlie the Conservative assisted places scheme and New Labour's means testing of university tuition fees. However, New Labour abolished the former while embracing the latter. The 75 pence increase in pensions was clearly justified in terms of principled arguments, but swiftly changed when New Labour's famous concern with focus groups curiously failed to predict the anger among recipients.

Conclusions

This text has covered a great deal of ground in a relatively high-speed tour. We have attempted to place a very diverse set of material within a coherent framework. This preliminary account is necessarily better on indicating problems than pointing to solutions. Indeed, the main conclusion is that we know relatively little about basic questions of the 'what?, when? and why?' of welfare change. In places we have given some provisional verdicts on these issues. Others may disagree with these. It is possible that we may disagree with some of them in the future.

We have suggested that analysing recent changes in social policy or the new politics of the welfare state may require new approaches. This is not a new insight. Writing an introduction to the 1964 version of *Equality*, which was first published in 1931, Richard Titmuss wrote that its author, Richard Tawney, realized that he was daunted by the complexities of the modern world of statistical fact. The simpler tools of measurement and analysis used by himself and others in the past were no longer adequate. Ancient inequalities had assumed subtler and more sophisticated forms, in part the product of far-reaching technological, social and economic changes (in Tawney 1964: 10–11). Social policy has tended to focus on the new 'designer labels' of the welfare state, without really asking more fundamental questions (what?, when? and why?) about substantive issues. At the age of 80, Tawney considered learning new tricks beyond him. However, in moves from the old (Richard-ism – Tawney/Titmuss) to the new (Tony-ism – Blair/Giddens), it may be necessary for all students of social policy ('still a student, getting over my education' in Tawney's phrase) to acquire them.

Further reading

Robert Goodin and Deborah Mitchell (eds) (2000) *The Foundations of the Welfare State*. Cheltenham: Edward Elgar.
Brings together many classic articles in three volumes. Covers a wide variety of material from the Old Poor Law to the 'third way'.

Ramesh Mishra (1981) *Society and Social Policy*, 2nd edn. Basingstoke: Macmillan. Still well worth reading for its discussion of more traditional welfare explanations, such as citizenship, industrialization, functionalism and Marxism. The chapter on functionalism provides material that allows a decision about to what extent the newer explanations of welfare change have functionalist elements.

Maurice Mullard and Paul Spicker (1998) *Social Policy in a Changing World*. London: Routledge.
Covers a wide variety of traditional and more recent perspectives on social policy in an accessible account. It tends to sacrifice depth for breadth.

Christopher Pierson and Frank Castles (eds) (2000) *The Welfare State Reader*. Cambridge: Polity Press.
This collection manages to limit itself to a single volume of classic articles on different aspects of the welfare state.

REFERENCES

Abercrombie, N. and Warde, A. (2000) *Contemporary British Society*, 3rd edn. Cambridge: Polity Press.

Abrahamson, P. (1999) The welfare modelling business, *Social Policy and Administration*, 33(4): 394–415.

Alber, J. (1988) Is there a crisis of the welfare state?, *European Sociological Review*, 4: 181–203.

Alcock, P. (2001) The comparative context, in P. Alcock and G. Craig (eds) *International Social Policy*. Basingstoke: Palgrave.

Alcock, P. and Craig, G. (eds) (2001) *International Social Policy*. Basingstoke: Palgrave.

Alt, J.E. (1979) *The Politics of Economic Decline*. Cambridge: Cambridge University Press.

Ashford, D.E. (1986) *The Emergence of the Welfare States*. Oxford: Blackwell.

Baker, J. (1979) Social conscience and social policy, *Journal of Social Policy*, 8(2): 177–206.

Baldwin, P. (1990) *The Politics of Social Solidarity*. Cambridge: Cambridge University Press.

Barlow, A. and Duncan, S. with Edwards, R. (2000) The rationality mistake: New Labour's communitarianism and 'Supporting Families', in P. Taylor-Gooby (ed.) *Risk, Trust and Welfare*. Basingstoke: Macmillan.

Barry, B. (1999) *Welfare*, 2nd edn. Buckingham: Open University Press.

Bauman, Z. (1998) *Work, Consumerism and the New Poor*. Buckingham: Open University Press.

Beck, U. (1992) *Risk Society: Towards a New Modernity*. London: Sage.

Beck, U., Giddens, A. and Lash, S. (1995) *Reflexive Modernization*. Cambridge: Polity Press.

Bell, D. (1960) *The End of Ideology*. Glencoe, IL: Free Press.

Bell, D. (1973) *The Coming of Post-Industrial Society*. New York: Basic Books.

Beresford, P. (1997) The last social division? Revisiting the relationship between social policy, its producers and consumers, in M. May, E. Brunsdon and G. Craig (eds) *Social Policy Review 9*. London: Social Policy Association.

Beresford, P., Green, D., Lister, R. and Woodward, K. (eds) (1999) *Poverty First Hand: Poor People Speak for Themselves*. London: CPAG.

Bevan, A. (1978) *In Place of Fear*. London: Quartet Books.

Beveridge, W. (1942) *Social Insurance and Allied Services* (The Beveridge Report). London: HMSO.

Beveridge, W. (1948) *Voluntary Action*. London: Allen & Unwin.

Blackman, T. and Palmer, A. (1999) Continuity or modernisation? The emergence of New Labour's welfare state, in H. Dean and R. Woods (eds) *Social Policy Review 11*. Luton: Social Policy Association.

Blair, T. (1998) *The Third Way*. London: Fabian Society.

Blair, T. (2001) Third way, phase two, *Prospect*, March.

Blair, T. and Schroder, G. (1999) *Europe: The Third Way/Die Neue Mitte*. London: Labour Party.

Bonoli, G. (1997) Classifying welfare states: a two-dimension approach, *Journal of Social Policy*, 26(3): 351–72.

Bonoli, G. (2001) Political institutions, veto points and the process of welfare state adaptation, in P. Pierson (ed.) *The New Politics of the Welfare State*. Oxford: Oxford University Press.

Bonoli, G. and Palier, B. (2001) How do welfare states change?, in S. Leibfried (ed.) *Welfare State Futures*. Cambridge: Cambridge University Press.

Bonoli, G., George, V. and Taylor-Gooby, P. (2000) *European Welfare Futures*. Cambridge: Polity Press.

Bosanquet, N. and Townsend (eds) (1980) *Labour and Equality*. London: Heinemann.

Boyne, G. (1998) Public services under New Labour: back to bureaucracy?, *Public Money and Management*, 18(1): 43–50.

Bradshaw, J. and Deacon, A. (1986) Social security, in P. Wilding (ed.) *In Defence of the Welfare State*. Manchester: Manchester University Press.

Brenton, M. (1985) *The Voluntary Sector in British Social Services*. Harlow: Longman.

Bridgen, P. and Lowe, R. (1998) *Welfare Policy under the Conservatives 1951–1964*. London: Public Record Office.

Briggs, A. (1961) The welfare state in historical perspective, *Archives Européene de Sociologie*, 2(2): 221–58.

Brown, G. (1999) Equality – then and now, in D. Leonard (ed.) *Crosland and New Labour*. Basingstoke: Macmillan.

Brown, J. (1995) *The British Welfare State*. Oxford: Blackwell.

Bryson, L. (1992) *Welfare and the State*. Basingstoke: Macmillan.

Burchardt, T. (1997) *Boundaries between Public and Private Welfare*. London: Centre for Analysis of Social Exclusion, London School of Economics.

Burchardt, T. and Hills, J. (1999) Public expenditure and the public/private mix, in M. Powell (ed.) *New Labour, New Welfare State?* Bristol: Policy Press.

Burchardt, T., Hills, J. and Propper, C. (1999) *Private Welfare and Public Policy*. York: Joseph Rowntree Foundation.

Burden, T., Cooper, C. and Petrie, S. (2000) *Modernising Social Policy: Unravelling New Labour's Welfare Reforms*. Aldershot: Ashgate.

Burrows, R. and Loader, B. (eds) (1994) *Towards a Post-Fordist Welfare State?* London: Routledge.

Cahill, M. (1994) *The New Social Policy*. Oxford: Blackwell.

Carr, E.H. (1990) *What is History?*, 2nd edn. Harmondsworth: Penguin.

Carrier, J. and Kendall, I. (1973) Social policy and social change, *Journal of Social Policy*, 2(3): 209–24.

Carrier, J. and Kendall, I. (1977) The development of welfare states: the production of plausible accounts, *Journal of Social Policy*, 6(1): 171–90.

Carrier, J. and Kendall, I. (1986) Categories, categorizations and the political economy of welfare, *Journal of Social Policy*, 15(3): 315–35.

Carter, J. (ed.) (1998) *Postmodernity and the Fragmentation of Welfare*. London: Routledge.

Carter, N., Klein, R. and Day, P. (1992) *How Organisations Measure Success*. London: Routledge.

Castles, F. (2001a) On the political economy of recent public sector developments, *Journal of European Social Policy*, 11(3): 195–211.

Castles, F. (2001b) The dog that didn't bark: economic development and the postwar welfare state, in S. Leibfried (ed.) *Welfare State Futures*. Cambridge: Cambridge University Press.

Castles, F. and Mitchell, D. (1992) Identifying welfare state regimes: the links between politics, instruments and outcomes, *Governance*, 5: 1–26.

Castles, F. and Pierson, C. (1996) A new convergence? Recent policy developments in the United Kingdom, Australia and New Zealand, *Policy and Politics*, 24(3): 233–45.

Cerny, P. (1997) Paradoxes of the competition state, *Government and Opposition*, 32(2): 251–74.

Challis, L., Fuller, S., Henwood, M. *et al.* (1988) *Joint Approaches to Social Policy*. Cambridge: Cambridge University Press.

Clarke, J. and Newman, J. (1997) *The Managerial State*. London: Sage.

Clarke, J., Cochrane, A. and McLaughlin, E. (1994) Introduction, in J. Clarke, A. Cochrane and E. McLaughlin (eds) *Managing Social Policy*. London: Sage.

Clarke, J., Gewirtz, S. and McLaughlin, E. (eds) (2000) *New Labour, New Managerialism*. London: Sage.

Commission on Social Justice (1994) *Social Justice: Strategy for National Renewal* (Chair: Sir G. Borrie). London: Vintage/IPPR.

Community Development Project (1977) *Gilding the Ghetto*. London: HMSO.

Corrigan, P. (1979) Popular consciousness and social democracy, *Marxism Today*, 14–17.

Cressey, P. (1999) New Labour and employment, training and employee relations, in M. Powell (ed.) *New Labour, New Welfare State?* Bristol: Policy Press.

Crosland, C.A.R. ([1956] 1964) *The Future of Socialism*. London: Jonathan Cape.

Crouch, C. (1997) The terms of the neo-liberal consensus, *Political Quarterly*, 68: 352–60.

Crouch, C. (1999) Employment, industrial relations and social policy, *Social Policy and Administration*, 33(4): 437–57.

Crowther, M.A. (1988) *Social Policy in Britain 1914–1939*. Basingstoke: Macmillan.

Culpitt, I. (1999) *Social Policy and Risk*. London: Sage.

Cutler, T. and Waine, B. (1997) The politics of quasi-markets, *Critical Social Policy*, 17: 3–26.

Cutler, T. and Waine, B. (1998) *Managing the Welfare State*. Oxford: Berg.

Cutler, T. and Waine, B. (2000) Managerialism reformed? New Labour and public sector management, *Social Policy and Administration*, 34(3): 318–32.

Daly, M. (2000) *The Gender Division of Welfare*. Cambridge: Cambridge University Press.

Daunton, M. (ed.) (1996) *Charity, Self-interest and Welfare in the English Past*. London: UCL Press.

Davies, H., Nutley, S. and Smith, P. (2000) *What Works?* Bristol: Policy Press.

Deacon, A. (2000) Learning from the US?, *Policy and Politics*, 28(1): 5–18.

Deacon, A. and Mann, K. (1999) Agency, modernity and social policy, *Journal of Social Policy*, 28(3): 413–35.

Deacon, B. (1983) *Social Policy and Socialism*. London: Pluto Press.

Deacon, B. with Hulse, M. and Stubbs, P. (1997) *Global Social Policy*. London: Sage.

Dean, H. (2000) Managing risk by controlling behaviour, in P. Taylor-Gooby (ed.) *Risk, Trust and Welfare*. Basingstoke: Macmillan.

Dell, E. (2000) *A Strange Eventful History: Democratic Socialism in Britain*. London: Harper Collins.

Dennis, N. (1997) *The Invention of Permanent Poverty*. London: Institute of Economic Affairs.

Department for Education and Employment (2001) *Schools – Building on Success*. London: Stationery Office.

Department of Health (1997) *The New National Health Service*. London: Stationery Office.

Department of Health (1998) *Our Healthier Nation*. London: Stationery Office.

Department of Health (1999) *Saving Lives*. London: Stationery Office.

Department of Health (2000) *The NHS Plan*. London: Stationery Office.

Department of Social Security (1998) *New Ambitions for Our Country*. London: Stationery Office.

de Swann, A. (1988) *In Care of the State*. Cambridge: Polity Press.

de Swann, A. (1992) Perspectives for transnational social policy, *Government and Opposition*, 27(1): 33–52.

Digby, A. (1989) *British Welfare Policy*. London: Faber & Faber.

Dolowitz, D., Greenwold, S. and Marsh, D. (1999) Policy transfer: something old, something new, something borrowed, but why red, white and blue?, *Parliamentary Affairs*, 52(4): 719–30.

Downs, A. (1957) *An Economic Theory of Democracy*. London: Harper Collins.

Drake, R. (2001) *The Principles of Social Policy*. Basingstoke: Palgrave.

Drakeford, M. (2000) *Privatisation and Social Policy*. Harlow: Longman.

Driver, S. and Martell, L. (1998) *New Labour: Politics after Thatcherism*. Cambridge: Polity Press.

Driver, S. and Martell, L. (2000) Left, right and third way, *Policy and Politics*, 28(2): 147–61.

Dwyer, P. (2000) *Welfare Rights and Responsibilities*. Bristol: Policy Press.

Ebbinghaus, B. and Manow, P. (eds) (2001) *Comparing Welfare Capitalism*. London: Routledge.

Ellison, N. (1999) Beyond universalism and particularism, *Critical Social Policy*, 19(1): 57–85.

Enthoven, A. (1999) *In Pursuit of an Improved NHS*. London: Nuffield Trust.

Esping-Andersen, G. (1990) *The Three Worlds of Welfare Capitalism*. Cambridge: Cambridge University Press.

Esping-Andersen, G. (ed.) (1996) *Welfare States in Transition*. London: Sage.

Esping-Andersen, G. (1999) *Social Foundations of Postindustrial Economies*. Oxford: Oxford University Press.

Esping-Andersen, G. (2000) The sustainability of welfare states into the twenty-first century, *International Journal of Health Services*, 30(1): 1–12.

Etzioni, A. (1996) *The Spirit of Community*. London: Fontana.

Exworthy, M., Powell, M. and Mohan, J. (1999) The NHS: quasi-market, quasi-hierarchy, quasi-network, *Public Money and Management*, 19(4): 15–22.

Ferlie, E., Ashburner, L., Fitzgerald, L. and Pettigrew, A. (1996) *The New Public Management in Action*. Oxford: Oxford University Press.

Ferrera, M. and Rhodes, M. (eds) (2000) *Recasting European Welfare States*. London: Frank Cass.

Ferrera, M., Hemerijck, A. and Rhodes, M. (2001) Recasting European welfare states for the twenty first century, in S. Leibfried (ed.) *Welfare State Futures*. Cambridge: Cambridge University Press.

Field, F. (1996) *Stakeholder Welfare*. London: Institute of Economic Affairs.

Field, F. (2000) *The State of Dependency*. London: Social Market Foundation.

Finlayson, G. (1994) *Citizen, State and Social Welfare in Britain 1830–1990*. Oxford: Clarendon Press.

Fitzpatrick, T. (1996) Postmodernism, welfare and radical politics, *Journal of Social Policy*, 25(3): 303–20.

Fitzpatrick, T. (2001) *Welfare Theory*. Basingstoke: Palgrave.

Flora, P. and Alber, J. (1981) Modernization, democratization and the development of welfare states in Europe, in P. Flora and A. Heidenheimer (eds) *The Development of Welfare States in Europe and America*. London: Transaction Books.

Flora, P. and Heidenheimer, A.J. (1981) The historical core and changing boundaries of the welfare state, in P. Flora and A. Heidenheimer (eds) *The Development of Welfare States in Europe and America*. London: Transaction Books.

Flora, P. with Kuhnle, S. and Unwin, D. (eds) (1999) *State Formation, Nation Building and Mass Politics in Europe*. Oxford: Oxford University Press.

Flynn, N. (1997) *Public Sector Management*. London: Prentice-Hall/Harvester Wheatsheaf.

Flynn, R., Williams, G. and Pickard, S. (1996) *Markets and Networks: Contracting in Community Health*. Buckingham: Open University Press.

Foster, P. and Wilding, P. (2000) Whither welfare professionalism?, *Social Policy and Administration*, 34(2): 143–59.

Foucault, M. (1979a) *Discipline and Punish: The Birth of the Prison*. Harmondsworth: Penguin.

Foucault, M. (1979b) *The History of Sexuality. Vol. 1: An Introduction*. Harmondsworth: Penguin.

Foucault, M. (1986) *The Uses of Pleasure*. Harmondsworth: Viking.

Foucault, M. (1988) *The Care of Self*. London: Allen Lane.

Foucault, M. (1991) Governmentality, in G. Burchell, C. Gordon and P. Miller (eds) *The Foucault Effect: Studies in Governmentality*. Hemel Hempstead: Harvester Wheatsheaf.

Fraser, D. (1984) *The Evolution of the British Welfare State*, 2nd edn. Basingstoke: Macmillan.

Freedland, J. (1998) *Bring Home the Revolution*. London: Fourth Estate.

Fukuyama, F. (1992) *The End of History and the Last Man*. London: Hamish Hamilton.

Fukuyama, F. (1999) *The Great Disruption*. London: Profile Books.

Furniss, N. and Tilton, T. (1977) *The Case for the Welfare State*. Bloomington, IN: Indiana University Press.

Galbraith, J.K. (1958) *The Affluent Society*. London: Hamish Hamilton.

Galbraith, J.K. (1967) *The New Industrial State*. London: Hamish Hamilton.

Gamble, A. and Wright, T. (1999) The New Social Democracy, in A. Gamble and T. Wright (eds) *The New Social Democracy*. Oxford: Blackwell.

Garrett, G. (1998) *Partisan Politics in the Global Economy*. Cambridge: Cambridge University Press.

George, V. and Wilding, P. (1984) *The Impact of Social Policy*. London: Routledge & Kegan Paul.

George, V. and Wilding, P. (1985) *Ideology and Social Welfare*. London: Routledge & Kegan Paul.

George, V. and Wilding, P. (1993) *Welfare and Ideology*. Hemel Hempstead: Harvester Wheatsheaf.

George, V. and Wilding, P. (1999) *British Society and Social Welfare*. Basingstoke: Macmillan.

Gewirtz, S. (1999) Education Action Zones: emblems of the Third Way, in H. Dean and R. Woods (eds) *Social Policy Review 11*. Luton: Social Policy Association.

Geyer, R. (1998) Globalization and the (non) defence of the welfare state, *West European Politics*, 21(3): 77–103.

Geyer, R. (2000) *Exploring European Social Policy*. Cambridge: Polity Press.

Giddens, A. (1984) *The Constitution of Society*. Cambridge: Polity Press.

Giddens, A. (1994) *Beyond Left and Right*. Cambridge: Polity Press.

Giddens, A. (1998) *The Third Way*. Cambridge: Polity Press.

Giddens, A. (2000) *The Third Way and Its Critics*. Cambridge: Polity Press.

Giddens, A. (ed.) (2001) *The Global Third Way Debate*. Cambridge: Polity Press.

Gilbert, B. (1970) *British Social Policy 1914–1939*. London: Batsford.

Gladstone, D. (ed.) (1995) *British Social Welfare: Past, Present and Future*. London: UCL Press.

Gladstone, D. (1999) *The Twentieth-Century Welfare State*. Basingstoke: Macmillan.

Glennerster, H. (1995) *British Social Policy Since 1945*. Oxford: Blackwell.

Glennerster, H. (1999) A third way?, in H. Dean and R. Woods (eds) *Social Policy Review 11*. Luton: Social Policy Association.

Glennerster, H. (2001) Social policy, in A. Seldon (ed.) *The Blair Effect*. London: Little, Brown & Co.

Glennerster, H. and Hills, J. (1998) *The State of Welfare*, 2nd edn. Oxford: Oxford University Press.

Glennerster, H., Power, A. and Travers, T. (1991) A new era for social policy: a new enlightenment or a new leviathan?, *Journal of Social Policy*, 20: 389–414.

Glyn, A. (ed.) (2001) *Social Democracy in Neoliberal Times: The Left and Economic Policy since 1980*. Oxford: Oxford University Press.

Goodin, R.E. (1988) *Reasons for Welfare*. Princeton, NJ: Princeton University Press.

Gough, I. (1979) *The Political Economy of the Welfare State*. London: Macmillan.

Gough, I. (1991) The UK, in A. Pfaller, I. Gough and G. Therborn (eds) *Can the Welfare State Compete?* Basingstoke: Macmillan.

Gould, A. (1993) *Capitalist Welfare States: A Comparison of Japan, Britain and Sweden*. Harlow: Longman.

Gould, J. (1998) *The Unfinished Revolution*. London: Little, Brown & Co.

Green, D. (1993) *Reinventing Civil Society*. London: Institute of Economic Affairs.

Green, D. (1996) *Communities without Politics*. London: Institute of Economic Affairs.

Green, D. (1998) Mutuality and voluntarism: a 'third way' of welfare reform, in E. Brunsdon, H. Dean and R. Woods (eds) *Social Policy Review 10*. London: Social Policy Association.

Green-Pedersen, C., van Kersbergen, K. and Hemerijk, A. (2001) Neo-liberalism, the 'third way' or what? Recent social welfare policies in Denmark and the Netherlands, *Journal of European Public Policy*, 8(2): 307–25.

Gribbins, J. (1998) Postmodernism, poststructuralism and social policy, in J. Carter (ed.) *Postmodernity and the Fragmentation of Welfare*. London: Routledge.

Grice, A. (1997) Blair aims for DIY welfare state, *Sunday Times*, 9 November.

Habermas, J. (1976) *Legitimation Crisis*. London: Heinemann.

Hadley, R. and Hatch, S. (1981) *Social Welfare and the Failure of the State*. London: Allen & Unwin.

Hadot, P. (1992) Reflections on the notion of the 'cultivation of the self', in T. Armstrong (ed.) *Michel Foucault Philosopher*. Hemel Hempstead: Harvester Wheatsheaf.

Hage, J., Hanneman, R. and Gorgan, E. (1989) *State Responsiveness and State Activism*. London: Unwin Hyman.

Hansard (2001) House of Commons Debate on Queen's Speech, 20 June.

Hantrais, L. (2000) *Social Policy in the European Union*, 2nd edn. Basingstoke: Macmillan.

Harris, D. (1987) *Justifying State Welfare*. Oxford: Blackwell.

Harris, J. (1977) *William Beveridge: A Biography*. Oxford: Clarendon Press.

Harris, J. (1992) War and social history: Britain and the Home Front during the Second World War, *Contemporary European History*, 1(1): 17–35.

Harvey, D. (1989) *The Condition of Postmodernity*. Oxford: Blackwell.

Hay, C. (1996) *Re-stating Social and Political Change*. Buckingham: Open University Press.

Hay, C. (1998) Globalisation, welfare retrenchment and the 'logic of no alternative', *Journal of Social Policy*, 27(4): 525–32.

Hay, C. (1999) *The Political Economy of New Labour*. Manchester: Manchester University Press.

Heclo, H. (1981) Towards a new welfare state?, in P. Flora and A. Heidenheimer (eds) *The Development of Welfare States in Europe and America*. London: Transaction Books.

Heffernan, R. (2000) *New Labour and Thatcherism*. Basingstoke: Macmillan.

Hennessy, P. (1992) *Never Again: Postwar Britain, 1946–51*. London: Cape.

Heron, E. and Dwyer, P. (1999) Doing the right thing, *Social Policy and Administration*, 33(1): 91–104.

Hewitt, M. (1991) Bio-politics and social policy: Foucault's account of welfare, in M. Featherstone, M. Hepworth and B. Turner (eds) *The Body: Social Processes and Cultural Theory*. London: Sage.

Hewitt, M. (1992) *Welfare, Ideology and Need*. Hemel Hempstead: Harvester Wheatsheaf.

Hewitt, M. (1994) Social policy and the question of post-modernism, in R. Page and J. Baldock (eds) *Social Policy Review 6*. Canterbury: Social Policy Association.

Hewitt, M. (2000) *Welfare and Human Nature*. Basingstoke: Macmillan.

Hewitt, M. (2001) New labour, human nature and welfare reform, in R. Sykes *et al.* (eds) *Social Policy Review 13*. Bristol: Policy Press.

Hewitt, M. and Powell, M. (1998) A different back to Beveridge?, in E. Brunsdon, H. Dean and R. Woods (eds) *Social Policy Review 10*. London: Social Policy Association.

Higgins, J. (1981) *States of Welfare*. Oxford: Blackwell.

Hill, M. (1993) *The Welfare State in Britain*. Cheltenham: Edward Elgar.

Hills, J. (1997) *The Future of Welfare*. York: Joseph Rowntree Foundation.

Hillyard, P. and Watson, S. (1996) Postmodernism and social policy: a contradiction in terms?, *Journal of Social Policy*, 25(3): 321–46.

Himmelfarb, G. (1995) *The De-moralisation of Society*. London: Institute of Economic Affairs.

Hirst, P. (1994) *Associative Democracy*. Cambridge: Polity Press.

Hirst, P. (1999) Has globalization killed social democracy?, in A. Gamble and T. Wright (eds) *The New Social Democracy*. Oxford: Blackwell.

Hirst, P. and Thompson, G. (1996) *Globalization in Question*. Cambridge: Polity Press.

HM Treasury (1999) *Access to Financial Services: The Report of Policy Action Team 14*. London: HM Treasury.

HM Treasury (2001) *Savings and Assets for All*. London: HM Treasury.

Hofferbert, R. and Budge, I. (1993) The party mandate and the Westminster model, *British Journal of Political Science*, 22(2): 151–82.

Hoggett, P. (1994) The politics of modernisation of the UK welfare state, in R. Burrows and B. Loader (eds) *Towards a Post-Fordist Welfare State?* London: Routledge.

Hoggett, P. (2001) Agency, rationality and social policy, *Journal of Social Policy*, 30(1): 37–56.

Hoggett, P. and Thompson, S. (1998) The delivery of welfare: the associationalist vision, in J. Carter (ed.) *Postmodernity and the Fragmentation of Welfare*. London: Routledge.

Holliday, I. (2000) Productivist welfare capitalism: social policy in East Asia, *Political Studies*, 48: 706–23.

Holman, R. (1993) *A New Deal for Social Welfare*. Oxford: Lion.

Holman, R. (1995) Family man, *New Statesman and Society*, 8 December.

Hughes, G. and Lewis, G. (eds) (1998) *Unsettling Welfare*. London: Routledge.

Hutton, W. (1999) *The Stakeholder Society: Writings on Economics and Politics*. Cambridge: Polity Press.

Institute for Public Policy Research (2001) *Building Better Partnerships*. London: IPPR.

Institute of Economic Affairs (1967) *Towards a Welfare Society*. London: IEA.

Inglehart, R. (1990) *Culture Shift in Advanced Industrial Society*. Princeton, NJ: Princeton University Press.

Inglehart, R. (1997) *Modernization and Postmodernization*. Princeton, NJ: Princeton University Press.

Iversen, T. (2001) The dynamics of welfare state expenditure: trade openness, deindustrialisation and partisan politics, in P. Pierson (ed.) *The New Politics of the Welfare State*. Oxford: Oxford University Press.

Jefferys, K. (1999) *Anthony Crosland: A New Biography*. London: Richard Cohen Books.

Jenkins, S. (1995) *Accountable to None: The Tory Nationalisation of Britain*. London: Hamish Hamilton.

Jessop, B. (1994) The transition to post-Fordism and the Schumpeterian workfare state, in R. Burrows and B. Loader (eds) *Towards a Post-Fordist Welfare State?* London: Routledge.

Jessop, B. (1999) The changing governance of welfare, *Social Policy and Administration*, 33(4): 348–59.

Johnson, N. (1987) *The Welfare State in Transition*. Brighton: Wheatsheaf.

Johnson, N. (1990) *Reconstructing the Welfare State*. Hemel Hempstead: Harvester Wheatsheaf.

Johnson, N. (1999) *Mixed Economies of Welfare*. Hemel Hempstead: Prentice-Hall.

Johnson, P. (1996) Risk, redistribution and social welfare from the Poor Law to Beveridge, in M. Daunton (ed.) *Charity, Self-Interest and Welfare in the English Past*. London: UCL Press.

Jones, C. (1985) *Patterns of Social Policy*. London: Tavistock.

Jones, C. and Novak, T. (1999) *The Disciplinary State*. London: Routledge.

Jones, K. (2000) *The Making of Social Policy in Britain*, 3rd edn. London: Athlone Press.

Jordan, B. (1998) *The New Politics of Welfare*. London: Sage.

Kennett, P. (2001) *Comparative Social Policy*. Buckingham: Open University Press.

King, D. (1999) *In the Name of Liberalism*. Oxford: Oxford University Press.

King, D. and Wickham-Jones, M. (1999) Bridging the Atlantic: the Democratic (Party) origins of welfare to work, in M. Powell (ed.) *New Labour, New Welfare State?* Bristol: Policy Press.

Klein, R. (1985) Public expenditure in an inflationary world, in L. Lindberg and C. Maier (eds) *The Politics of Inflation and Economic Stagnation*. Washington, DC: Brookings Institute.

Klein, R. (1993) O'Goffe's tale, in C. Jones (ed.) *New Perspectives on the Welfare State in Europe*. London: Routledge.

Klein, R. and Millar, J. (1995) Do-it-yourself social policy, *Social Policy and Administration*, 29: 303–16.

Korpi, W. (1979) *The Working Class in Welfare Capitalism*. London: Routledge & Kegan Paul.

Korpi, W. (1989) Power, politics and state autonomy in the development of social citizenship, *American Sociological Review*, 54(3): 309–28.

Krieger, J. (1986) *Reagan, Thatcher and the Politics of Decline*. Cambridge: Polity Press.

Krieger, J. (1999) *British Politics in the Global Age*. Cambridge: Polity Press.

Kuhnle, S. (ed.) (2000) *Survival of the European Welfare State*. London: Routledge.

Kumar, K. (1995) *From Post-Industrial to Post Modern Society*. Oxford: Blackwell.

Labour Party (1997) *New Labour Because Britain Deserves Better* (1997 General Election Manifesto). London: Labour Party.

Labour Party (2001) *New Ambitions for Britain* (2001 General Election Manifesto). London: Labour Party.

Land, H. (1999) New Labour, new families?, in H. Dean and R. Woods (eds) *Social Policy Review 11*. Luton: Social Policy Association.

Lash, S. and Urry, J. (1987) *The End of Organized Capitalism*. Cambridge: Polity Press.

Lavalette, M. and Mooney, G. (eds) (2000) *Class Struggle and Social Welfare*. London: Routledge.

Laybourn, K. (1995) *The Evolution of British Social Policy and the Welfare State*. Keele: Keele University Press.

Le Grand, J. (1982) *The Strategy of Equality*. London: Allen & Unwin

Le Grand, J. (1991) The state of welfare, in J. Hills (ed.) *The State of Welfare*. Oxford: Clarendon Press.

Le Grand, J. (1997) Knights, knaves or pawns? Human behaviour and social policy, *Journal of Social Policy*, 26(2): 149–69.

Le Grand, J. (1998) The Third Way begins with CORA, *New Statesman*, 6 March, pp. 26–7.

Le Grand, J. and Bartlett, W. (eds) (1993) *Quasi-Markets and Social Policy*. Basingstoke: Macmillan.

Leibfried, S. (2000) National welfare states, European integration and globalization, *Social Policy and Administration*, 34(1): 44–63.

Leibfried, S. (ed.) (2001) *Welfare State Futures*. Cambridge: Cambridge University Press.

Leonard, D. (ed.) (1999) *Crosland and New Labour*. Basingstoke: Macmillan.

Leonard, P. (1979) Restructuring the welfare state, *Marxism Today*, 7–13.

Leonard, P. (1997) *Postmodern Welfare*. London: Sage.

Levitas, R. (1996) The concept of social exclusion and the new Durkheimian hegemony, *Critical Social Policy*, 16(1): 5–20.

Levitas, R. (1998) *The Inclusive Society?* Basingstoke: Macmillan.

Lewis, J. (1995) *The Voluntary Sector, the State and Social Work*. Aldershot: Edward Elgar.

Lewis, J. (1999) Voluntary and informal welfare, in R. Page and R. Silburn (eds) *British Social Policy in the Twentieth Century*. Basingstoke: Macmillan.

Ling, T. (2000) Unpacking partnerships, in J. Clarke, S. Gewirtz and E. McLaughlin (eds) *New Mangerialism, New Welfare?* London: Sage.

Lipsky, M. (1980) *Street Level Bureaucracy*. New York: Russell Sage Foundation.

Lister, R. (2000) To RIO via the Third Way, *Renewal*, 8(4): 9–20.

Loader, B. and Burrows, R. (1994) Towards a post-Fordist welfare state?, in R. Burrows and B. Loader (eds) *Towards a Post-Fordist Welfare State?* London: Routledge.

Loney, M. (1986) *The Politics of Greed*. London: Pluto.

Lowe, R. (1999a) *The Welfare State in Britain Since 1945*, 2nd edn. Basingstoke: Macmillan.

Lowe, R. (1999b) Introduction: the road from 1945, in H. Fawcett and R. Lowe (eds) *Welfare Policy in Britain: The Road from 1945*. Basingstoke: Macmillan.

Lowndes, V. (1999) Managing change in local governance, in G. Stoker (ed.) *The New Management of British Local Governance*. Basingstoke: Macmillan.

Lund, B. (1999) Ask not what your community can do for you: obligations, New Labour and welfare reform, *Critical Social Policy*, 19(4): 447–62.

Lyotard, J-F. (1984) *The Postmodern Condition* (trans. G. Bennington and B. Massumi). Manchester: Manchester University Press.

Macadam, E. (1934) *The New Philanthropy*. London: Allen & Unwin.

MacGregor, S. (1999) Welfare, neo-liberalism and new paternalism: three ways for social policy in late capitalist societies, *Capital and Class*, 67: 91–118.

Mandelson, P. and Liddle, R. (1996) *The Blair Revolution: Can New Labour Deliver?* London: Faber & Faber.

Mann, K. (1998) 'One step beyond': critical social policy in a 'postmodern world', in J. Carter (ed.) *Postmodernity and the Fragmentation of Welfare*. London: Routledge.

Marquand, D. (1988) *The Unprincipled Society*. London: Cape.

Marquand, D. (1992) *The Progressive Dilemma*, revised edn. London: Heinemann.

Marquand, D. (1998) The Blair paradox, *Prospect*, May: 19–24.

Marsh, D. (1980) *The Welfare State*. London: Longman.

Marsh, D. and Rhodes, R. (eds) (1992) *Implementing Thatcherite Policies*. Buckingham: Open University Press.

Marshall, T.H. (1963) *Sociology at the Crossroads*. London: Heinemann.

Marshall, T.H. (1970) *Social Policy*, 3rd edn. London: Hutchinson.

Marshall, T.H. (1981) *The Right to Welfare*. London: Heinemann.

Marsland, D. (1996) *Welfare or Welfare State?* Basingstoke: Macmillan.

Marwick, A. (1990) *British Society since 1945*. Harmondsworth: Penguin.

May, M. and Brunsdon, E. (1999) Commercial and occupational welfare, in R. Page and R. Silburn (eds) *British Social Policy in the Twentieth Century*. Basingstoke: Macmillan.

McKibbin, R. (1997) Very Old Labour, *London Review of Books*, 3 April, pp. 3–6.

McLaughlin, E., Trewsdale, J. and McCay, N. (2001) The rise and fall of the UK's first tax credit, *Social Policy and Administration*, 35(2): 163–80.

Midwinter, E. (1994) *The Development of Social Welfare in Britain*. Buckingham: Open University.

Miliband, D. (1994) From welfare to wealthfare, *Renewal*, 2: 87–90.

Mishra, R. (1981) *Society and Social Policy*, 2nd edn. London: Macmillan.

Mishra, R. (1984) *The Welfare State in Crisis*. Brighton: Wheatsheaf.

Mishra, R. (1990) *The Welfare State in Capitalist Society*. Hemel Hempstead: Harvester Wheatsheaf.

Mishra, R. (1999) *Globalization and the Welfare State*. Cheltenham: Edward Elgar.

Moran, M. (2001) The rise of the regulatory state in Britain, *Parliamentary Affairs*, 54(1): 19–34.

Morgan, K. (1985) *Labour in Power 1945–1951*. Oxford: Oxford University Press.

Moses, J., Geyer, R. and Ingebritsen, C. (2000) Introduction, in R. Geyer, C. Ingebritsen and J. Moses (eds) *Globalization, Europeanization and the End of Scandinavian Social Democracy?* Basingstoke: Macmillan.

Mullard, M. and Spicker, P. (1998) *Social Policy in a Changing Society*. London: Routledge.

Murray, C. (1984) *Losing Ground*. New York: Basic Books.

Murray, C. (1996) *Charles Murray and the Underclass: The Developing Debate*. London: Institute of Economic Affairs.

Myles, J. (1998) How to design a 'liberal' welfare state, *Social Policy and Administration*, 32(4): 341–64.

Navarro, V. (1999a) Is there a third way? A response to Gidden's *The Third Way*, *International Journal of Health Services*, 29(4): 667–77.

Navarro, V. (1999b) The political economy of the welfare state in developed capitalist countries, *International Journal of Health Services*, 29(1): 1–50.

Navarro, V. (2000) Are pro-welfare state and full-employment policies possible in the era of globalization?, *International Journal of Health Services*, 30(2): 231–51.

Nettleton, S. and Burrows, R. (1998) Individualisation processes and social policy, in J. Carter (ed.) *Postmodernism and the Fragmentation of Welfare*. London: Routledge.

Newman, J. (2000) Beyond the new public management? Modernising public services, in J. Clarke, S. Gewirtz and E. McLaughlin (eds) *New Managerialism, New Welfare?* London: Sage.

Newman, J. and Clarke, J. (1994) Going about our business? The managerialism of public services, in J. Clarke, A. Cochrane and E. McLaughlin (eds) *Managing Social Policy*. London: Sage.

O'Brien, M. and Penna, S. (1998) *Theorising Welfare*. London: Sage.

O'Connor, J. (1973) *The Fiscal Crisis of the State*. New York: St. Martin's Press.

Offe, C. (1982) Advanced capitalism and the welfare state, *Politics and Society*, 2(4): 479–88.

Offe, C. (1996) *Modernity and the State*. Cambridge, MA: MIT Press.

Ohmae, K. (1990) *The Borderless World*. London: Fontana.

O'Malley, P. (1992) Risk, power and crime prevention, *Economy and Society*, 21(3): 252–75.

Orloff, A.S. and Skocpol, T. (1984) Why not equal protection? Explaining the politics of public social spending in Britain 1900–1911 and the United States 1880s–1920, *American Sociological Review*, 49: 726–50.

Orwell, G. ([1941] 1982) *The Lion and the Unicorn: Socialism and the English Genius.* Harmondsworth: Penguin.

Osborne, D. and Gaebler, T. (1992) *Reinventing Government: How the Entrepreneurial Spirit is Transforming the Public Sector.* Reading, MA: Addison-Wesley.

Owen, D. (1965) *English Philanthropy 1661–1960.* Oxford: Oxford University Press.

Page, R. (1995) The attack on the British welfare state – more real than imagined? A Leveller's tale, *Critical Social Policy*, 15: 220–8.

Page, R. (1996) *Altruism and the British Welfare State.* Aldershot: Avebury.

Penna, S. and O'Brien, M. (1996) Postmodernism and social policy: a small step forwards?, *Journal of Social Policy*, 25(1): 39–61.

Perkin, H. (1989) *The Rise of Professional Society.* London: Routledge.

Pestoff, V. (1998) *Beyond the Market and State.* Aldershot: Ashgate.

Peters, B.G. (1999) *Institutional Theory in Political Science.* London: Pinter.

Peters, T. and Waterman, R. (1982) *In Search of Excellence.* New York: Harper & Row.

Petersen, A. (1997) Risk, governance and the new public health, in A. Petersen and R. Bunton (eds) *Foucault: Health and Medicine.* London: Routledge.

Petersen, A., Barnes, I., Dudley, J. and Harris, P. (1999) *Poststructualism, Citizenship and Social Policy.* London: Routledge.

Pfaller, A., Gough, I. and Thurborn, G. (eds) (1991) *Can the Welfare State Compete?* Basingstoke: Macmillan.

Pierson, C. (1994) Continuity and discontinuity in the emergence of the 'post-Fordist' welfare state, in R. Burrows and B. Loader (eds) *Towards a Post-Fordist Welfare State?* London: Routledge.

Pierson, C. (1996) Social policy, in D. Marquand and A. Seldon (eds) *The Ideas that Shaped Post-War Britain.* London: Fontana.

Pierson, C. (1998a) *Beyond the Welfare State*, 2nd edn. Cambridge: Polity Press.

Pierson, C. (1998b) Theory in British social policy, in C. Pierson and N. Ellison (eds) *Developments in British Social Policy.* Basingstoke: Macmillan.

Pierson, C. (2001) *Hard Choices.* Cambridge: Polity Press.

Pierson, P. (1994) *Dismantling the Welfare State.* Cambridge: Cambridge University Press.

Pierson, P. (1996) The new politics of welfare, *World Politics*, 48: 143–79.

Pierson, P. (ed.) (2001) *The New Politics of the Welfare State.* Oxford: Oxford University Press.

Pinker, R. (1979) *The Idea of Welfare.* London: Heinemann.

Political and Economic Planning (1937) *Report on the British Social Services.* London: PEP.

Pollitt, C. (1993) *Managerialism and the Public Services.* Oxford: Blackwell.

Popper, K. (1968) *The Logic of Scientific Discovery.* London: Hutchinson.

Powell, M. (1995a) The strategy of equality revisited, *Journal of Social Policy*, 24(2): 163–85.

Powell, M. (1995b) Did politics matter?, *Urban History*, 22(3): 384–403.

Powell, M. (1997a) *Evaluating the National Health Service.* Buckingham: Open University Press.

Powell, M. (1997b) An expanding service: municipal acute medicine in the 1930s, *Twentieth Century British History*, 8(3): 334–57.

Powell, M. (1998) In what sense a national health service?, *Public Policy and Administration*, 13(3): 56–69.

Powell, M.A. (ed.) (1999a) *New Labour, New Welfare State?* Bristol: Policy Press.

Powell, M.A. (1999b) New Labour and the third way in the British NHS, *International Journal of Health Services*, 29(2): 353–70.

Powell, M.A. (2000a) New Labour and the third way in the British welfare state: a new and distinctive approach?, *Critical Social Policy*, 20(1): 39–60.

Powell, M. (2000b) Something old, something new, something borrowed, something blue: the jackdaw politics of the third way, *Renewal*, 8(4): 21–31.

Powell, M. (ed.) (2002) *Evaluating New Labour's Welfare Reforms*. Bristol: Policy Press.

Powell, M. and Boyne, G. (2001) The spatial strategy of equality and the spatial division of welfare, *Social Policy and Administration*, 35(2): 181–94.

Powell, M. and Hewitt, M. (1998) The end of the welfare state?, *Social Policy and Administration*, 32(1): 1–13.

Putnam, R. (2000) *Bowling Alone: The Collapse and Revival of American Community*. New York: Simon & Schuster.

Raban, C. (1986) The welfare state – from consensus to crisis?, in P. Lawless and C. Raban (eds) *The Contemporary British Welfare*. London: Harper & Row.

Rake, K. (2001) Gender and New Labour's social policies, *Journal of Social Policy*, 30(2): 209–31.

Rawnsley, A. (2001) *Servants of the People*. Harmondsworth: Penguin.

Rhodes, M. (1996) Globalization and West European welfare states, *Journal of European Social Policy*, 6(4): 305–27.

Rhodes, M. (2000) Reconstructing the British welfare state, in F. Scharpf and V. Schmidt (eds) *Welfare and Work in the Open Economy, Vol. 2: Diverse Responses to Common Challenges*. Oxford: Oxford University Press.

Rhodes, R. (1997) *Understanding Governance*. Buckingham: Open University Press.

Rhodes, R. (2000) The governance narrative, *Public Administration*, 78(2): 345–63.

Riddell, P. (1991) *The Thatcher Era*, 2nd edn. Oxford: Blackwell.

Riddell, P. (1997) New labour message sounds reassuringly old, *Times*, 30 September.

Ritzer, G. (1996) *The McDonaldisation of Society*. London: Sage.

Robson, W.A. (1976) *Welfare State and Welfare Society*. London: Allen & Unwin.

Rodger, J. (2000) *From a Welfare State to a Welfare Society*. Basingstoke: Macmillan.

Rose, R. (1984) *Do Parties Make a Difference?*, 2nd edn. London: Macmillan.

Rose, R. and Shiratori, R. (1986) Introduction, in R. Rose and R. Shiratori (eds) *The Welfare State East and West*. Oxford: Oxford University Press.

Ross, F. (2000) Beyond left and right: the new partisan politics of welfare, *Governance*, 13(2): 155–83.

Ruane, S. (1997) Public–private boundaries and the transformation of the NHS, *Critical Social Policy*, 17(1): 53–78.

Rys, V. (1964) The sociology of social security, *Bulletin of the International Social Security Association*, January/February.

Sako, M. (1992) *Prices, Quality and Trust*. Cambridge: Cambridge University Press.

Sassoon, D. (1999) European social democracy and New Labour, in A. Gamble and T. Wright (eds) *The New Social Democracy*. Oxford: Blackwell.

Sartre, J-P. (2001) Existentialism and humanism, in S. Priest (ed.) *Jean-Paul Sartre: Basic Writings*. London: Routledge.

Saunders, P. (1981) *Social Theory and the Urban Question*. London: Hutchinson.

Savage, S. and Atkinson, R. (eds) (2001) *Public Policy Under Blair*. Basingstoke: Palgrave.

Saville, J. ([1957/58] 1983) The origins of the welfare state, in M. Loney, D. Boswell and J. Clarke (eds) *Social Policy and Social Welfare*. Milton Keynes: Open University Press.

Scarborough, E. (2000) West European welfare states: the old politics of retrenchment, *European Journal of Political Science*, 38: 225–59.

Scharpf, F. and Schmidt, V. (eds) (2000a) *Welfare and Work in the Open Economy, Vol. I: From Vulnerability to Competitiveness*. Oxford: Oxford University Press.

Scharpf, F. and Schmidt, V. (eds) (2000b) *Welfare and Work in the Open Economy. Vol. 2: Diverse Responses to Common Challenges*. Oxford: Oxford University Press.

Schottland, C. (1967) *The Welfare State*. New York: Harper & Row.

Schwartz, H. (2001) Round up the usual suspects!, in P. Pierson (ed.) *The New Politics of the Welfare State*. Oxford: Oxford University Press.

Selbourne, D. (1994) *The Principle of Duty*. London. Sinclair Stevenson.

Seldon, A. (ed.) (1996) *Re-Privatising Welfare*. London: Institute of Economic Affairs.

Shakespeare, T. (2000) The social relations of care, in G. Lewis, S. Gewirtz and J. Clarke (eds) *Rethinking Social Policy*. London: Sage.

Shaw, E. (1996) *The Labour Party since 1945*. Oxford: Blackwell.

Shin, D-M. (2000) Economic policy and social policy: policy linkages in an era of globalization, *International Journal of Social Welfare*, 9(1): 17–30.

Skelcher, C. (1998) *The Appointed State*. Buckingham: Open University Press.

Smith, S.J. and Mallinson, S. (1997) Housing for health in a post-welfare state, *Housing Studies*, 12: 173–200.

Social Exclusion Unit (1998) *Bringing Britain Together*. London: Stationery Office.

Sokal, A. (1996) Transgressing the boundaries: towards a transformative hermeneutics of quantum gravity, *Social Text*, 46–7: 217–52.

Spicker, P. (1988) *Principles of Social Welfare*. London: Routledge.

Squires, P. (1990) *Anti-Social Policy*. Hemel Hempstead: Harvester Wheatsheaf.

Stephens, J. (1979) *The Transition from Capitalism to Socialism*. London: Macmillan.

Stephens, J., Huber, E. and Ray, L. (1999) The welfare state in hard times, in H. Kitschelt, P. Lange, G. Marks and J. Stephens (eds) *Continuity and Change in Contemporary Capitalism*. Cambridge: Cambridge University Press.

Stoker, G. (ed.) (1999) *The New Management of British Local Governance*. Basingstoke: Macmillan.

Sullivan, M. (1992) *The Politics of Social Policy*. Hemel Hempstead: Harvester Wheatsheaf.

Sullivan, M. (1996) *The Development of the British Welfare State*. Hemel Hempstead: Harvester Wheatsheaf.

Sutherland, S. (chair) (1999) *With Respect to Old Age: A Report by the Royal Commission on Long Term Care*. London: Stationery Office.

Swank, D. (2000) Political institutions and welfare state restructuring, in P. Pierson (ed.) *The New Politics of the Welfare State*. Oxford: Oxford University Press.

Sykes, R., Palier, B. and Prior, P. (eds) (2001) *Globalization and European Welfare States*. Basingstoke: Palgrave.

Tawney, R.H. ([1931] 1964) *Equality*. London: George Allen & Unwin.

Taylor-Gooby, P. (1985) *Public Opinion, Ideology and State Welfare*. London: Routledge & Kegan Paul.

Taylor-Gooby, P. (1988) The future of the British welfare state: public attitudes, citizenship and social policy under the Conservative governments of the 1980s, *European Sociological Review*, 4: 1–19.

Taylor-Gooby, P. (1991) *Social Change, Social Welfare and Social Science*. Hemel Hempstead: Harvester Wheatsheaf.

Taylor-Gooby, P. (1994) Postmodernism and social policy: a great leap backwards?, *Journal of Social Policy*, 23(3): 385–404.

Taylor-Gooby, P. (1997) In defence of the second-best theory: state, class and capital in social policy, *Journal of Social Policy*, 26: 171–92.

Taylor-Gooby, P. (ed.) (2000) *Risk, Trust and Welfare*. Basingstoke: Macmillan.

Taylor-Gooby, P. and Lawson, R. (1993) Where we go from here: the new order in welfare, in P. Taylor-Gooby and R. Lawson (eds) *Markets and Managers*. Buckingham: Open University Press.

Temple, M. (2000) New labour's third way, *British Journal of Politics and International Relations*, 2(3): 302–25.

Thane, P. (1996) *Foundations of the Welfare State*, 2nd edn. Harlow: Longman.

Thelen, K. and Steinmo, S. (1992) Introduction, in S. Steinmo, K. Thelan and F. Longstreth (eds) *Structuring Politics*. Cambridge: Cambridge University Press.

Thomson, S. (2000) *The Social Democratic Dilemma*. Basingstoke: Macmillan.

Thompson, G., Frances, J., Levacic, R. and Mitchell, J. (eds) (1991) *Markets, Hierarchies and Networks*. London: Sage.

Thompson, S. and Hoggett, P. (1996) Universalism, selectivism and particularism, *Critical Social Policy*, 16(1): 21–43.

Timmins, N. (1996) *The Five Giants*. London: Fontana.

Titmuss, R. (1950) *Problems of Social Policy*. London: HMSO.

Titmuss, R. (1963) *Essays on the Welfare State*. London: Allen & Unwin.

Titmuss, R. (1968) *Commitment to Welfare*. London: Allen & Unwin.

Titmuss, R. (1971) *The Gift Relationship*. New York: Pantheon Books.

Tomlinson, J. (1998) Why so austere? The British welfare state of the 1940s, *Journal of Social Policy*, 27(1): 63–77.

Tomlinson, S. (2001) *Education in a Post-Welfare Society*. Buckingham: Open University Press.

Tonnies, F. (1955) *Community and Society*. London: Routledge & Kegan Paul.

Townsend, P. (1995) Persuasion and conformity: an assessment of the Borrie Report on Social Justice, *New Left Review*, 213: 137–50.

Townsend, P. and Bosanquet, N. (eds) (1972) *Labour and Inequality*. London: Fabian Society.

Toynbee, P. and Walker, D. (2001) *Did Things Get Better?* Harmondsworth: Penguin.

Turner, B. (1994) *Orientalism, Postmodernism and Globalism*. London: Routledge.

van Oorschot, W. (2000) Who should get what and why?, *Policy and Politics*, 28(1): 33–48.

Vandenbroucke, F. (1999) European social democracy: convergence, divergence and shared questions, in A. Gamble and T. Wright (eds) *The New Social Democracy*. Oxford: Blackwell.

Veit-Wilson, J. (2000) States of welfare, *Social Policy and Administration*, 34(1): 1–25.

Walker, A. (1997) The strategy of inequality, in A. Walker and C. Walker (eds) *Britain Divided*. London: CPAG.

Walker, R. (1999a) The Americanization of British welfare: a case study of policy transfer, *International Journal of Health Services*, 29(4): 679–97.

Walker, R. (ed.) (1999b) *Ending Child Poverty*. Bristol: Policy Press.

Walsh, K. (1995) *Public Services and Market Mechanisms*. Basingstoke: Macmillan.

Watson, S. (2000) Foucault and the study of social policy, in G. Lewis, S. Gewirtz and J. Clarke. (eds) *Rethinking Social Policy*. London: Sage.

Webster, C. (1994) Conservatives and consensus, in A. Oakley and A.S. Williams (eds) *The Politics of the Welfare State*. London: UCL Press.

Whelan, R. (1996) *The Corrosion of Charity*. London: Institute of Economic Affairs.

Whelan, R. (1999) *Involuntary Action*. London: Institute of Economic Affairs.

White, S. (1998) Interpreting the 'Third Way', *Renewal*, 6: 17–30.

White, S. (ed.) (2001) *New Labour: The Progressive Future*. Basingstoke: Macmillan.

White, S. (in press) *The Civic Minimum*. Oxford: Oxford University Press.

Whiteside, N. (1996) Creating the welfare state in Britain 1945–1960, *Journal of Social Policy*, 25(1): 83–103.

Whitty, G. and Power, S. (1999) New Labour's education policy: first, second or third way?, *Journal of Education Policy*, 14(5): 535–46.

Wicks, M. (1987) *A Future for All*. Harmondsworth: Penguin.

Wilding, P. (1982) *Professional Power and Social Welfare*. London: Routledge & Kegan Paul.

Wilding, P. (1992) The British welfare state: Thatcherism's enduring legacy, *Policy and Politics*, 20: 201–12.

Wilensky, H. (1975) *The Welfare State and Equality*. Berkeley, CA: University of California Press.

Williams, F. (1989) *Social Policy: A Critical Introduction*. Cambridge: Polity Press.

Williams, F. (1999) Good-enough principles for welfare, *Journal of Social Policy*, 28(4): 667–88.

Williams, K. and Williams, J. (eds) (1987) *A Beveridge Reader*. London: Allen & Unwin.

Wright, A. (1996) *Socialisms*. London: Routledge.

Yeates, N. (1999) Social politics and policy in an era of globalization, *Social Policy and Administration*, 33(4): 372–93.

Yeates, N. (2001) *Globalization and Social Policy*. London: Sage.

INDEX